I Take Just Pride

*How a Fraternity Reinvented Itself,
Why a Professor Joined*

S<small>COTT</small> C<small>ONROE</small>

Box Grove Communications
Cortland, New York

ISBN 13: 978-0-9626536-3-6
ISBN 10: 0-9626536-3-2

Library of Congress Control Number 2007925932

Cover illustration and design by Steve Perina

Book design by BookMasters, Inc.

Printed by BookMasters, Ashland, OH

For my parents, Barbara and Bruce

And the men of Phi Kappa Tau

Creed of Phi Kappa Tau

Phi Kappa Tau, by admitting me to membership, has conferred upon me a mark of distinction in which I take just pride. I believe in the spirit of brotherhood for which it stands. I shall strive to attain its ideals, and by so doing to bring to it honor and credit. I shall be loyal to my college and my chapter, and shall keep strong my ties to them that I may ever retain the spirit of youth. I shall be a good and loyal citizen. I shall try always to discharge the obligation to others which arises from the fact that I am a fraternity man.

—Roland Maxwell, 1950

Table of Contents

PREFACE   x

PROLOGUE   xiii

PART I: A MARK OF DISTINCTION
         (OR, THE DIFFERENT PATH IS TOUGH)

Chapter 1–Saying No (Summer 1998/Winter 1999)   3
Chapter 2–Cliff's Edge (Fall 1999)   11
Chapter 3–Friends on a Mission (Spring 2000)   17
Chapter 4–Call Me Professor (Spring 2000)   21
Chapter 5–Colony (Fall 2000)   28
Chapter 6–Homecoming (Fall 2000)   32
Chapter 7–Fat Albert and Other Follies (Fall 2000)   34
Chapter 8–Finding New Blood (Winter 2001)   41
Chapter 9–Identity (Winter 2001/Winter 1974)   44
Chapter 10–Old Words (Winter 2001)   53

PART II: ADMITTING ME TO MEMBERSHIP
          (OR, OLD GUY TAKES A RISK)

Chapter 11–Brian's Battle (Winter/Spring 2001)   57

Chapter 12–Muscle Matters (Spring 2001)   65

Chapter 13–Gut Check (Spring 2001)   69

Chapter 14–Cleaning Up (Spring/Summer 2001)   74

Chapter 15-Home (Summer/Fall 2001)   79

Chapter 16–The Booze Question (Fall 2001)   84

Chapter 17–Shattered Day (Fall 2001)   87

Chapter 18–Goal Attained (Fall 2001)   89

PART III: THE OBLIGATION TO OTHERS
(OR, LEARN TO BE PART OF SOMETHING)

Chapter 19–Up in the Air (Fall 2001)   97

Chapter 20–Ambition (Fall 2001)   100

Chapter 21–Late Bid (Fall/Winter 2001)   107

*Chapter 22–How Rush Imitates Life
   (Fall/Winter 2001)*   116

Chapter 23-Generations (Spring 2002)   128

Chapter 24–Commitment (Spring 2002)   135

Chapter 25–The Tough Man (Spring 2002)   139

Chapter 26-Trophies (Spring 2002)   145

Chapter 27–Men from the Past (Summer 2002)   148

Chapter 28–Meet the Cousins (Summer 2002)   158

Chapter 29–A President's Choices (Fall 2002)   166

Chapter 30–Sex Talk (Fall 2002)   172

Chapter 31–Grading My Brothers (Fall 2002)   178

Chapter 32-Jocks (Fall 2002)   185

Chapter 33–Local Custom (Fall 2002)   189

Part IV: The Spirit of Youth
(Or, Better Get Used to Change)

Chapter 34–Rebellion (Winter 2003)   197

Chapter 35–Turmoil (Winter 2003)   200

Chapter 36–The Value of Lou (Spring 2003)   205

Chapter 37–Recovery (Spring 2003)   210

Chapter 38–Departure (Spring 2003)   215

Chapter 39–Summer of the Future (Summer 2003)   220

Epilogue   228

Appendix   239

Acknowledgments   243

Bibliography   245

Preface

I did not set out to join a college fraternity in middle age. That would never have occurred to me. To spend time with a society of college students and get to know its members, yes, maybe—I often did that kind of story as a journalist. I once skated with a Division I college hockey team, in warm-ups of a game, a couple of days after practicing with them and learning to put on the gear (I returned to reality during the National Anthem, when I was in the locker room, changing back to street clothes). Hanging out was something I did well. I had spent parts of eight years hanging out in fraternities when I met Phi Kappa Tau. I was offered the chance to join fraternities but did not, for it seemed too ridiculous. That time of my life was gone.

Once I did become a Phi Tau, I had to learn how to tell people about it. I break the news to associate brothers (pledges), usually after they accept their bids. For them it's just one more thing to absorb about this entity they've joined. It's trickier with people my age. I gauge whether fraternities are even a subject for conversation, then work through steps: I'm an advisor, my fraternity is easy to work with, it actually initiated me in 2001. Twelve hours before I turned 46. Yes, they offered and I decided to accept, not an automatic decision. No, it is not like the film comedy *Old School*—I rarely drink with them, am not part of rush, and my slice of the fraternity is pretty narrow. I gain from it what I can, given the age gap. The person I'm telling this to might look as if I had lost my senses. Or they might smile as they hear another baby boomer story of self-discovery.

I finally decided to talk about this on paper, and about the men who made it possible and what they wanted to accomplish, when I was pitching a book about how fraternities were being forced to adapt to a changed society or die out. An agent or editor said, "Wait, you belong to one now? I want to hear about that." Problem: while I had notebooks full of interviews and observations everywhere but at Phi Tau, I had never planned to write about the Phi Taus. I thought it was a conflict of interest. So this is a memoir, bolstered by interviews and journals, and ending in 2003.

I am still, at this writing, an advisor to the chapter and a part of things generally. My age is showing somewhat; at the house I often feel like a visitor from another country. I have written about the current brothers a little in the Epilogue, but otherwise I have left them alone. My Phi Tau chapter changes every semester, sometimes every few months, so I am lucky if I can keep up let alone portray the men accurately. We like each other most days.

In these pages there are no composite characters, although there are a couple of composite situations. I also have changed some names for privacy reasons. I did so reluctantly, for in over 25 years as a journalist—thousands of stories—only once or twice did I not use real names.

I wrote the following story for myself, my fraternity brothers of all ages, anyone who once belonged to a fraternity (or sorority, a different thing), and anyone who didn't but is curious. I wrote it with my fellow baby boomers in mind, but I would be glad if anyone gained from reading it. The North-American Interfraternity Conference, the umbrella organization for 64 national fraternities, says it has 5,500 chapters spread over 800 campuses, the number of either shifting as chapters fold or are re-born, as ours was. That doesn't include the "local" fraternities, entities unto themselves with one to three chapters. The NIC says about 350,000 men (and some women, if a chapter is co-ed) belong to fraternities. Millions have joined since fraternities were founded from the mid-19th century to the mid-20th. That's a lot of people who followed my path, though only a few walked it after college, as I did.

Many people disdain, dislike, or disregard fraternities. The reasons are many and real, from traumas and tragedies born of recklessness, to images of drunken idiocy that fill popular culture, to just the alien notion of finding friends formally. Plenty of men quit during pledging or after initiation. They lose whatever they saw and felt when they said yes to the bid, or the chapter's internal culture shifts, or the sheer experience of belonging becomes too much. It can be tiresome, to be surrounded by dozens of men who know so much about your life and comment on it, or pressure you to do something you don't want to.

Colleges question fraternities' value socially or educationally, rightfully so. For every wonderful thing fraternities do, something else happens that a college administrator must explain to parents, alumni, mayors.

Yet too often fraternities are reduced to a one-dimensional story line in the news media and popular culture. Again, this is partly their own fault—some don't see themselves as anything more than partying and friendship. When they do try to explain what else they offer, people don't always listen, leery of being conned.

So I want to tell my side of this story but also the men's. This generation called Millennials has much to be admired about it, even when they baffle or frustrate my generation. The men in this book accomplished something and I want it to be known.

We were together at times and headed in different directions at other times, even before graduation took everyone off into the world. We recruited men who would not make the fraternity their whole life, who wanted an anti-fraternity, and that was how we wanted it. The other side of that was days when I wished we were more together.

This is one slice of my life. I am telling stories about a family, in a sense: people who argue, don't always know or forgive each other as much as they should, people who laugh in the shared warmth of a weekly meeting or a bar. I was there enough to think I can tell this story, at least from my viewpoint. I hope I have done it justice.

Prologue
Ithaca, New York 1994–1995

This story begins with an ending.

A partnership dissolved, an old family business closed, a beloved pet had to be put down, a flame on a candle was blown out. That Saturday morning in November 1994 felt like all those things for the men gathered a few blocks from Cornell University, at a small mansion they had once called home.

There were seven of them sitting around a heavy wooden table in 106 The Knoll's book-lined, elegant Chapter Room, where this chapter of Phi Kappa Tau national fraternity met every week and where this Board of Governors, composed of alumni (with the chapter president and treasurer present as de facto members) met every month. Reminders of the past—plaques, framed copies of the charter that made the chapter's existence legal and official—hung on two of the walls. A fireplace graced a third wall, with a lighter area in the wood where a historic plaque had hung for years but was now missing, presumed stolen. The men were in their late twenties and early thirties, not gray-haired yet but with careers and spouses, now sober with the sad decision they had to make.

For a few years they had been kidding themselves that this thing could still work out. The chapter, once 30 strong in their time—a bit small for a Cornell fraternity but able to function financially—had shrunk to 10 members. A fraternity is a business on one level, and this business was failing.

The only hope was that they, and their national headquarters in Ohio, could start over. A colony could be formed from men who wanted to re-build, rooted in Phi Tau history and traditions, and build it strongly enough to endure—to do more than party, to stay out of trouble with the law and university, to sustain itself.

The Alpha Tau chapter of Phi Tau (referred to from now on as Phi Tau) had prided itself on being a place for those who never expected to join a fraternity. Its men were not smooth, had not been prom kings and class presidents in high school, would not have gotten a chance at most of Cornell's 42 fraternities. And that was fine. They rejected what they saw as mindless obedience to the cult of cool, of status, of looking good and blindly following everyone else.

Yet this was indeed a fraternity. The brothers put new members through pledging, said the creed, sent annual reports to national and Cornell. They did a little of what would be considered hazing. The end of pledging involved a trick where pledges were told to bring a goldfish to the house, put it in a glass of water, and swallow it. The pledges were blindfolded, and glasses of water with raw eggs floating in them were substituted for the goldfish glasses. That was what the pledges swallowed. As hazing went, it was pretty tame. The brothers enjoyed notoriety where they could get it. They had their Nuts and Bolts Party, where each man received a bolt and each woman a nut, and they had to see whose nut screwed on whose bolt. Enraged feminists raised hell about that one, which pleased the men.

But a fraternity still needed to function as a whole, and the men here had become a collection of individuals. Some of them were too caught up in engineering or pre-medical studies to give the chapter much of their time. There were more offices than men to hold them, and the president and treasurer ended up having to run the thing. The last rush had yielded just three new members, where the Cornell average was about 13 or 14.

The men had not played the game, of connecting to the powers that be whether you want to or not.

Pat Madden made the motion to dissolve the chapter. A computer consultant from Boston, Class of 1988, he had seen this day coming for a while and now it was time to get this over with. Chairman Jack Zinn got a second. The vote was unanimous.

Their only solace was that Phi Tau wasn't closing for the reasons most fraternities did: death, rape, injury to a pledge, or too much bad behavior for too long. The times were too litigious and American society was too down on anything all-male, no longer as tolerant of the good old boy network. Women had been asserting themselves. No, this was a case of weak organization. "We were not a problem child," one of the board members, an engineer named Bob Cundall, told me 12 years later. The Phi Taus of 1994 just did not find enough men who wanted to be part of them. Perhaps they did not see the need to actually strategize and sell themselves during rush, or did not know how.

Phi Tau's low membership meant little money to manage the property and the building, which had been the chapter's home since 1906, interrupted only by a few years in World War II when it served as military housing. Few men also meant little money to fund parties, which were costly now that Interfraternity Council required they be managed by caterers who ID'd the students, poured the beer, and absorbed much of the liability. The men in the house had to pay to get in, just as guests did.

Jack Zinn notified national headquarters and Cornell's Greek Life office about the board's decision. The national staff had not asked for the chapter to be folded, they would have kept trying to revive the chapter rather than dissolve it, but they understood. The chapter's relationship with national was weak. To the brothers, national was this distant entity that sent someone to visit the chapter once a year or so, a fellow called a consultant who was just out of college; three of them covered the more than 85 chapters. Consultants gauged how each chapter was doing, internally and with its campus The Cornell Phi Taus had concluded that national mostly was interested in how many warm bodies they had, meaning how much money the chapter generated in annual national dues. The chapter's bonds with Cornell were weak as well. The men had stopped sending someone to weekly IFC meetings. The IFC, governing body for most fraternities (the black and Latino fraternities had their own council) seemed pretty useless to the men, just a group that helped the administration tighten its rules and policies every year until the fraternities in particular boiled with frustration.

The Phi Taus chose not to play the game, which was a mistake. Every fraternity needed to play the game a little.

Fraternities had arrived at Cornell in 1868, when groups of men from Zeta Psi and Chi Phi flipped a coin to see who would establish a chapter first. Zeta Psi won the toss but Chi Phi—according to its own lore—went ahead that night and formed its chapter anyway. The two had feuded or at least ignored each other ever since. The university had not yet graduated its first class when those two chapters arrived. They were followed by more in the next few years, until Cornell quickly had 10. Fraternities had been around for 40 years already (not counting Phi Beta Kappa, an honorary society that had begun as a fraternity at William and Mary in 1776). The Cornell system grew as the university did, men needing places to live and a network of friends to help them both in college and afterward. Fraternity membership appealed to people who had always been achievers and planned to run the country. There had been more than 50 fraternities in the early 1960s. Their alumni went on to be CEOs, politicians, industry leaders. There were the Coors family of Coors Brewing Co., the Johnsons of Johnson Wax, National Hockey League Commissioner Gary Bettman (rush chair, alumni chair, and IFC finance chair), writer Kurt Vonnegut Jr., and hundreds more.

The Cornell Phi Tau chapter's most prominent alumni were in banking, business, and finance. The chapter was young. Two small local fraternities named Skull and Bandhu had formed in 1901 and 1902 respectively, merged after World War I to form a local called Phi Delta Sigma, which petitioned to join Phi Tau national in 1930 and was accepted—the 43rd Phi Tau chapter, Alpha Tau. The petition in its blue cover lay on a shelf in the Chapter Room, looking fairly new 65 years later.

The board also agreed that the current brothers could continue to live at 106 The Knoll, an unusual step. Most men did not react well to being told they were failures, and when fraternities folded the brothers often damaged the house, so the alumni often made them move out and closed it up, even put plywood across windows. The Phi Taus stayed through May.

The university went on, as it will. The campus was stunning, with gardens and trees from around the nation, green quads, spires and stone. In Collegetown, the bars and restaurants and apartments along the south edge of campus, students hurried from class to home and back in a steady stream of preoccupied, bright, sometimes wealthy and well-dressed youth. The football team was losing its last four games but would have a winning record. The seniors were going to rush the field after the last home game, as they had rushed the field after the first home game as freshmen. Hockey season was starting, the only sport students really cared about, and students thought about going after those season tickets.

The saddest day for the alumni came that May. They packed up the memorabilia, the charters and plaques and secret ritual items and composite portraits, and the painting that hung above the mantle in the dining room, of a former Skull and later faculty mentor. They brought it to a storage facility on Ithaca's west side. "Not many guys showed up to do it," Bob remembered. "It was the most poignant moment." The alumni hired a company to manage the property, which was rented out the next year.

By then, there was some other news.

The national Phi Tau's CEO and chapter development staff agreed with the board that the chapter could be re-colonized. This candle could be lit again. They set the date for 2000. But national would manage the process. With a re-colonization, it was best to let a few years go by, enough of a gap between the past and whatever lay ahead that the colony could start anew. The chapter would be more like a traditional fraternity, national said. That hurt the recent alumni and current brothers. "They don't want us to interact with the new members [coming in 2000] because I guess they're afraid the bad karma will [seep] into the new members," the chapter president told the student newspaper, the *Cornell Daily Sun*.

"We talked a lot about how, when our fraternity would be brought back, it would be in a form we wouldn't recognize," Bob Cundall said. "More frat-like. That's what works." It was hard to swallow, even if the alumni knew that over the years the chapter had gone through different internal cultures. A fraternity culture shifts every few years with the constant flow of new men with new ideas and goals. The alumni resolved to tell the new men about their traditions as soon as national allowed—about their feud with neighboring Delta Chi, and their names for all the rooms (Presidential Suite, Gandhi's Room, Tailor Shop, Crow's Nest). Phi Tau would no longer be the place where men who didn't want to be frat boys could find a home.

But that would not be entirely true, as it turned out.

Northern New York, Fall 1995

It was Bid Night for the fraternities. I could tell because guys were puking their drinks of celebration out of the attic window down the block from my apartment. The puke landed on dirt that used to be the front lawn.

I strolled down the sidewalk and one of the men said, "Hey, Scott" the way a cop tells bystanders at an accident, "Please move along."

I understood. I was an ally at times, an older guy who actually respected the idea of a fraternity even if I had never belonged to one. But I was also an enemy, as part of SUNY College at Potsdam's administration. I saw too much and was never sure what to do with what I thought I saw. My job was public relations writer and occasional spokesman, but I also volunteered as advisor to Interfraternity Council, governing body for the college's six fraternities. I took the role fairly seriously, even if I was between a rock and a hard place. The college wanted the fraternities (and sororities) to clean up their act. The fraternities wanted to be left alone. I had grown up in Potsdam, 20 miles from the Canadian border, a frozen place of hockey and lonely hamlets, and people knew me so I heard about a lot. One minute a fraternity and I could be fine with each other, the next minute I'd be asking for an explanation, maybe telling the man in charge of the Greek system about it. I wasn't paid to do this but I really wanted to help both sides.

The puking was funny but embarrassing. I wanted the fraternities to be so much more than they were, to have a better sense of what they could offer. They put images of guys puking in toilets on the cover of their rush materials. I said couldn't they find a better image, like intramural sports or their brotherhood dressed formally, looking handsome and adult? Wouldn't they attract more guys if they emphasized other sides of themselves? They listened, at least, but they were college men, wanting to do things their way.

I'll call this fraternity the Gray Wolves instead of by their Greek letters, since there will be plenty of Greek letters in this story and it can get confusing. These men were a "local" fraternity, meaning they were not a national fraternity, which has dozens of chapters. The gray wolf was their emblem (they wouldn't tell me why). The Gray Wolves rented this house, and inside composite portraits and banners hung on the walls, but there were no Greek letters outside. Greek-letter societies at the two colleges in Potsdam (SUNY and Clarkson University) could not display letters on a house unless it was in a certain village zone or they had existed before 1979. This fraternity fell into neither category. The 20 men used my high school classmate Jerome Lyman's former house. Jerome, enormously popular president of our junior class and the National Honor Society, lived in Chile now as a vice president of McDonald's. His family was scattered through the region. When he came home for reunion I told him not to drive past his old house, but he did and he was appalled at what a wreck it had become.

That night I walked around the neighborhood. Order of Prometheus was dark; the men always went to their advisor's house in the country for Bid Night party, and took away everyone's car keys. A couple of other fraternities were just raging away, but behind their walls.

At the Gray Wolves' house I stopped to talk to Phetus, their president, who stood on the front porch. Phetus was a junior who looked 17 and loved the band Phish, hence his nickname and its spelling. "We got six pledges," he said. He knew I cared.

I was getting used to living here again, after 17 years as a newspaper writer and photographer in the Syracuse area a few hours south, the last decade as a sports writer. My sister Laurie and her family were around the corner. An obstetric nurse, she helped to deliver babies so everyone knew her. People remembered me from high school or my sports writing years. "I saw you walking down Elm Street," they would tell me. I was adjusting to PR work, to wearing a shirt and tie every day, to being a team player. I had e-mail for the first time. I owned my first personal computer, a MacIntosh Performa. I missed the call of stories—I had lived for stories, had married my career instead of anyone who could love me back—but I was learning to be content with finding them for other people in my former profession.

The college's written policy on advising student groups said I was to guide but not really lead, and I was to avoid anything that put me at legal risk. Yet I wanted to know the fraternity world here, this variation of what I had seen at other colleges. Before coming here I had always worked as a journalist, so I went where I pleased and asked about anything I felt like. I had a beer with the Gray Wolves one spring afternoon and the next day I was told to watch it, that kind of thing got you fired. Sometimes I dropped by fraternity parties before they really hit stride. I understood a line needed to be kept between me and students but had trouble seeing it. No doubt the men laughed about my showing up, and wondered if I was trouble.

The Bid Night party got louder. Men yelled above me, big men rocking the house. Phetus smiled at me, gauging my mood. He was calm and pleasant. He played the president's role well. He planned to attend law school. I said good night, stay out of trouble.

While I had not belonged to one in college, I had always believed in fraternities' potential to help a man grow, not to mention their power to watch each other's backs. Between SUNY Potsdam, Clarkson across town, and St. Lawrence University and SUNY Canton down the road, there were more than 25 fraternities. I heard about brawls between them, or between them and sports teams. They got busted for loud parties. Even in quiet times the men bent rules every way they could. A house had "ghost pledges," pledges not registered with the college because they did not meet minimum grade standard for pledging; then their pictures would be on the composite when we had no record of their even receiving a bid. Or, in a complication I saw nowhere else, Potsdam students would do a dual degree with Clarkson and become Clarkson students for one year—while serving as officers of Potsdam fraternities or sororities. We had no jurisdiction over them, so we told them to step down, but they saw no conflict. Or the director of campus life would say he saw 10 guys walk past his house in the country last night, obviously stranded out there and made to hoof it back to the village—hazing. I would work with these situations, and sometimes I would alert the dean of students about potential problems. But I was not a spy for the college so I often tried to warn the men when they were walking a line—tried to be an educator.

The tables in the student union were another example. Each fraternity had a table that it had occupied at lunchtime for years (they did not have cooks so they ate in the dining halls and student union). This year the African-American students had decided their customary table in a corner was no good and had taken over the Gray Wolves' table, which was at the center and front. The fraternity responded by having one of its guys sit in an empty seat, then another and another as the black students left, until the table was 50-50 and finally all Gray Wolves. I warned the dean of students that a problem was brewing but he refused to believe anyone had their own table. The situation finally blew up into a shouting and shoving match.

People should listen to me some of the time. I wasn't always full of it.

The IFC had not been especially pleased to have an advisor, when I signed on a year ago. They were used to just a name on paper to appease the college. The IFC president my first semester was glad for my presence but he held a wide campus view, for he was also student government president and a live-in manager of the student union. The others stared at me that first meeting, and a guy with shaggy blond mane said, "You'd have more credibility with us if you pledged one of our houses."

Interesting idea. I had been dinged the few times I rushed fraternities 20 years earlier at tiny, expensive, elite St. Lawrence. It hurt like hell, to put myself there to be chosen, to be judged as a man or person from how I looked (skinny, bespectacled), how I acted (a bit awkward, a bit too honest), and what I had done (yearbook, Student Council, class officer, hockey and track manager—not impressive at SLU). The first house I tried was a jock house, all football players and wrestlers, and rumored to have tough pledging. They seemed to speak their own language to each other. I did not try houses where I had a good shot. I wanted to reinvent myself. The jock house said no, which back then meant I found an empty mail box when bids came out. Other mail boxes had white envelopes: bids, a door opening. I rushed the preppy house next, then the ultra-cool house. Finally I accepted a "social bid" at Sigma Pi, meaning I was welcome at closed parties but not pledged or initiated.

Now a man offered a bid 20 years later in Potsdam—and he was a Sigma Pi, from this college's chapter.

I was not surprised that a man could join a fraternity long after college. I had seen it and heard about it at a summer academy for Greek advisors. The term was "alumni initiate." But I didn't know how young men decided to tap an older man for membership or what led him to say yes. I thought both sides had to know each other for a year or so first. A Cornell fraternity had initiated its chef after four years. A fraternity here had initiated a member's father, the college's dining services director, after a couple of years. This bid offer felt too easy. I wanted real brotherhood, if it truly existed.

"What will this entail?" I asked.

"It'll be the most fun you'll be glad you never have to go through again. What time do you go to bed?"

I said 11 o'clock.

"Not anymore."

"A bid, just like that? Your house doesn't even know me."

"Yeah, but I can get you a bid."

Why do it? If not actual brotherhood, what? Research! I had spent three years gathering material for a book about how fraternities were adapting (or not) to the new America of the 1990s, the lawsuit-happy and politically correct America. I had observed life at Cornell University and Colgate University fraternities, and since moving back to Potsdam I had spent time at St. Lawrence, at the very jock house that had first rejected me in 1974. I was there as they led the fight to keep the wrestling team, which SLU dropped despite its success. I interviewed brothers and alumni, ate dinner at houses, and tried to sense what it was like to live among dozens of other men, go through ceremonies, earn your way as a pledge. I asked men of my generation what they had gained by belonging. Some of them said they had gained little, that it was just something else they did in college. Some had hated it. Others said it shaped their whole way of dealing with the world, especially in business or politics or law. At reunions they still stuck together, laughing over their old stories.

The jock house had welcomed me because, as a sports writer in Syracuse and as an alumnus from St. Lawrence's glory years in sports, I had written about or photographed or partied with many of their alumni: a potential ally. SLU was imposing changes on its Greek system, making students wait until sophomore year to pledge, putting in tougher policies to govern them. The men bitterly resented it. A senior said maybe I should get a bid now, or at least see pledging so people would know it wasn't so awful. This was the most secretive fraternity I had met or have met since. While the motion did not pass—all of their votes had to be unanimous— the split was 50-50. That shocked me, that they were so worried as to possibly let an outsider observe some of their pledging.

Now, this offer came from a SUNY Potsdam fraternity.

I said no, I would lose my job. I also didn't trust these men yet. They offered me a bid again the next semester, and this time I asked a senior administrator for her opinion. "You would gain a valuable window into student culture," she said, "but you'd put yourself at legal risk." I said no again.

I was here partly because of restlessness with my last job as a sports writer. I had worked nights and weekends, observing life and writing about other people, while coaches and teachers made a difference in young lives. They guided athletic boys being raised by single mothers, kids caught between divorcing and over-worked parents, kids feeling lost. I just wrote about it. I wanted to get in the battle, and ended up with this PR job in my hometown. I brought my fraternity story with me. The college fraternity was dying, or so I had heard for several years. America wanted fraternities to tame their ways or be gone. But if this was death it was slow, like a huge old oak rotting inside. It seemed more like a massive game: colleges tighten rules, students get around them, colleges add rules, students (resentful as all hell now) escape them.

In Potsdam fraternities did not have the same sense of history as houses at private colleges did. I felt some heritage in their houses, and certainly their pledges had to memorize facts, but it was not the same. Their friendships flowed strong. So did their feuds. Fraternities feuded and made up, occasionally fought in the bars downtown, showed their letters on colorful jackets. Along with the rowdiness they could do good works as well. They all did some community service—another demand from the college—and the Gray Wolves staged bed races in downtown Potsdam to raise money for the local hospital.

The men listened to me a little and did some of what I advocated, which made the college see me a success. I had come to believe I was some sort of Youth Whisperer, able to talk to the young. A conceit—I had not begun to master the art of telling college students what I thought.

One day SUNY Potsdam's president passed me a letter from an alumnus, a college president himself. It said he was disgusted with his fraternity's alumni newsletter because the men referred to pledges as "scrotes." He said we needed to do something about this "sick organization." The brothers shrugged it off. "These older guys don't understand, times have changed," the chapter president told me. "Our culture is different." Culture, yes. I heard that a lot. It sounded like an excuse.

My big boss, the vice president for advancement, had been IFC president here, and he respected Greeks but could not tolerate this. We let the Greek-letter societies use our mailing system for these newsletters, and in return we demanded change. The scrotes newsletter became more professional and cleaner. Another house that told alumni to come back so they could chase helpless women and vomit off the back porch had to revise its writing.

Trying to advise students could leave a person frustrated. We had to take ourselves seriously but also chill out. Too often it was easy to think, am I a fool? Are all of my experiences so worthless? Then I would remember what I was like at 19 or 20, and forge onward.

People of my generation asked me why we had fraternities anymore. It seemed silly, elitist, and old-style. I wondered if it was even possible for college-age men to change so they would fit what this new society demanded. I mean, a male is hard-wired a certain way. Fraternities could unleash what was dark and ugly about a young man, as well as what was noble and strong.

"Tell me, what purpose do they serve?" a colleague in campus life would ask. "How can you justify their existence?"

I said, "You can learn a lot by belonging to one."

"About what? How much beer you can pound down? Taking advantage of women?"

My research had confirmed for me that Greeks had something to offer, but it was a bit like my sports days, covering sports I had not played and sounding as if I knew what I was talking about. I had thought about running track but not tried it. I had long ago gotten accustomed to rough male humor but had never belonged to any group of men. My friends did not test my loyalty. We did not call each other brothers.

For me, for many of us, it all melted together and made us feel under attack: wrestling programs being dropped around the nation to make way for women's sports; girls demanding to compete on boys' teams; fraternities under fire, traditions tossed out; and our employers sending us to diversity workshops where men sat in a circle of women and talked about how they learned to be a man and who taught them. Women sat in circles of us, and we switched it up: white and black and brown, educated or not, rich or not. We said what the facilitators wanted us to and got out of there. Male-dom had been turned on its head, and we could say nothing, just hunker down.

Yet fraternities deserved to be in trouble. They had gotten away with awful things for years. They loved booze too much. They could warp a man with their collective pull toward the easy, the low end, the group's wishes. We were all afraid, we adults who worked at the colleges, that someone would die.

That fall I got involved with a task force on Greek life at our college, created by the vice president for enrollment management and student services. She wanted us to look hard at everything about the Greeks.

I was crossing the Academic Quad a couple of days later when six or seven guys from different fraternities surrounded me and began yelling. Their eyes were alive with anger, their fists clenched.

"Goddamn college! Leave us alone!"

"What are you going to do, get rid of us? We know the college wants us gone."

They had heard about other colleges, especially in the Northeast, that had dissolved their fraternities. This new and ever-growing online system, the World Wide Web, brought them news. Colleges were taking away fraternities' houses, making men wait until sophomore year to rush, abolishing whole systems. Whatever was fun, colleges could just take it away.

Stunned, I said nobody knew what this task force would do. We didn't have an agenda. Maybe we would find that the Greek system was doing better than we thought.

"You might gain from this," I said. "We might come up with suggestions, ways to improve what you already have. Besides, it doesn't hurt to look at yourself. Everybody should, from time to time."

My heart was pounding a little, but I liked this talk across generations. I was in the game, like those teachers and coaches.

The men's anger faded. They seemed glad to think about what I said. I went on my way across the expanse of lawn while the pack of them drifted toward a classroom building, muttering. How volatile this fraternity thing was, how pressured we all felt to find answers to it, how much they wanted to exist while so many people wanted them gone. So many questions about why fraternities should still exist, and my travels around upstate New York, with side trips to Texas and Vanderbilt, had yielded partial answers. I felt the bonds among these guys, at least in my intellect, not really with my heart.

The next year, I would be offered a bid yet again, as a graduate student at Cornell.

Before classes started I introduced myself to the president of Cornell's Sigma Pi chapter. He saw me as a potential resource. The chapter had kicked out 16 members, leaving only 11, so they were starting over. But the chapter president and I both made mistakes, pushed the idea and the process too hard and fast. I saw ritual I should not have. The men told him to tell me to take a hike. I resolved that if I ever again advised a fraternity, I would discourage the men from offering me membership. I was supposed to be beyond all that.

But I still liked the idea, and what was that about?

Hadn't I outgrown such a notion?

Was this some baby boomer itch to re-make the past?

What appealed to me was the challenge a fraternity could present to my self as a man, who I was, what kind of friend. The idea lay there in me and would not be ignored.

PART I

A Mark of Distinction

(Or, the Different Path is Tough)

ONE
Saying No
(Summer 1998/Winter 1999)

Kate called to me from the front porch of her Collegetown house one summer afternoon. I was always glad to see her. Kate had been my right-hand student in my first semester of teaching news writing, when I was a graduate student. I was new not just to lecturing but to managing a classroom. She interpreted students for me. Now she was going to be a senior and I was revising my master's project so I could get that Ivy League degree in August and figure out what came next.

A stocky young man, with red hair, was drinking a beer, a Rolling Rock. Kate said, "This is my brother Tom."

Tom wasn't shy either. "Want a beer?" he said to me. I said sure. I seldom socialized with students but what the heck, it was summer. He pulled out a cigar and started tearing off the plastic wrapping. "Want a cigar? They're primo."

I said no thanks and asked where he went to college.

"I don't, I'm still in high school."

I quickly excused myself and practically ran up the street.

Tom actually had graduated a semester early and spent the spring at Penn State. He would enroll at Cornell in the fall, as a major in my department, communication.

I retreated to my single-bedroom apartment, in an old building—a former fraternity house—off North Campus. My lease was up but I planned to stay and live off my savings while I applied for newspaper and PR jobs, pitched ideas to magazine editors, and kept sorting through my fraternity research.

I didn't see Tom again until the fall. He was always upbeat, I noticed. I wanted to be that upbeat.

* * *

December came and bitter young men carried boxes of their belongings out of a fraternity house not far from my apartment. All 40 members of this house, which I will call DRI, had quit rather than "go dry" at their national leaders' order.

Going dry meant no alcohol on the premises and therefore no parties. The men could drink elsewhere, but that wasn't enough. Other fraternities had gone dry too. Lawsuits flew at them, and colleges accused them of encouraging alcoholism or at least enormous amounts of drinking. The others at Cornell that were supposed to go dry had been given reprieves until such time as a high percentage of the IFC was dry, which was nowhere in sight. But not DRI. The DRI brothers had tried to have rush against the backdrop of this change in their culture, and had attracted only a handful of pledges because freshmen wanted a place to drink. The men debated what to do next. They were not raging party animals but they had their fun. Every spring they staged Medieval Madness: pledges in kilts and carrying torches out front, and a draw bridge lowered in front of the castle-like house. Their Christmas party was legendary, an inferno of booze. Several of the brothers were rugby players and several were varsity soccer players, so they had a jock vibe of wildness.

DRI asked to become a local fraternity for a while. Cornell said yes but the alumni said no, we can't absorb your liability. The men split over what to do. Half wanted to soldier on and half said the hell with this, we are not dry. Finally all the DRI brothers quit and looked for other places to live. I asked if they wanted their pictures taken in front of the house but they said no, they wanted nothing to do with Greek life anymore.

Before they packed up, they held their Christmas party. Few guests were invited. Word had spread through campus that week that DRI was going out with the party to end all parties, and the alumni had said no way, so the men had let it be known that the party was private.

A huge evergreen tree filled one end of the Great Hall, and in a corner a brother chose tapes to blast through the house. Guests were greeted by a rugby player so tough and intense that the team had voted him Most Likely to Be Made into an Action Figure, who informed them that the only drink served that night would be Mad Dog 20–20. When you finished a bottle, you waited until everyone was watching and then threw it in the fireplace and heard the soft "whok" of breaking glass, as the men roared.

The party raged into the night, and then the mood shifted to ugly. Someone jumped from a balcony onto the Christmas tree, which shook and then fell. A tall senior pulled an exit sign off a door frame. Someone painted on the library wall. This was a common pattern for young men: release anger through destruction.

The damage to the house came to $15,000. The DRIs had to fix what they could or be sued. The furious alumni took the furniture out of the Great Hall.

DRI national decided to recruit new men and pledge them right away, instead of waiting and re-colonizing. Two men from national headquarters in Oxford, Ohio, came to campus for January 1999 rush and set up shop in the Great Hall. Hundreds of freshmen and a few sophomores wandered the streets around campus, looking at the fraternities, and a few stopped at DRI. The weather was unseasonably warm for upstate New York, melting the previous week's snow into little streams in the gutters and beckoning the teenagers outside to try three, four, maybe more fraternities, invited by upperclassmen, maybe courted since last fall, or just randomly tasting each fraternity's collective personality. Classes had not started yet and bids would not go out for more than a week, so life consisted of small talk over chips and soda (hot food in some houses), house tours, shaking hands endlessly, then at night a visit by "contact teams" from the fraternities that informed the kids where they stood, offered sales pitches, or told them to look elsewhere (the ding squad). New blood, new friendships, some rejection, many decisions, and lives changed. DRI was different. Whoever joined now would re-define fraternity as more than a place to drink.

It was a tough sell.

The Cornell freshmen, who were bright (90 percent ranked top 10 percent in their high school class), accustomed to pecking orders and status signs, now looking for a home, asked each other about this notion. A few ventured into the foyer, then into the Great Hall, and listened as the DRI staff talked about a new kind of fraternity, populated by men who wanted something ambitious. The theory was that such men were out there. To survive, to be relevant in a complex time when the student body was more diverse, fraternities reached out to a wider range of men. Cornell was one-third Greek, so what about the other two-thirds of the men? The trick was to communicate that a fraternity need not be a bunch of drunken louts in a pack. Dartmouth—whose fraternity system had inspired the iconic film *Animal House*—had just announced that its fraternities had to go, and was bracing for a battle against pro-Greek alumni.

New kinds of fraternities were needed, or the traditional kind had to be altered.

The men from DRI weren't just offering the company line. One had seen a brother die from drinking, when he was in college down south. The two told the freshmen, "We need to get in touch with the fraternity's principles. This is an opportunity for friendship, a guide to living." The freshmen might have known a little about fraternities and therefore grasped why one might go dry, but they were not sold. Politely, they nodded and then departed. Every other house said no problem, we drink and we party, we just manage the parties well. The law can't really be enforced. There are always manufactured IDs or trying to pass yourself off as someone else who is legal, or you just don't register the party and hope you don't get caught. Cornell rush being cutthroat, maybe a few fraternity men told the freshmen that a dry house was weak, join us on a road trip to the casino near Utica. Or we'll smuggle you into a bar in Collegetown. We'll have a few brews at our off-campus annex, a house rented by seniors. We'll get to know you drunk as well as sober.

What kind of man you are.

Cornell allowed DRI to extend its recruiting period beyond the ending date for everyone else, to maybe snag freshmen who had not found a fraternity or had skipped rush. It was daunting to start a fraternity that was different and build it to last. The stakes were higher for everyone as it was, since many houses were not satisfied with last year's crop after rush was shortened from two weeks to one. A fraternity that had a live-in advisor, as ordered by its alumni and encouraged by the university for all fraternities, said other houses used that fact to coax kids away. "They've got, like, an RA."

DRI's cultural shift was welcomed by the administration. Cornell liked chapters making over themselves. Three had re-colonized in recent years. Another had built a new house after fire destroyed the old house.

Our society told its colleges to tame those boys, but could it really be done, at an age when young adults test themselves and rebel against older people? Were men too hard-wired by their biology to rein in their aggression and energy?

Should fraternities be taken so seriously, or were they ultimately just places to live, party, and make friends?

If fraternities ever had real value, educationally or otherwise, did they still?

✶ ✶ ✶

Cornell sprawls across three campuses on East Hill, called North, Central, and West. North and West are residential. Central Campus overlooks Cayuga Lake and the small city of Ithaca. Collegetown borders Cornell on the southeast. Farmland lies to the north and east, leafy streets of faculty and student houses to the south and west. The fraternities and sororities—a total of more than 60, varying as houses close or come back—sit here and there among the streets, clustered. The university has four public colleges alongside the endowed ones, making a hybrid of the patrician and privileged with the middle-class and farm. Cornell has as much in common with Ohio State or Iowa as it does Harvard. In fact, its president that year had been president at Iowa. It is a hyper-active, uptight place where students fret over a B-plus (I love it anyway). Cornell looks rural but is actually urban: cut-throat, cold, impersonal. So it was a natural place for fraternities to take root in the 1800s and thrive, even in times when they were out of fashion, even with the scrutiny in the 1990s. Cornell prizes achievement, and ways of distinguishing yourself from everyone else, and status, and anything that leads to a career running the world or working for those who do.

From that first coin flip between Zeta Psi and Chi Phi in 1868, fraternities had grown at Cornell. They bought or built houses of their own, and recruited pledges in groups—pledge classes—to keep them clean (before that, boys pledged practically as they stepped off the train upon arriving at campus). A collection of stories about Cornell, published in 1898, let me hear the fraternity members talk in an almost British manner, about stout fellows and men who are "sporty" (they like their alcohol). Some of their ways were rooted in the Masonic movement. They had begun as white-only, all WASP with maybe a rare Catholic member, forcing Jews and blacks to start their own fraternities, but that ended in the 1960s. Their memberships had risen and fallen over the decades, suspended totally during the wars—the military had used fraternities to house troops—and declined in the late 1960s through the 1970s, when they were seen as Establishment and uncool. They returned to strength in the 1980s.

Alumni tended to say their fraternity days had much to do with who they were now. The man taking over as CEO of Johnson Wax, Herbert Fisk Johnson II (known as Fisk), had belonged to Chi Psi fraternity, like his father and grandfather. He held five degrees from Cornell, three in physics. His becoming a Chi Psi was not automatic. Arriving on campus in the fall of 1975, he'd hated the place and was about to transfer when he decided to accompany a friend on a tour of fraternities. They wandered past his father's and he decided to check it out. "I felt right at home," Johnson told me. I asked what he had learned as a brother that he continued to use in managing his huge family corporation. He said, "Everything."

Fraternities offered shelter from Cornell's campus life, with its crushing workload, and from the university's sheer size, about 13,500 undergraduates—not Illinois or Texas, but big. They offered connection to students who prized status, pecking orders, heritage. Fraternities here were less visible—Cornell men did not wear their Greek letters much—and when they feuded or fought, it was out of the public eye. "Nobody wants to jeopardize that Ivy League degree," a fraternity president told me once. I could see it. The expectations on fraternities had grown, with the creation in 1997 of the Strategic Plan, a structure for managing chapters that laid out academic, community service, and leadership goals to be met each year. Chapters were supposed to have faculty advisors, and live-in advisors. Not every chapter adhered to it very well, but the plan was there, and every chapter was assessed at the end of the year by how well it met university expectations.

✶ ✶ ✶

Tom accepted a bid from a fraternity that had several Navy ROTC men among its members. His parents, both Cornell graduates, approved. His father had not joined a fraternity but his mother still loved her sorority. Tom was the child of politicians, and inclined toward politics himself, though he had not been interested in student government at his suburban Philadelphia high school. Two other Navy men pledged with him: Chaz, a blond fellow from Florida, and Shane, who was from Michigan.

Chaz lasted about two days. The hazing began immediately, and while he understood the idea of putting people through physical and mental tests to see how tough they were, how committed, he did not see the value of this. Tom and Shane didn't either but decided to stick it out.

The pledge period was supposed to last 10 weeks, and every week brought new surprises. Tom was awakened in the middle of the night and told to report to the house, where he was screamed at while he and the other pledges stood, blinking, in a line. The men yelling at him were drunk and enjoying their power. In the back Tom saw the senior who had recruited him, who he had respected. That was fading rapidly.

One night the pledges did NOP—Night of Porn, a tradition. They sat watching porn on TV and could not move. If they did, they were struck by thrown objects. It went on for a couple of hours.

Tom thought of the Navy men who ordered him around with his fellow midshipmen. The man in charge was a 13-year Marine veteran, the gunnery sergeant. He knew what he was doing, Tom thought, not like these idiots.

The upbeat quality I saw in Tom when I met him was no illusion; he recovered quickly from setbacks. He was a wonderful companion who enjoyed finer things, like sailing (which he taught), learning to judge wine using all five senses, telling stories, beer, his family's Pocono cabin. He did not like school at all, never had. He saw little connection between his courses and the real world. He did enough to get by. But he understood the power of connections and saw it here, in a fraternity.

But this—being screamed at, up until all hours, having things thrown at him—was not what he'd hoped for.

The theory behind hazing is multi-faceted. If people are abused physically and mentally over weeks, they will be worn down and can then be built up again in spirit, in a way that fits the fraternity. The abuse—which varies with the fraternity, some being fairly benign—also makes a man show his loyalty, commitment to becoming part of the house, humility, ability to laugh off problems. It is also hoped that pledges will bond under duress, becoming closer friends and brothers as they help each other get through the torment. Their anger toward the brothers grows until the end, the final week, after which they are embraced into the fraternity and must not hold a grudge. It's a nice theory, but the reality is more complicated.

Men have tested each other's will and toughness for centuries. Many societies have rites of passage, times when boys become men and girls become women, and hazing is a natural extension. Fraternities began to incorporate hazing into their culture not long after they formed in the 19th century, adapting practices common in British public schools (where younger boys were subservient to older boys), adding tricks learned in Civil War military camps. Hazing lay deep in the male psyche. Many sports teams make rookies do menial tasks or put up with abuse. So do longtime male domains such as firefighting and police. College faculty even made new faculty stand in the dining hall and sing their alma maters, at the start of the 20th century. But by now, 1999, hazing had claimed lives and damaged bodies, because unlike societies where men guided boys, these practices were managed by men not much older than the pledges, sometimes carried away with their power. They did not always watch over the proceedings too closely, and accidents happened.

Another night, Tom and a couple of fellow pledges kidnapped a senior and were chased through Ithaca by brothers. Tom was driving, and he blew a stop sign as he tried to get away. A cop could see me, he thought, and I could get arrested and lose my ROTC scholarship. This sucks.

Tom knew about proving yourself. He had played football in high school, served as a co-captain. He started at center—a pulling center, escorting the quarterback down the field.

He stayed in the fraternity for five weeks to make sure he wasn't weak. Then he told the chapter president and pledge educator (the position formerly called pledge master or pledge whip) that he was done. Shane followed him, although Shane would pledge again in the fall and rise to become the fraternity's president.

Disappointed, Tom turned away from fraternities. For sophomore year he got an apartment with Chaz and a couple of other friends, and put it behind him.

TWO
Cliff's Edge
(Fall 1999)

My toes rested against the cliff's rough gray edge as I stared down at the murky brown water. I wanted to jump but could not.

Risk had never been my thing.

The water flowed only 25 feet below, and was plenty deep, and people were waiting for me to go. A couple dozen jumpers, from maybe 16 years old to 23, mostly male, lined the gorge near Ithaca on a late afternoon in September. They waited to jump or dive, as young people had been doing in Ithaca's gorges for decades, taking pleasure in the adrenaline rush and feat of bravery. All summer, into the fall, people did this every sunny day. It was illegal but the Cornell Police usually just gave everyone warnings. Our towels were draped over the metal fence around the cliff. Our jeans and shirts lay in small piles; my glasses lay on mine. A waterfall nearby roared so that we could barely hear each other, and mist came to us on the breeze.

"C'mon, Scott, don't think about it. Just go," called a student neighbor who had walked here with me, had jumped already, and now sat on a ledge below. I could see him if I squinted. *Yes, go.* I never would have done this at his age but I would now.

Good old Scott, chicken shit. Not athletic.

Look at me, chunky middle-aged dude among the (mostly) washboard stomachs, wearing plain old blue shorts among the guys in funkier shorts with their boxers sticking out around the waist, the current fashion. At least I had my big calves, courtesy of some Scottish Highlander ancestor.

I almost went, stopped.

"I'm going, and I'm a girl," yelled a young woman across the way.

"That's great, miss," I called back. "Doesn't have any impact on me—I'm past all that." *Though I might jump for your mother,* I thought. She jumped.

11

"I can't believe you're waiting for me," I said to the friend crouched on the ledge below.

"I can't believe I am either," he said.

"I don't know why I can't go."

"You'll go when you're ready."

I wanted to fall through space, to leave behind the despair that I'd been barely keeping at bay. My master's degree had not yet paid off. Lacking a clear direction, I was applying for jobs in public relations, magazine editing, even—God forbid—newspapers. I tutored foreign graduate students in writing their dissertations. I cashed bonds and sold stocks to pay my rent. I published a few articles. A man whose business was failing paid me to help him write letters to old clients. A professor in my department who specialized in risk communication paid me to research how farmers could be encouraged to be more safe, farming being one of the two most dangerous occupations in America (along with construction). An old friend from St. Lawrence had hired me to write a book about his son, a national champion wrestler at Ohio State, to be published by the family in time for Christmas.

In the past month I had finished as the runner-up for an editing job at Georgia and as a finalist for another at Penn State. Now I was runner-up for a public relations job at a community college, a job I had developed as a part-time employee. I knew that when a door closes, another opens, and I had not wanted the job much anyway. It did not pay well. But still.

I wanted to feel alive. No, that's too dramatic. I just wanted to risk my body, to defy fate, to fight my anxiety. Even my Cornell degree was a liability and boon at once. It got me interviews but turned off some employers, as if an Ivy Leaguer would be too much to handle.

I stepped off the cliff, arms to my side, feet flat. I hit and sank deeper than expected, stroked quickly to the surface, and gazed up as if from the bottom of a huge bowl of rock, as people cheered. I was thrilled.

A few weeks later I stood on a stone bridge at the mouth of that gorge, looking down from 33 feet, frozen. Two 18-year-old boys joined me, both over six feet tall and leanly muscled, striding onto the bridge as if they owned it. I had talked to them before. One, shoulders adorned with tattoos of snowflakes and waves, had imitated my perfect diction. They always seemed defiant here in Cornell's shadow, as if they would never belong. The tattooed one went to community college and was a pro snowboarder; he could dive and do flips off the bridge. They were part of a growing breed I'd encountered as a sports writer: athletic males raised by single women. "He's never had a male presence in his life," Tattoo Man's mother had told me. But under the tough exterior he didn't drink or smoke, and was becoming a Christian.

They jumped while hugged together, came apart in mid-air, hit the water sideways, and surfaced laughing. Seeing my hesitation, one of them said, "Want to jump with me, bear-hugging?" He meant it quite innocently. Apparently he would break the impact for me with his body. "No, thanks," I said. "I appreciate the offer, though." I finally jumped and seemed to hang in the air forever. I thought my form was fine, but hit my chin on the water and had whiplash for a day. Not as thrilling.

The teenager left me wondering, not for the first time or the last, what went on inside young people's heads.

✶ ✶ ✶

I was alone a great deal, a lifelong habit that had started to bother me. Friends were scattered because I had moved around or life had taken them away, or I had let them go. I didn't look for a life partner as hard as I should have, and didn't let it consume me. I had always enjoyed being alone, reading, or wandering with my camera, or in the darkroom. It was in my genes—an aunt and grandmother were the same way. And I was a writer, an outsider.

Probably it was just an inability to grow up and seek responsibility, move myself into love and fatherhood. I didn't particularly want children, though I felt lucky to have my nieces and nephew, helped look after them, remembered their birthdays.

At the same time I didn't want to latch onto something and wrap my life around it. I was the center of my world. I had long denied that, but steadily it screamed at me from deep down: change. In my working life, I was fed up with being a doormat, a supporting player, a hard-working man who was too diplomatic or lacking in courage to really matter. What to do? I didn't really want journalism, with all its cynical, soul-eating qualities. I wasn't sure journalism would take me back now that I'd been tainted, had worked as a flack: a PR person. Journalists were too in love with the dark and dirty, PR people too eager to scrub away complication. Yet I had to do something, and soon.

✶ ✶ ✶

An apple pie cooled on a windowsill just inside Chef's kitchen at Cornell's Zeta Psi fraternity chapter. Chef's cigarette lay next to it. I tried the

back door to see if it was unlocked, and it was. I stepped into this fraternity I had been visiting off and on for seven years, into the domain of this
middle-aged man who was part of it.

Zeta Psi was both open, allowing me to come and go practically as I
pleased, and closed, declining to let me see pledging activities. During the
pledge period, at the end of dinner I had to leave because the Zetes were
doing some pledge activity. It could not have been much, because they let
me go to the third floor, where I could hear laughter. They never seemed
to consider how rude it was to make a guest depart, and I simply accepted
it—the journalist is not part of what he writes about. The other choice was
to leave the house.

They were a mix of varsity athletes and guys who never touched a
weight, the handsome and the average, the charmer and the guy who was
unlikely to get a bid anywhere else, an "acquired taste" accepted by his
brothers but difficult to explain to outsiders. Over the years I had known
many of them. A Republican senior who had interned with U.S. Senator
Alfonse D'Amato cursed as he watched Bill Clinton take the White House
in 1992 and then fidgeted as he waited to see if D'Amato would win re-
election (he did, narrowly). Another senior's sunny calm turned to surli-
ness as graduation approached and he fretted about his lack of a job,
waiting to see if the CIA was going to hire him. The house manager,
charged with managing the property, moved out because his girlfriend
told him to choose her or Zeta Psi. The Zetes had at least one man of every
race, which made them diverse even for Cornell, one of the more diverse
universities in the nation. They kept a mattress on the roof in the spring,
for hooking up with ladies, and ran a wire from their third floor to the sidewalk out front, where they would launch a fork to slide down and break a
water balloon over an unsuspecting passerby. One night several of them
went to a brother's senior art exhibit—silver gelatin prints—but there was
a keg outside the gallery door and they hunkered around it, never setting
foot inside.

The Zetes maintained their own vision of what was cool. They
greeted the slender little chemistry major with the acid wit, who might
not pass muster elsewhere but became a valued part of them. One of their
resident studs was a blond Californian who received a few dollars every
month from a childhood movie role.

There I met for the first time a man who had been initiated long past
his college years: Chef, a few years younger than me, about 35, who had
been the fraternity's chef for nine years. A former stockbroker who had
turned to cooking to make a living, he was hired by Cornell at another

house and then came to Zeta Psi, where the men were unhappy with their cook. The first night Chef made dinner, a brother asked him to step into the dining room—and the men applauded him.

Chef loved making the best food he could for the men, to give them something after a long day of classes, and they loved him. He drank with them at their parties, cooked extra for big events such as Homecoming, and had his wife and daughters help with house functions involving alumni. During Senior Week, he hosted the seniors at his family's fishing camp on Lake Ontario.

Now Chef moved quickly among two ovens and two stoves, preparing rolls and the entrée and salad. Two Zetes sat on a counter near the window where the pie cooled, one puffing on his own cigarette. Brothers often hung out in the kitchen between classes and dinner, hearing Chef expound on politics and the 1970s and Cornell itself. He was a big man with a booming laugh and a ponytail. After his initiation, I kept asking him what it was like, to be brought into a circle of men half his age. "It's just been a tremendous part of my life," he said. "I'm a lucky man." Then one of the men, or sometimes an alumnus, would say, "Well, he's not really a brother." But he was. Chef was just as much at home as any of the 20-year-olds. On his birthday, the men followed the same custom they did with each other, carrying him upstairs—not easy, for he was 200 pounds—and sticking his head in a urinal, the classic swirlie.

Tex sauntered in. He was a football player from Texas who had come to Cornell determined that he would not "do a fraternity—I would not be a 'fratty' like the guys I saw back home." But friends on his hall were having such fun as Zeta Psi pledges that he asked for a bid and got one. The brothers saw him as a future president but he said rush chair fit him better. In some act of defiance he had made himself look like white trash: long hair and long sideburns. It didn't hurt his appeal. Tex worried about his engineer father, who could be downsized (that great cold word) any year. Tex asked how I was doing, I said I was looking, and he said, "Don't go back to the machine." He meant the traditional workplace. "Don't do it, man."

I glanced at Chef. He shrugged. He'd left all of that behind. A sign above the kitchen door said, "Chef's Place."

Chef's ability to fit in here fascinated me. I sometimes thought about the bid offers at SUNY Potsdam and the near-offers elsewhere. Chef was like an older brother to these guys. Being here with him was like stepping into some alternate reality where society's rules for what is normal for a certain age, had been suspended. Countless friends and former colleagues my age would not understand such a thing. But I saw so many relationships that defied norms, especially on a university campus, where whatever barriers lay between adults and young adults could fade in an instant.

✶ ✶ ✶

My communication department at Cornell had a party and I went because I needed to be seen, to be out in the world. The freelance writing was interesting but there was too little of it.

A professor glared at me and said he hated a letter I had written to the Ithaca newspaper, complaining about drivers who didn't use turn signals. I'm like that: I use turn signals. I also stop for stop signs, don't run red lights, and don't let people turn left when I have the right of way. I said too bad, but why didn't he signal to other drivers what he was doing? That was communication.

The department chair said someone was taking a medical leave for spring semester. Would I like to teach Science Writing for Public Information? I had done some grading for that course and knew what it entailed: writing for science and engineering majors mostly, with brochure and newsletter projects. Lots of writing. I said yes.

I was employed again.

THREE
Friends on a Mission
(Spring 2000)

The three freshmen had been talking and decided it was time for action. Their names were Jeff, Jay, and Alan, nicknamed "Train" (I never asked why). Cornell's fraternity rush was done and while they had looked at fraternities, they had not joined any. Now it was February and they were talking about getting a house or apartment off campus, but they had an idea. During rush they'd attended an information session for a fraternity, Phi Kappa Tau, gone for five years and starting up again.

They walked down the hall to a room belonging to another freshman named Adam. He liked what they were going to do. I'll make the call, Jay said, and on Adam's wall phone dialed the number of Phi Kappa Tau national headquarters in Oxford, Ohio.

The four were part of a loose group of friends in Mary Donlon Hall who had either not bothered with rush or had not found what they wanted among the houses they visited—had not liked enough men, had not identified with whatever personality they found in each house, had not believed anyone who said there was no hazing. But the notion of belonging to a fraternity nagged at them and they remembered the information session.

About 11 to 15 freshmen were very or mildly interested. Among them were two of Jay's three roommates, who were from Southern California and Buffalo, and several other guys he had met while watching baseball last fall in a lounge. He was a New York Mets fan and the Mets were playing the Atlanta Braves. Train was an Asian-American from SoCal who majored in hotel administration, Adam was a business major from a town nearby, and Jeff was an industrial and labor relations major from Long Island. Their group also included an Indian biological engineering major from nearby Rochester (Nieraj), a muscular fellow from Massachusetts who did not drink because his body was a temple and who was going to major in natural resources (Magnus), a blond guy from suburban Philadelphia (JB),

17

and a Latino guy from Westchester County with a smooth manner and big smile (Andres, called Dre). Jeff had two classmates at Cornell from his Long Island high school and they were part of this too: Joe and Rob, known as Komo (a shortening of his last name). Joe and Jeff had feuded over a girl in high school but were on good terms now. There were two other Long Islanders named Dennis (Dream) and Paul (Paulie).

At the center of it all was Jay: sharp-tongued wiseguy, quick and decisive, whose stocky build did not hint at what a fine athlete he was. They followed his lead. When he did not get a bid from a fraternity he was rushing, they turned to him.

The information session had been given by two young men, Gabe and Winky, who were about 23 and spoke like salesmen, and an alumnus of the defunct chapter named Pat Madden. Make this chapter whatever you want, they said. We want this to be a strong chapter that is different, that doesn't have hazing and does lots of community service and has campus leaders. Other than that, build it as you wish. This is your chance to be founding fathers (they didn't add that founding fathers was not quite right, since Phi Tau national already had four of those who had started this thing in 1906).

"Make your mark, gentlemen."

Phi Tau's national leaders had decided it was time. They would find an "interest group" which would become a "colony," re-building the chapter with a fusion of what the men wanted with what national expected and taught from both traditions and fresh ideas. Phi Tau's national leaders had concluded, like many of their brethren at other national fraternities, that the times demanded change if Greeks were to not just endure but grow. Since 1906 the fraternity had founded more than 140 chapters, but they had collapsed left and right until now 85 remained. Strong in the Midwest and South—Ohio and Kentucky especially—Phi Tau had only a handful of chapters in New York, and some of them were struggling. Cornell's chapter might mark a comeback, and it wouldn't hurt to have a chapter in the Ivy League again. At the same time, the national leaders were trying to re-define the whole thing around the slogan "Building Men of Character."

Fraternities in the South and Midwest tend to recruit and pledge freshmen in the fall, but in the Northeast freshmen must get through their first semester before committing themselves to a Greek organization. Cornell's rush in January 2000 presented an opportunity to find new blood. This was why Gabe and Winky had talked to freshmen in Mary Donlon Hall. Like DRI the year before, the two men didn't find many takers. They even walked through the residence halls, handing out flyers.

Now Jay spoke to Gabe, who was director of chapter services. We have a group that's interested, Jay said. Gabe and Winky returned to Ithaca the next week, and for a week they met with the men. They laid out just what this enterprise would require: the forming of a "colony" that would eventually prove its strength at managing itself, attracting new members, and holding higher standards, until it got back chapter status. Eleven men signed on, although two dropped out quickly.

I did not know them then and had never heard of Phi Tau. This part of the story comes from what they told me.

They agreed that they would bring new members into the fold without hazing because hazing had no purpose. They would require each member to do 15 hours of community service per semester. They would seek men who did not want the typical frat boy thing, who would be classy, especially with women.

The nine set about recruiting more men. They met in the dining hall a hundred yards away, and in a basement room at Mary Donlon, and elected officers. As vice president they chose Komo, a neuroscience and psychology major who was quite structured and could get irritated quickly when the room erupted into chaos. Jay's roommate from SoCal, named Garrett, became secretary and a sophomore named Tope became treasurer because he knew money, having sold a dot-com before the dot-com crash. They added a social chair for whenever they started having parties, not to mention mixers with sororities: Magnus. A philanthropy chair would coordinate community service (Nieraj), and a rush chair would direct the finding of new blood (Andres). And at the top, Jay became president.

JB knew a sophomore from home that might be interested, who had quit a fraternity last year: Tom. After Tom decided to give fraternity life another try, he brought in two other sophomores from Navy ROTC, one of them Chaz, and with them came a sophomore from Florida. By early April they had 21 members.

I can picture them now, a group that walked together everywhere, all talking at once like a flock of crows. They sounded 35 years old at times, indeed they always seemed mature, to have taken on this task. Joe always said they weren't so much mature as consumed by the sheer challenge of what lay ahead. No question they represented not just Cornell students—toward the top of the class in high school, belonging to all sorts of clubs, hoping their Ivy League degree would bring them riches—but their generation as well, the Millennials, just arriving in college. I have read the profile of this generation and it basically fits the founding group: collaborative, high expectations of themselves and others, deeply informed, accustomed to the wonders of online technology, supremely confident at least on the outside. Every opinion mattered and everyone was heard, even if they should have stayed quiet. Not many of them had cell phones yet but that would change, and they were far more at home with new technologies than I would ever be, as instant messaging and cell phones with cameras would come along. I don't think they knew much about fraternities, but they learned.

A colony needed to be nurtured and given a foundation, so that the members could steer through problems. It was amazing how quickly a colony or young chapter could go sour. A couple of weak leaders, poor teaching of new members, guys losing faith in the plan: in no time any of these could pull a new chapter into trouble. They would start doing the same stupid, crude, insensitive things lesser chapters did, partying out of control, letting house business or community service slip away, not caring, breaking the law.

Gabe and Winky said little about the chapter's alumni. The colony would need to establish an alumni relations program and begin reaching out to the 500 chapter alumni, most of whom had heard little from the place in years. But alumni were also a problem for a colony. Wanting to please these older men who could offer stories (and money), young men might adopt traditions that national staff didn't want them to. Men from the Cornell Phi Tau's era of "anti-fraternity," the 1980s and 1990s, were especially not welcome yet. Let the colony first learn national history, and the history of fraternities in general. Let the colony write its constitution and figure out how to manage itself. Later, the men could decide what if anything they wanted to adopt from that time.

At the front of the room for these meetings, Jay exuded confidence and decisiveness. Men followed him. He was Jewish, like one-quarter of Cornell's students, but this did not seem a large part of his identity. He had tried out for club lacrosse, with Magnus, but they had concluded that most of the men who got to play were either seniors or from a certain fraternity. Jay's biggest hero was his father, a jewelry store owner who had gone into politics and gotten elected town councilman. Their township in Nassau County was especially blue-collar, and Jay could slip between a tough-guy manner, aiming profanity at his friends, and then suddenly grin and show his intelligence with a well-considered response. He always had that warmer side beneath his gruffness.

Gabe and Winky pushed them to adopt two slogans: "Men of Character" and "A Cut Above." They would not be frat boys.

Did these men understand how ambitious they were? Did it matter? They were caught up in the task before them, eager to create something that would last after they graduated. Cornell is so huge and imposing, its Nobel and Pulitzer winners, its world-class research centers. Most people there feel like barnacles on a whale.

FOUR
Call Me Professor
(Spring 2000)

My life changed because I was too lazy to bring a lunch, requiring a trip to Trillium Dining Hall below my office, for soup and coffee and maybe a half-moon cookie.

Near the tall windows I saw Tom eating. He wore his Navy khakis, this being Wednesday. April was starting, so outside it felt warmer. Tom greeted me and I asked what was new.

"I've joined a fraternity, a new one starting up," he said. "Phi Kappa Tau."

Yes, the student newspaper had carried an article about it. I had visited maybe a dozen Cornell fraternities and knew the system well but had never heard of this one. I was unaware that Tom had pledged elsewhere the year before and then quit.

"We don't have the house—we're just a colony, so we won't get the house back until we get our charter back," he said.

A colony, huh. Some colonies lasted only a couple of years before going bad—gaining (or learning from alumni) habits and customs that got them in trouble. But some grew into strong chapters.

"Say, don't you do research on fraternities?" Tom said. "Don't you know a lot about fraternity issues?"

I guessed I did.

"Would you like to speak at our weekly meeting? We meet on Sunday nights."

Sure, I said. It seemed like a chance to organize my thoughts and lecture about something besides writing.

Phi Tau had been gone for five years and the new version would be a different kind of fraternity. Tom mentioned the non-hazing, service-oriented, higher-standard vision of these men. It sounded like a smart strategy, if idealistic.

✶ ✶ ✶

Calculators—why were there calculators in a writing class?

Ah, yes, engineering students and their problem sets. I stared up at the corner of the small auditorium, at the group I had dubbed the Party of Five, and they saw me and put away the calculators. My lecture today would be about brochure design and, in my usual shift of gears within a period, punctuation. I did not want to cover punctuation, because college students, especially Ivy League students, should know it. But in the age of Spell Check and writing software, of high schools that stressed structure and content but not the finer points, punctuation and word usage were dying arts.

I was teaching at Cornell for the first time in a year and a half, pleased to have a steady paycheck. There I was, facing mostly biology and engineering students, a clientele I didn't associate with writing. The two lectures had 39 and 41 students, way bigger than a writing class should be, but I was just happy to have work again. Communication 260, Science Writing for Public Information, was about conveying scientific and technical material to people who didn't know much about it. I liked most of the students even if they could be more intense than what I was accustomed to, the pre-med students especially. I loved writing and wanted them to love it, even if most were here just for graduation requirements and grades. My science background was slim, so I said I was an English major and writer, and made them meet me halfway. Most weren't accustomed to a professor who knew their names and something about them, asking questions from 10 feet away. They knew big lecture halls.

I talked about punctuation—road signs to lend order, pieces of a system for conveying ideas—and then brochure design and the use of visuals. I collected their weekly writing assignment, slipped my notes and folders into a nylon pouch, and headed across the Ag Quad to my building. Man, this was tougher than I remembered. These kids were so bright, and I was struggling to relate my material to the engineers. I had not faced many battles over grades, maybe because I was giving out a lot of A's. In fact, I could tell that the grades were too high—more than half of the students were carrying an A or A-minus. That would not sit well with the department or Cornell. Next semester the syllabus would have to be tweaked, the course more difficult, my grading standards higher—if the ill lecturer did not return and if I were hired back. Unable to afford Ithaca, I had moved 25 miles northeast to the small city of Cortland, where I knew hardly anyone. And here I was, pleased to have even a one-semester appointment.

I had forgotten the hostility (mine and theirs), the contest of wills, my wanting something and their not wanting to do it or understanding why it mattered. Having read that students now were spoon-fed everything, I didn't want to teach that way, but I wasn't always as clear as they needed me to be either. Every week's pile of papers hit me with unclear word combinations, poor endings, misspelled words, until it was like static on the radio and I heard nothing else. Yet I was grading gently, having forgotten that toughness works better. I did let a couple of them do projects over again rather than give them an F, something their engineering faculty would have sneered at. The Ruth Strodt Rule, I called it, after the math professor at St. Lawrence who had allowed me to take a final exam between semesters after I missed it, rather than flunk me.

* * *

The colony met in a science seminar room right out of the 1930s that smelled of chalk and much-polished wood. Through the closed door I saw young men wearing coat and tie sitting around four tables put together to make one large table. Tom appeared in the hallway as I waited, followed by a dark-haired fellow he introduced as Jay, the freshman who was the colony's president. I was accustomed to dealing with seniors and juniors, wise elders who would teach freshmen how to manage the organization, its budget, its parties, and how to recruit new members and make them part of the brotherhood. A second-semester freshman as president—that would take some time to absorb.

In a corner sat a bespectacled, good-looking man in his mid-twenties: LeGrand, the chapter advisor, who worked in Greek alumni relations for Cornell. He was not a Phi Tau; in college he had belonged to Lambda Chi Alpha. I thought, how perfect for the university, to have its thumb on this new fraternity from the start, and how unfortunate for me that my audience would include a man who had actually belonged to a fraternity. I was a semi-fraud, as with my old job of newspaper sports writer, where I wrote about sports I had never played. But LeGrand just listened politely.

I spoke for maybe 15 minutes and then took questions. I said fraternities were under fire from a society where the lawsuit ruled, where young men were expected to show they valued more than just other men like themselves, where young people were told to have fun but at the same time be adult. I outlined the history of national fraternities. In a way, the Phi Taus were like a fraternity of the early decades, where groups of men gathered to discuss current literature and politics that was forbidden in the classroom, meeting—like the men in front of me—wherever they could. They wrote creeds and rituals, adopted ancient Greek ideals for living, enjoyed brandy and cigars. They founded other chapters of their fraternities at campuses that wanted them, and broke off to form new fraternities.

I said that in the early 20th century, freshmen had to fight their way onto campus. This was called rush, a word that today means recruiting new members. I told them about hazing's origins. Later, after World War Two, men came to college on the GI Bill and added what they'd learned in boot camp, although some said no, they'd already gone through hell and wouldn't let younger guys do anything to them.

The Phi Taus drank in everything I said. Around the table I saw with my baby boomer sensibility the mix of them, from thin to athletic, white and brown and black. They seemed very young and kind of geeky—a harsh outlook on my part.

The questions came at me, mostly from a black fellow.

"How should we try to recruit new guys?"

"If hazing is so bad, why do fraternities do it?"

"Why are fraternities singled out as targets?"

I stuck with a neutral tone. The truth was, I had begun as an objective researcher who saw why fraternities were hated and was leery of how they could form a pack mentality and demand blind loyalty. Yet I had begun to believe in what a fraternity could be, from my travels.

As I drove home, watching for deer along the country roads, I thought about my Monday morning lecture. I always felt under-prepared on Mondays. I mulled over some cases of students missing class or performing badly. Some students were chewed up by Cornell or by their own lives. There was the senior who never knew what was going on; I suspected the death of her father the previous fall was affecting her. There was the senior who showed up two weeks late because his parents were divorcing and he was trying to referee. He never did give the course much effort, pouring his energy into his role as pledge educator. There was the fraternity president whom I had known since his freshman year, when I did a focus group on his hall about Greek images. There were nine men who thought about going to the same fraternity, a "package deal," then split among four fraternities and, for two of them, remaining independent. There was the junior who had a strong "A" going and then vanished for two weeks, until I decided it was my business and tracked him down. There was the senior who was taking a year's worth of credits at once, with a wife, baby, and business to occupy what other time he had.

Was this really my job, to care? No, but I did.

Phi Tau drifted in and out of my thoughts.

These men had lofty ideals, like the well-behaved boy in school. It would be interesting to see how this colony fared.

* * *

Tom asked if I would serve as Phi Tau's faculty advisor. Cornell's administration wanted every fraternity and sorority to have one, along with the chapter advisor. I said yes, if I were hired for the fall. I had not set out to teach at a college but now I wanted to. The communication department was part of the College of Agriculture and Life Sciences, Cornell being New York's land-grant university. My writing courses—the one I taught now and the magazine class I had taught before—would be part of an English or journalism department elsewhere, but here they were remnants of a "communication arts" department that was morphing into social sciences.

Tom invited me to the colony's barbecue the first Saturday in May. This was Phi Tau's traditional Spring Weekend; the men were honoring a custom. I said yes.

The last day of classes was Slope Day, a remnant of the Spring Weekend celebrated when the legal drinking age was 18. Thousands of students skipped class to drink on a quarter-mile slope on Central Campus. Cornell had hoped to rid itself of this party day, but it remained, so the university grudgingly supplied medical and police personnel, water, and volunteers to patrol for problems. I was a volunteer. I flowed with the day, firmly mellow, carrying water for students who told me they wanted a different kind of liquid. My own students were freaked out that I would see them drunk, a common reaction on the rare times I encountered them in the bars next to campus. They would stare, look away, then maybe absorb my being a person outside of the classroom, and be polite. Amateur time: students who seldom drank pounded down gin and vodka. For two hours, I checked on students who were sleeping or passed out, to make sure they wouldn't choke on their own vomit. I didn't see the Phi Taus anywhere nor did I look for them.

The next afternoon I found the Phi Taus in a park on Cayuga Lake's south end. The men were playing softball and ultimate frisbee, shirts against skins. I found Tom, who had taken over the grill to cook hot dogs and hamburgers. A handful of alumni were there, veterans of the 1980s, come back to look over this group who were going to re-found their fraternity chapter. These men worked mostly in computer-related fields. Jay and the other Phi Tau officers introduced themselves and made small talk.

I said hello too and added that I might be the faculty advisor next year.

"You might be?"

"Well, I'm confident I will be," I said.

"A faculty advisor? We had one but we hardly ever saw him."

The young Phi Taus were friendly to the alumni but unsure, for these were the men who had lost the chapter. Cornell students don't like failure. Yet I understood how a fraternity could fade, how over time the men would lose or reject what earlier generations had done, how a couple of weak years—few pledges, poor leadership—could send the whole chapter on a downward spiral. These alumni had kept alive the hope that the fraternity they loved, where they had grown up, could come back.

Across the park the guys battled at ultimate frisbee, sending the white disc coasting against the blue sky. An alumnus joined them, which they liked. Maybe I should jump in there. No, the sidelines were a comfortable place for me. I had spent my life observing, recording, the manager of sports, the photographer. I observed but did not always learn, one minute wise and clear in my thinking, the next minute muddled. I saw without seeing.

Did I want to be a fraternity advisor again? I had done alright at SUNY Potsdam. I tried to keep the peace and help the fraternities understand the townspeople, alumni, and college itself, and work with them. But I kept my distance, following the college's policy that an advisor to a student group needed to be hands-off, but with some guidance. That was a problem with fraternities: You couldn't leave them to their own devices.

What I might gain, I could only guess.

Part of me said a fraternity advisor really needed to be more successful, tougher at confrontation, and maybe a father himself. Aw, the hell with that. In many ways I was a fine specimen of middle age, loaded with experience. My friendships were strong but fewer than in my youth. I took my family for granted, loved my siblings' children but was glad to leave them when my visit was over. I liked being alone, too much. Finding a soul mate had never been a high priority for me, but now I found that people almost preferred that you had married and divorced a couple of times to never marrying, as if anyone who had not married had not really grown up. I lived with it. I was either a tough survivor or an unstable mess, depending on the person. In my cynical moments, it seemed inevitable that every man of my generation would be laid off, or be jobless for some reason, or suffer a blow to his business. Changing careers, getting a degree late in life: the way of the future.

These Phi Tau men were caught up in the struggles of their age group and, as if they needed more, the building of a fraternity—discovering just what they'd gotten into. They did not have time to think about how I might help them. That day, it just seemed that advising a fraternity would be good for me, and besides, this fraternity seemed tame enough, even boring. Whatever messiness developed would be LeGrand's deal, not mine. He was their teacher and coach.

Tom amused me, even as I respected his outgoing ways. This colony would need him.

The Phi Taus' mix of men appealed to me. I had seen plenty of fraternities where the men look like they walked out of a clothing catalogue, all teeth and sharp cheekbones and chiseled bodies. If someone who didn't look that way got in, it was because of an ally or some quality that the brotherhood liked. A fraternity that accepted all manner of men usually struggled. Over time it might change as the brothers sought out good-looking men, and those men nudged the chapter in their own direction. "You don't look for guys like yourself, you look for guys you wish you were," a Cornell fraternity member once told me. "Then those guys take over. As a senior you belong to a house that would not accept you if you rushed now." Once initiated, a man is always a brother, but that doesn't mean he's part of that inner core that pushes the thing. The Phi Taus established that they valued how a man carried himself and what he stood for, who he was deep down, more than how he looked.

My own life, I kept to myself. I would say that I covered sports, and mention professional athletes I had interviewed. I would present myself as a successful man. The men never asked me much about myself in the first couple of years, out of indifference or politeness. They were learning so many truths about themselves that they didn't worry about me.

Yes, working with a fraternity might be good for me. It would give me credibility as I wrote my book about fraternities. I felt no bond with these men. I liked their commitment to recruiting all kinds of members. We fit each other. But mostly they were just guys that I would advise about school.

FIVE
Colony
(Fall 2000)

Winky was shorter than I was but muscular, and he radiated confidence. We met for breakfast at Trillium one Wednesday in September. Jay the Phi Tau president was there too, in fact this was supposed to be a meeting with him. But national wanted to know more about me, and Winky was making one of his periodic drives through the area, as one of national's traveling consultants.

I had class in a half hour or so. I had been re-appointed to my lecturer position in the Department of Communication for the fall semester. The other lecturer had not returned from medical leave. More good news: I could limit the science writing lectures to 25 students. The bad news: I had four lectures adding up to 95 students—four in a row, with a lunch break. I'd beefed up the standards in science writing. A future law student said my standards were still too low. As usual, students tried to get out of doing assignments, or shone brilliantly. A few said they liked writing better after hearing about it from me.

I could officially become Phi Tau's faculty advisor. The Phi Taus returned ready to work. Their house at 106 The Knoll still rented out, they met in several different classrooms and lived in residence halls near each other on North Campus. Like other fraternities they began to recruit new men in August, when the 18-year-olds walked in small herds from orientation events at the Arts Quad, to Collegetown, hoping to find a bar that would let them in or parties in houses—the "fraternity annexes." Rush chairs waited along the sidewalk, cups in hand, inviting freshman males up to the annex house. A keg on a porch looked like an apple core coated with ants, as students swarmed around it, until city police would appear and chase everyone off. As the semester wore on, fraternities met prospects in class or through female friends, or open houses, or weekly drinking sessions. The Phi Taus would be a colony until they could show national that they were on their way. Then they would move into their house, and have their charter presented to them.

Jay said nothing that morning. He and I would never have so much as a conversation during his term as president. I learned later that he was nervous about having a writer inside the fraternity.

"Do you understand how much work it is to be a fraternity advisor?" asked Winky.

Looking at the clock—I hated to be late—I said I thought so. He asked if I was going to write about the men. I said no, I would just use them as a layer of reference in my research (this book came about only because they said it could).

"Being an advisor can be very rewarding," he said. "You might become close to the men. My chapter had an advisor who had us over for dinner, and regarded us almost as his sons."

I said I understood. I told myself that would probably not happen to me.

Winky asked Jay to get him a guest pass to a fitness center.

"You're not big enough to work out there," Jay said. That gym was used mostly by men who were especially intense. Winky, who was indeed big enough, glared at him. Jay grinned insolently. I was to see that grin many times.

Whatever else led to my becoming faculty advisor, I never heard. I suppose Jay, LeGrand, and the Board of Governors chair approved it. Most fraternities were happy just to find faculty who would have anything to do with them. My duties were vague: be a resource in academics and write recommendation letters. Sounded easy enough.

✳ ✳ ✳

JB played and sang in a rock band, and we went to see a performance at a place called The Nines. Underage people could be there but not drink, although the men ordered pitchers of beer using fake ID. Maybe one of the juniors was 21 but I doubted it. I sat with them but didn't drink. I had not bought the beer for them, so I wasn't going to be punished if anything happened; I had only to mind my status as advisor. Most fraternity advisors I knew did not drink with their men, even when the men asked them to. I already had, a little.

The Nines was tough on underage drinkers. The staff would take a beer from a student's hand and tell him or her to hit the road. Most students believed drinking was their right, part of college, and they resented being monitored this way. To them anybody who stopped them from drinking was a villain, period. I didn't point out that every year bars closed—people lost their businesses—because students saw the law as just inconvenience.

The Phi Taus were coming into focus for me, even if I attended their meetings only twice a month. Beyond their range of ethnicities they could be broken down in other ways. Most were from families of two or three children, where I'd grown up with families of five or six. I was the oldest of four. In time the colony would have men who were the only child in their families. Three of the men didn't drink and one was vegetarian. A few were Catholic (Hitman ushered at a church in town). They were mostly well-off, sons of professional people, except for a few blue-collar men like Joe and Dream. Two were varsity athletes, on the track and soccer teams. Dream was an intramural official.

They wrote a constitution so they would have officer descriptions and procedures for voting on everything, getting this ambitious vision of a fraternity firmly in their hearts and minds, not easy because they were critical. They were tough on each other, calling out each other on every mistake or action that deviated from this plan of theirs. "Founders" was a misnomer but it sounded sexier than Re-Founding Group or Colonists. They kept each other in line. In time I would learn that they were not all friends, more like business partners in a way, learning to trust each other and gaining a sense of each other's abilities. Every fraternity is like this to an extent, and in every fraternity, friendships form and fade. Somehow I wanted these men to be different but they were not, not in that sense.

The group called themselves an anti-fraternity, a term that sounded brave but was not accurate. An anti-fraternity was more like the old version of Phi Tau that had collapsed. The men used the label because they weren't sure what else to call this thing they had set in motion.

The men met in classrooms at that science building. Afterward they often gathered at a place called The Chariot, below street level in the lower part of Collegetown, to eat pizza and corn nuggets—corn kernels roasted into a hard treat.

✶ ✶ ✶

The colony added one more member: a sophomore friend of Dream's who chose Phi Tau over the fraternity where Tom and Chaz had depledged.

The men did the ceremony themselves for the first time, at a townhouse where Train, Dre, and Adam lived. The sophomore had no idea it was coming. Hitman and Dream had painted their faces in a tribal manner, big swaths of brown around their eyes and cheeks, which was not part of the national way. LeGrand and I were watching from the kitchen, and LeGrand just shrugged and said we can persuade them to do this with more dignity next time. He was more hands-on than I was, he would tell them when they messed up and how they should be doing things, but that day belonged to them.

SIX
Homecoming
(Fall 2000)

The Friday of Homecoming Weekend, Phi Tau had a wine and cheese reception for alumni at a house in Collegetown where one of the juniors, Tope, lived. The men were a bit anxious, so as an elder who had worked with alumni in a previous job, I actually put in my two cents. I said to just listen to the older men's stories, get a feel for what the fraternity was like in their time, be nice to their wives (who, if unhappy, might dissuade their husbands from returning in the future), and abstain from drinking. I said some of the men had married women from nearby Wells College, who could tell as many stories about Phi Tau as they could.

The alumni walked in and looked around uncertainly, so I met them at the door along with Jay and Tom. As with the barbecue in April, these men were from the 1980s. One of them, Bob Cundall the engineer, asked, "Are these guys going to be swallowing goldfish, the way we did during pledging?" I said no, whatever traditions the new men adopted from the old would be up to them, but silly hazing stunts were out.

The alumni asked me what they should do about drinking wine in the same room with current Phi Taus who weren't drinking with them. "You didn't buy the alcohol," I said, and added that while it was best to avoid situations where underage guys were drinking, you couldn't always—a beer might appear in a freshman's hand when you didn't expect it. "The guys won't drink while you're here," I said. "My approach for several years now has been to stay maybe a half hour, maybe an hour, at any fraternity function."

So we did. As the alumni and I left, the guys were playing video games in the living room and, in a sort of quiet defiance, had beers in their hands.

* * *

Homecoming also meant our first tailgate before the football game, another chance to mingle with alumni and hang out with each other. And that was where we first met Lou.

While I waited for a hamburger I saw several students nearby who were painting "GO CORNELL!" in red letters on their bare chests, one letter per man. The only Phi Tau was Chaz, now a junior; the rest were his Navy ROTC buddies except for this fellow with a red "E" on his chest and stomach, a freshman who looked like an athlete. He was grinning as if this were his fantasy of college life come true and these were the best guys in the world.

Waving smoke from the grill away from my face, I asked someone who he was. A rushee, maybe, I was told. Lou looked too much like a jock to fit in. Our colony had a few athletes, and we liked sports fine, on ESPN or wherever. We had just begun to enter teams in intramural football and soccer. Several guys camped out for hockey season tickets and went to most games. But this freshman looked like the kind of frat guy we wanted to avoid. Of course, we already had guys who liked their booze; I just hadn't quite seen that side of us yet.

The men were pushing hard for Lou to rush Phi Tau when January arrived. It wasn't just that they liked him. They were worried that nobody would want to join their colony.

✳ ✳ ✳

I was invited to dinner with the chapter and alumni. The day before, Zeta Psi had asked if I would be faculty advisor. I had heard of people who advised more than one fraternity, so I said yes. An hour before the dinner, Tom gave me a ride to my parking lot. I told him about Zeta Psi.

His jaw tightened. He looked straight ahead through his Jeep Cherokee's windshield.

"I don't like it," he said. "You are our advisor. I don't think you should be some freelance advisor."

"Well," I said, surprised, "I could say no."

Tom said, "It's not brotherhood."

Brotherhood? Nobody had ever challenged me to be a brother. I decided he was right. I said I would go right to Zeta Psi and tell the president I could not do it. Tom said, "Don't let me pressure you." I said no, I would end the situation right now. He nodded. Zeta Psi was nearby. The president understood right away why I was saying no. I drove to the restaurant downtown and joined everyone.

That was the beginning of my thinking about what it meant to be a friend, a brother, a person who cared. This was the first time I began to really feel Phi Tau.

Maybe I was too skeptical. Maybe I should give this brotherhood thing a try, even as an advisor. It would mean surrendering part of myself to a greater whole. I never really had done that.

SEVEN

Fat Albert and Other Follies

(Fall 2000)

"**A**lright, let's get going. Shut the hell up."

Jay waited for quiet, standing at the front of the room. Then the men stood and recited Phi Tau's creed to start their weekly meeting. I remained silent—the creed had little to do with me. It was a warm Sunday night, and we were gathered in a basement classroom in that same old building where I'd met them.

We went through the agenda, hearing reports. The social chair spoke of possible sorority mixers and drinking events at Tom and Chaz's apartment. The treasurer asked for receipts from officers, the alumni relations chair described attempts to find and contact brothers from the past, and the philanthropy chair listed community service projects. I don't recall hearing anything from the new member educator, because their program was being developed. They did not have a house manager or a steward (the man who works with the cook to manage the kitchen and menu) because they did not live in the house yet.

My role was still vague, which in some ways didn't bother me. Better not to be telling them how to live or behave, for students resented that and Americans in general seemed to resist any authority more than ever. I was glad to let LeGrand handle the molding of these young minds.

The colony's constitution was coming along. So was the non-hazing new member program. Maybe they had toyed with trying a hazing event, to see what it was like—after all, didn't most fraternities do it?—and then dismissed the idea. They listened to LeGrand on the fine points of what their fraternity would be about. He pushed them toward crafting a pledge program devoid of anything resembling hazing, even such seemingly benign events as scavenger hunts or pledges interviewing brothers about themselves, because he knew that scavenger hunts can be about stealing property and that interviews can become a form of imposing power on a pledge. LeGrand critiqued the men's progress, partly by preaching and

34

partly by asking them about their choices, letting them think through it. He was teaching—like me, except that I assigned grades.

LeGrand and I feared that once they tried hazing, the guys would be hooked, and that would start the proverbial slippery slope where they would develop newer and more brutal forms of hazing in the years ahead. That seemed to be the pattern in other chapters. Tom and Chaz's friend Shane had de-pledged from that other fraternity when they did, but had gone back. He told Tom that we would have hazing eventually, it was inevitable. Tom said, "Like hell." The Phi Taus joked about making pledges have sex with goats or sheep. For the next couple of years, they would make comments along the lines of "You'll need to choose your sheep," to see the associate members' reaction.

Jay asked for my faculty advisor's report. I found that addressing them made me nervous, maybe because this was an alien environment, not like my classroom. I reminded the guys that I could write recommendation letters, for jobs or graduate school, but since they were all sophomores and juniors, there was little call for that yet. "I'm available to talk to anyone about how they are doing in school," I said, knowing full well that in terms of grade point average, Phi Tau already was one of the higher-ranked fraternities. "I also have photos from the touch football game last week to give out." As I did everywhere, I had begun photographing their events.

The colony already had its own beer pong (or Beirut) champions, the team of Dream and Hitman. Dream was all brawn and emotion, very Italian. Hitman was a bundle of contrasts, equally intense about his engineering studies, drinking, and competing at anything. I constantly saw new sides to him. I once saw him carrying a trombone case—he played in a campus orchestra. The two made a raucous Beirut pair.

Tonight the men closed the meeting with a discussion about the T-shirt that would be sold to promote the week's big event, their first party. A party: Yes, the men were underage, but they were also restless to start being an actual fraternity. Phi Tau had rented another fraternity's house for the event.

The T-shirt mattered because fraternities use shirts to promote events and unify themselves. The Phi Taus knew they wouldn't use a raunchy or suggestive slogan, as many houses did. A T-shirt could be sold to promote the party, and then it would be seen around campus for the next couple of years, forming part of a house's image. Suggestive was fun, and people might laugh it off as the work of naughty college guys, but Phi Tau was too new and wanted to be different. The men chose an Eighties Night Out theme. They needed an image for the shirt's back, something emblematic of that decade. I thought immediately of two movies, *Ferris Bueller's Day Off* and *Back to the Future*. Someone nominated Ferris Bueller. They argued and spouted ideas, which Jay wrote on the blackboard. They could not agree.

"We are not leaving until you bitches decide on something," Jay said.

"C'mon, Jay," they said, groaning.

"No, I mean it. We need to have something tonight."

Finally, someone yelled out, "Fat Albert." No way, I thought. Bill Cosby's character was from the 1960s and 1970s. But the cry went through the room, yes, perfect, we all grew up with Fat Albert.

Where, I wondered, through cartoon re-runs? "I don't like this idea," I told Tom afterward.

"Neither do I," he said, looking grim. A caricature of a black man on a T-shirt would be asking for trouble from black students. Tom could see the repercussions and was calculating what to do. A day later, he reported the men had changed their minds. Fat Albert seemed potentially racist. They chose Ferris Bueller instead, so Matthew Broderick graced the shirt.

As would happen often over the years, while I was fretting over a situation and debating what to do, it blew over. The party was a success, I heard later. Fall parties are used as recruiting tools, and hopefully the guys attracted a few freshmen. It didn't sound like a big party, big being desirable—lots of women and freshmen—but it was a start. They needed to get the hang of parties: finding a theme that worked, getting out the word about who they were.

The men also held their first mixer with a sorority, again at someone else's house. Sororities could not host parties, if they belonged to the Panhellenic Association and adhered to national rules. In many municipalities, a houseful of women who hosted alcohol and men was technically a brothel.

✶ ✶ ✶

Hitman rolled out with the football in his right hand, Dream and Magnus in front to slow down the opponent fraternity. They weren't really blocking, as this was flag football. Jay and Adam ran downfield, looking back.

They were at the intramural fields off North Campus. The colony had entered its first intramural football team, in a fraternity division. Hitman was splitting quarterback duties with Jay.

Hitman saw Adam racing down the sideline and launched the ball. It slipped into Adam's hands but one of the opponents dove from his left and ripped the flag from the band of nylon around his waist. A couple more times we tried, but could not score. As the autumn sun faded into a smudge in the gray sky, and the lights came on, Phi Tau lost.

Phi Tau did not win much—not enough athletes, or maybe not enough experience at playing together. But through the sweat, the sight of the ball spiraling through the air, the mistakes and the little heroics— there they felt together. You could see it. They were becoming a unit. Football allowed them to prove they were like other fraternities at least in this respect.

At chapter Joe reported that we had won at something: bowling. We were undefeated. They all laughed at how they excelled at a nerd game.

Dream, who was sports chair, had started a new tradition: every week he named someone who had excelled in sports as his Dream Teamer of the Week. Starting the next spring, he would choose a brother as Dream Teamer of the Year for contributions to Phi Tau athletics. That night he gave the weekly award to Adam, who was as skilled at sports as he was quiet. And he was very quiet. Whoever sat next to him in chapter could always get a laugh by saying, "Sorry, couldn't hear you, Adam was making too much noise."

* * *

From the time Tom asked me to speak to the colony, I saw that he was setting the stage to succeed Jay as president in 2001. But it was not automatic. Tom was opposed to hazing but was pro-drinking—to the point where he promised to battle national headquarters on party policy and get a keg in every room, so to speak.

Tom expected to run unopposed. Nobody else wanted the job as much as he did. Then he heard that Jay, though tired of being in charge, was going to run again. Jay worried that Tom's attitude about partying would ruin things. Sensing doom, Tom went to Jay's room on North Campus and the two agreed that Tom would run unopposed if he promised to learn why drinking needed to be managed carefully. "Look, you have to be a hard ass," Jay told him. "You need to be the guy who enforces the rules."

The night of the vote for president and vice president, which always would be done before the other officers, the men discussed Tom for a while before voting him in. This was a crucial time for the fledgling fraternity and they were concerned. The wrong man could lead the colony astray, back toward "frat" values, before it was even two years old. Finally they decided Tom would be fine.

The fraternity president occupies a strange role, always filled with pressure, going back to the early decades of the 20th century, but carrying more now. He has always led the pack and served as its public face, sometimes as an alpha male who keeps everyone in line, sometimes as a well-spoken, presentable fellow. I have seen all kinds: the jocular pal to everyone, the firm-handed CEO, the quiet but respected leader by consensus, the man at the head of the house's central power group, or the man between all of the house's factions. He is the house parent, almost. It is he who gets called to the dean's office when someone causes trouble, and he who will most likely be arrested and sued over problems. He therefore has the last word on everything from how a party should be set up, to how squabbles should be settled, to how men behave toward each other and other students. He is the brothers' voice to the alumni who oversee the physical house and advise the chapter. He is the brothers' voice to any outside entity, and the conduit of information between them and the university and national headquarters.

The president is expected to stop, or at least try to stop, behavior that damages the fraternity or its image. Since our society became more litigious, that has meant applying a cautious and legalistic view to everything—reining in what fraternities used to get away with. The time when I really see a president under stress is during a party, where most of the people are underage and everyone knows it but acts as if the law never changed. Every argument, bit of horseplay among men, talk of sex, or call to drink more is a potential injury, death, lawsuit. I once asked a president how he could stand it when his house had parties, and whether the men understood the risk to him. He said they understood, and they generally liked him enough to make sure he wasn't put at risk, but of course as the night wore on and booze took over, they were all capable of doing something stupid. He just needed to do his best.

Not much has been written about President George W. Bush's days as president of his Delta Kappa Epsilon chapter at Yale. He sounds like a fun, amiable man's man who could settle disputes and be respected by everyone, a leader from the gut, with a sound grasp of how men think and talk to each other. Every fraternity president must have these qualities to an extent, or his reign is filled with problems.

Being president means learning to use whatever charisma you're born with, for you can rally men behind a cause, and turn them against people and the very identity they've been cultivating. That happened with new chapters: get the charter back, then immediately revert to frat-boy ways.

A party was one event that demanded the president be in charge and that the men support him. The catering system Cornell had created for its fraternity parties a few years earlier had lapsed in 2000, as the catering companies went out of business, undone by violations of their liquor licenses no matter how diligent they were. Some remnants were in place, such as a person to dispense booze, and a table of unsalted foods and non-alcoholic drinks off to one side. The president patrolled for problems, along with the social chair and risk manager. Sober monitors, usually six or seven per party, watched over everything as well—and hopefully they were sober.

The president could try to have fun at parties, but mostly that had to wait until he was out of office. Potential lawsuits loomed in every chaotic corner: man and woman arguing, woman slipping on a staircase, guys wrestling around. In the late 1990s, fraternity parties and behavior inspired millions in lawsuits against Cornell at any given time, and national headquarters made a large target as well. The president, the one likely to go to jail, had to keep his fingers crossed.

Adding to all of this, universities were concerned because drinking had become more alluring—forbidden, a challenge. Researchers were divided on whether students drank more than in my time. Some argued that more students were not drinking in high school, in fact were showing less interest in social groups like Greeks because they did not want to drink. Studies showed repeatedly that Greek membership led those who did not drink as freshmen to learn how, and those who did drink to do it more. It was pretty common to hear men needling those who didn't drink. Young people thought they understood how to be safe around alcohol and that they should be considered responsible. "We can be sent to war at 18 but we can't drink," they said. The Phi Taus were no different.

LeGrand began to meet with Tom and patiently review the legal risks of drinking, underage or otherwise. I don't know how close the colony came to shifting direction, for the colony was—and remains now, as a chapter—able to rise above any one leader's wishes. Tom was pretty astute. He heard and pondered the administration's views, and the law and case histories they were based on. He was thinking about law school or business school, after his four-year Navy commitment was done, and probably a political career ultimately. He believed, more than some of the men did, that the colony needed to focus not just on itself and having fun but on the larger picture. Tom saw why Cornell's rules had become so tough, and in time he shifted so far away from his belief in reckless partying that he worried about drinking all the time.

One trick to helping a colony sustain itself, become a chapter, and remain a strong chapter is recognizing key moments and trying to respond to them. Harder than it sounds, but it can be done.

The role of drinking, when to have alcohol as part of what we were doing, and managing parties would always be a major source of tension and debate.

EIGHT
Finding New Blood
(Winter 2001)

He was tall and slender, poised and almost elegant, with dark eyes that could be serious or just slightly lit with glee. Of Indian descent, he was from New Jersey and had just arrived at Cornell as a sophomore transfer, from California but originally from Rutgers University. And he was already a Phi Tau, having been initiated at Rutgers.

The question was, would Vijay want to join the colony? Transferring meant discovering how well you fit in your fraternity's chapter at your new school. Chapter cultures and personalities can differ radically within a national. He would be the only initiated brother in the mix, since the rest were far from ready to be welcomed into the fold, in national's view.

First Vijay had to decide to remain at Cornell. An engineer, he had asked to transfer to communication, but the College of Engineering wouldn't let him right away. He was upset enough that he told the communication faculty he might go home.

But Vijay stayed and decided to visit Phi Tau when rush began.

* * *

January 2001 rush meant the first true rush for the colony. Andres was in charge, as recruitment chair. The men planned to use their traditional house for their smokers. One problem: when they arrived that first Tuesday of rush, to set up, the students renting the house had not been informed. They were livid.

Tom stepped upstairs to speak with the couple of indignant occupants who were back early. He returned with word that the men could use only the first-floor foyer, dining room, and front porch for the smoker. The Newman Room was wall to wall with furniture and who knew what else. The Chapter Room was open. But there were no house tours, which hurt, since prospective members like to see where they will live.

41

106 The Knoll was small for a fraternity house, with enough living space for only 21 men, 24 if some doubles became triples. The mansion was looking shabby. The floors were hardwood but gouged and worn out. Spindles were missing from the central stairway's railing. The carpet was faded. The chandelier hung useless. There was no sign anywhere that said this was Phi Tau, so Chaz the Navy ROTC midshipman (about to be chosen battalion commander) made huge letters out of plywood. He, Tom, and Jeff tied them to the balcony over the front door.

Rush is a way for a fraternity to maintain not just membership but identity—or change it. Who would the Phi Taus find, to help them build their vision? They didn't want to project themselves as something they weren't, as was habit for many fraternities. But they worried that nobody would want what they did in a fraternity, so for some freshmen they were targeting—Lou and his buddies Ice and Ken—they exaggerated how much they partied. They had cultivated a strapping Long Islander they nicknamed Big Daddy, who looked more likely to fit the football houses.

How did the colony determine a way to conduct rush, that first January? About four of the men had gone through rush the previous year, and a couple of others had visited houses but not rushed seriously, yet they'd absorbed the schedule and nuances. LeGrand helped. Tom, as a veteran of two rush periods and friend of many Greeks, offered a plan he called "One Thousand Points of Light," where he outlined ways to make conversation and find out who a man was, plus tips on how to conduct yourself at a rush event— such as never letting a recruit stand there without someone to talk to.

They made one decision right away: rush would be dry. Since this was university and IFC policy, that seemed automatic, but most fraternities at Cornell had alcohol at night events after the smokers. A few tried to impress rushees by smuggling them into bars, a few had booze-soaked road trips, and most had power hours or other beer nights at their houses or annexes. Phi Tau was too new, and aiming toward chapter status, so wet rush was out.

✻ ✻ ✻

At the smoker the men saw Vijay. "He's so cool, is he too cool for us— will he want to be part of us?" they asked me. Already, a transfer from the Florida State chapter had met them and said no thanks. I said wait and see.

Out front, the guys grilled hot dogs and burgers. They were dressed business casual. Tom and Hitman, who was now vice president, parked themselves at the end of the driveway in canvas chairs, calling to the packs of freshmen who passed by, "Hey, guys, what's up? Why don't you go up to our house and have a burger?" Neighboring Delta Chi complained, so Tom encouraged freshmen to visit them next. The guys were a bit annoyed with Tom for being so accommodating. His outgoing manner often grated on them, but they needed him—many of them were introverted.

In time the Phi Taus would decide that their best approach was for each man to find someone like himself to replace him. They sought campus leaders, and tried to pinpoint potential leaders for the house. They were surprised when a few freshmen turned away from them, wanting a fraternity that hazed. Phi Tau signed nine men plus Vijay, who had decided that he liked this colony that would soon be a chapter. He wasn't as quiet as believed, he was a comedian, and in time he would blend with the founding group as if he had been there from the start. The men nicknamed him "Stamos" because like the actor John Stamos, he had thick, wavy hair.

Nine pledges was below the campus average of 13, and well below what national headquarters considered solid. But the men were pleased. They got Big Daddy, Lou, Ice, Ken. They added Neil, a sophomore who lived next door in the "crew house," a rental full of rowers. He'd been a coxswain (the person in the stern who steers the boat and determines the stroke rate) but had grown too big for the position. The selling point for the new men was the promise that they would also be founding fathers of the new Phi Tau chapter. I thought it was just a line. The Founders, the first 15 or so guys to create the colony, kept a firm grip on everything.

NINE

Identity

(Winter 2001/Winter 1974)

I stopped by Phi Tau's first smoker, curious to see how it would go. Smok-ers are gatherings where fraternity brothers and prospective brothers talk over chips and soda, sometimes hot food. The name smacks of a long-ago era of cigars and brandy. My research had caused me to hang out at smokers several times. I heard someone from another fraternity telling freshmen, "That's a new fraternity, and they have this sketchy old guy who hangs around." Every fraternity had to decide whether to bash others (called dirty rush) or just play up their own strengths. "You'll have 40 friends here who will support you" clashed with "Other houses say they're tight-knit but they really aren't." Or I heard, "You want to go where? Please. They're so lame. You belong with us."

But it often felt odd. Rush meant failure to me. I could remember it clearly.

* * *

My necktie was too long in the back so I pulled the Windsor knot apart and tried again, finally harnessing the blue-and-red-striped silken length against the collar of my white shirt. I grimaced at my face in the mirror: thin, not handsome but so be it, wire-rimmed glasses that finally had replaced my dark-rimmed ones from high school, brown hair curly in back but wavy on top, a bit of acne along my chin. It was early Febru-ary 1974 and I had just turned 18 two months ago, catching up with my fellow St. Lawrence University freshmen just as some of them turned 19.

Every room in Sykes Residence for Men, home to most of the 250 freshman males, had a sink and mirror. I checked my face. Shaved two days ago and didn't need to now. Someday I would shave every day, as some of my classmates already did. I tugged on my light-blue blazer and dark brown corduroy pants, and tied the laces on my good brown shoes, ready to face my possible future.

My single room was so small that even at 5-foot-7, I could put my feet against one wall and almost touch the other. I had a desk, typewriter, and book shelf, as befitted an English major who usually read two books at once (science fiction but lately some Updike). On a small table sat a record player with a radio, for my Stones and Beatles and Led Zeppelin. "Stairway to Heaven." The stairs were to my right as I stepped into the hall.

My neighbors were not going with me to fraternity rush. They thought I was crazy, a loner and individual like me trying to join a fraternity—aiming for, of all things, Beta Theta Pi the jock house, all muscle and swagger. Girls won't talk to you if you go Beta, they said. You're not like those guys, they said.

Call it reinventing myself.

Here I was both a native and a stranger. Canton, New York, lay between the Adirondacks to the east and the Canadian border to the north and west. The nearest cities of any size were Ottawa and Montreal. SLU—tiny, expensive, selective, nicknamed Larryland and Country Club of the North—was a pocket of wealth in this rugged land. My hometown, Potsdam, was just 11 miles to the north but I pretended it was 500 miles away. Yet my being a native carried no weight, not when so many kids were from prep school or were class presidents and star athletes. Now fraternity rush was here. Having been chosen for admission to this university, I would be judged again.

I knew what a fraternity was. Potsdam was dotted with these mansions displaying Greek letters, like fortresses along the border between the two colleges and the village's downtown. Every winter, ice sculptures sprouted on their lawns for Ice Carnival and in the warm months, snow fencing appeared around their yards, kegs were unloaded, and student bands sent a drum beat through the village. Men wearing jackets with funny symbols sewn into them—Greek letters, I learned—strutted around. One day men lined up on a sidewalk, marching, while another guy barked orders at them. This was part of a fraternity, proving your worth before you're finally in: pledging, getting hazed. Then there was the way my father, his older brother, and Grandpa Conroe spoke with great fondness of their fraternity at Alfred University.

A handful of guys at the other end of Bork Hall (a nickname chosen for its oddness, belonging to President Nixon's solicitor general, who had fired the attorney investigating the Watergate scandal) talked about Phi Kap, one of the fraternities across the street. Each of the seven fraternities had a distinct personality. Sigma Chi was ultra-cool, SAE was preppy, Sigma Pi was hard-partying and full of hockey players, Phi Sig was so on the fringe that it pledged women, ATO was long-haired counter-culture types, and Beta Theta Pi was ultra-secretive, hard-edged jocks who called non-Betas "nons," making it sound like "non-people." Phi Kap was nice guys, a few athletes. A senior in Phi Kap asked me to stop by but I said no thanks, I'm going Beta, and his look said I was a fool doomed for pain. Phi Kap was me, but I didn't want me.

For these two weeks of rush, smokers were a few evenings a week, ending with "preferential smokers" for guys the houses really were interested in. Before Beta's smoker I walked to a triple where a high school friend lived. He and one roommate were not rushing. The other roommate, a football player, was going to SAE with several other freshmen on the team, a defiance of tradition since most football players joined Beta. We were all slightly in awe of this roommate. He had stopped me cold the first day here, when I still thought my high school achievements were special. I'd been elected class treasurer, a Student Council homeroom rep, National Honor Society. This guy casually said he'd been football captain and class president at his suburban Buffalo school, which was more than four times the size of my school.

Oh.

St. Lawrence could do that to you. Honor society? I'd only made it as a senior after a disastrous fall from the honor roll the year before, and here were valedictorians or close. Student Council? My junior year homeroom chose me, to my shock, in an election without nominees—the 30 students just voted and even hinting that you wanted it could doom your chances. I'd tied and then won by two votes, a great day for a guy who used to be such a loner that he read books in the cafeteria during lunch. Now I met Student Council and class presidents throughout Sykes. Photography, my growing passion? Several freshmen had better cameras and knew more than I did, so I was learning from them. Sports? I managed track and hockey while these people heard the crowd's roar.

The third week at SLU, I ran for class president, 17 years old and speaking my mind. My obnoxious campaign posters criticized the hall councils. I lost. I had not run for president in high school. I didn't dazzle a room, was not one of the boys. My one stab at school-wide office (which did involve campaigning) ended when the principal canceled elections. Class officer votes didn't involve campaigning; we were nominated and the class voted. So I never learned how to sell myself that way.

Even if my friends were correct and I was not fraternity material, I wanted to take a stab at it. Fraternities accounted for 50 percent of the men here, and 95 percent of the parties. Men ruled this campus from the administration to the department chairs, to the fact that men had 12 varsity sports while women had three.

At 7 o'clock, while a lot of guys headed across the street to other fraternities, I walked in the other direction, to Beta Theta Pi.

✳ ✳ ✳

Beta lay beyond the administration building, on the edge of campus. A concrete path curved between trees and past a two-story white mausoleum sort of building the Betas called the Temple, which only they were allowed to enter (through a tunnel in the basement). Beyond lay the brick house with white pillars out front. In the back was a red fire engine the Betas rode to football games and parked beyond one end zone, the campus security officers just smiling at them. From inside came laughter and music. I pushed open the front door and stepped in.

Big men filled the living room, and "men" seemed like the word. Athletes lived here, scorers of touchdowns, hitters of home runs. I'd been to a few parties at this house. Not a drinker in high school, at college I immediately began drinking. I even blacked out at a morning party (8 a.m. Saturday) where the Betas served something from a metal vat—one cup and I was gone. I prayed the men didn't remember.

I greeted football players and wrestlers I had met as a photographer. They had cautioned me that Beta was very selective. I was surrounded by broad shoulders and self-assurance. Even my fellow freshmen acted at home, as teammates of Betas.

I hung out with a junior wrestler. I admitted that in high school I paid no attention to his sport as my best friends played, watched, and talked hockey, the ruling sport here next to Canada. One friend's father coached the local college team. They had an ice rink in their back yard, with snow banks for a penalty box and a tennis ball for a puck. Wrestlers tended to be poorer, and I thought the sport was silly. Now I admired their muscle, stamina, and courage.

The wrestler's brother, a freshman, knew everybody. I could sense that some guys would slide into fraternities without much effort. They knew people or simply had a way about them.

The Betas talked to me. I was not blown off. A few seemed indifferent, some struck me as real jerks, others were friendly enough. This whole thing was so weird, this notion that you could be friends with 50 other men automatically. Look at me, I thought, and feel who I am beyond the glasses and skinny frame.

What did I know about being a man? From my intellectual parents, who wanted us kids reading or out doing something instead of gazing at the TV, I had learned that being a man meant being well-rounded and dependable. We did chores, had paper routes at 4:30 a.m., washed dishes before we got a dishwasher. My mother, Barbara, was intelligent, warm-hearted, but tough. She worked in the village library to help pay for my college tuition. My father, Bruce, had started as a high school math teacher and become a guidance counselor, then a college counselor at Potsdam State (as we called it then). He was diplomatic and kind, and away during the week this year, finishing a doctorate that would help him become an administrator, while Mom managed the house and my three younger siblings. I admired my parents more than anyone. They had met on the way to kindergarten and been together since high school. They pushed us to try everything, to be athletes and musicians and artists, and with me they put up with all sorts of weird creative impulses and anti-social habits.

I watched the men around me. My best friend's hockey coach father was a town icon who could silence any of us boys with a look, and we were in awe. Another friend's father was a doctor who loved climbing mountains. Another was a small but intimidating man from New York City who gave driver tests. Beyond them, men were hunters and athletes and drinkers of beer. My dad was handy around the house, another badge of manhood that I did not have. He and Mom loved recreation, introducing us to skiing, waterskiing, and snowshoeing. Dad enjoyed teaching on the side and was respected by students, as I learned one day as I waited outside his office and heard a sobbing girl say, "At last, someone with answers." He was strong in ways that had nothing to do with brawn. I was much like him. I hoped the Betas grasped this.

"Why are you interested in fraternities?" someone asked. Because you have all the parties, I said, and beyond that it looks like people gain a lot from belonging to a fraternity.

"Why us?"

Good question. The Betas seemed bound by something stronger than mere friendship, always together, surrounded by women. This wasn't me, but I could use a little of it. So I answered, "Because you're leaders. You're special. You have a presence about you." I tried to find guys with "pull" to argue in my behalf during the discussions over who would receive a bid. I tried to see where guys might stand in my case. But it felt like hanging with guys in the hallways of high school to see if they'd invite me to be part of their group, or like applying to college again, or like taking a test, all at once and yet not like any of them.

The Betas knew I was a photographer and on the yearbook staff. I hadn't told the seniors and juniors on the yearbook that I was rushing, since they clearly disdained Greek societies.

"Yearbook, huh?"

The wise response would have been, "Because the editor is hot. I plan to lay out more than just pages." But I was too honest, so I vaguely said something about recording history in pictures and hoping to be editor in a couple of years. Bad response. A wiseass answer might have left them saying, "That kid's not as nerdy as he looks."

A few of the Betas didn't seem to fit, in build or demeanor. One resembled a minister, quite professorial. Someone said he didn't drink or swear. Yet the men clearly loved him.

The smoker ended and I left thinking my chances seemed good. Maybe I should try Phi Kap the next day. No, I didn't want to rush more than one house at once. It would be hard enough to meet most of the men at one house. Besides, it would be embarrassing to show up now.

That week someone asked if I grasped how tough Beta's hazing was rumored to be. I had tried to ignore that. I dreaded the idea. I'd never seen hazing but I'd heard it. Coming back from Lake Placid one Saturday, my high school's hockey players piled their blue gear bags at the middle of the bus and held initiation for rookies. I heard laughter and the hiss of athletic tape being wrapped around guys. The cheerleaders were riding with us that day, which wasn't the norm, and the wall kept them up front, sulking. As the manager I sat in the front too, also not part of whatever was happening. The girls wouldn't talk to me. Here in college, I heard, the hockey players pinned down rookies and shaved every part of their bodies, mimicking the pros' tradition.

Then there was Boy Scout camp. Our scoutmaster took us to Quebec, to Camp Tamaracouta, as a change of pace. The Canadian boys called us dumb Yankees and I responded by re-writing their national anthem, from "Oh Canada" to "Oh Bathroom Bowl." Forced to make peace, we joined the other troops in a camp tradition Knights of Tamara, a leadership honorary. Our troop leader represented us. All of the Knights coated themselves with butter and wrestled, two at a time, in a pit filled with cocoa powder. The boy with the least powder on him won. Our troop leader was strong and made it pretty far. Then they all swam the nearby lake one-handed, holding in their free hand a rock with their initials carved on it, and in the dusk they vanished into the woods on the far shore, to take part in some ceremony. I would have happily swum that lake with one hand, but wrestling mostly naked in front of a crowd did not appeal to me.

Nor had I given many public promises, which is where pledging began. National Honor Society had plucked me from a student assembly and had me take a pledge on the stage. Boy Scout meetings began with the oath, which sounded noble—sound mind and body, morally straight— but lost its appeal when I looked around the room at some of the wilder boys. We met on the second floor of the village fire station, a spittoon in every corner. Those were my two experiences with repeating a promise of who I would be.

✳ ✳ ✳

More smokers, then preferentials. As I passed Betas on the way to class, I gauged how they greeted me, if they did. One friend said don't act like you want it so bad, it can turn them off. My parents, Greeks in college, urged me to not take this thing so seriously. One unusually warm evening the campus went nuts with streaking, the new fad at colleges that we'd read about. Kids mooned people, and freshmen ran naked across campus and were caught by security then released when about 100 of us surrounded them and chanted, "Let them go." The Betas ran naked around the administration building, Vilas Hall, whose namesake was an ATO, the Betas' scorned neighbor. Could I have joined them? My quest at Beta seemed like a longshot but I pressed on. At the last preferential I turned on the charm.

Pledge Saturday dawned gray and forbidding. After 1 p.m. I began to check my slot in the mail room, seeking a small white envelope, stuck at a slant to fit: a bid. I would find out if my shot at reinventing myself had worked.

The mail room was right below my second-floor single. My first trip down, nothing. My second, nothing. Other guys pulled envelopes from their mail slots, pleased or nonchalant, as if they had been tipped off or just never worried about it.

My gut began to ache. I put on the Rolling Stones' *Goats Head Soup* album to light me up with its raunchier songs. C'mon, Beta, say yes. Down the hall, classmates adjusted their ties and jackets, white envelopes in hand. Parties commenced across the street. Sororities brought their pledges to serenade the fraternities. As freshmen accepted bids, they were greeted by choruses of joy and handed bottles of champagne to chug before going inside to take the oath. The celebrations grew and so did my despair.

A third trip: nothing in my mail slot. "Maybe they're late," another freshman said. "I've heard it happens. Who is it?"

"Beta."

"Oh. Uh, well, good luck."

Two hours passed and obviously I didn't have a bid. Furious and humiliated and sorrowful all in one hot stew, I practically ran downtown, about four blocks, past the fraternities and their damn parties. I hid in a movie theater, looking through a couple of tears at *American Graffiti* and feeling like Terry the Toad, the gawky character who chased after the other kids in that film.

Nobody offered an explanation. I simply didn't fit. It was a gamble and I knew it, but the ache wouldn't quit even when my parents said this wasn't the end of the world. At sports events, in bars, on campus some Betas said hello as if nothing happened and some looked away. One suggested I try again next fall, but I doubted that would happen. This felt too much like failure.

I encountered the university's president in my dorm one afternoon (I never heard why he was there). Dr. Piskor was a pleasant, round-faced man, sort of grandfatherly. He asked how my freshman year was going. Good, I said, and then blurted, "except I didn't get into a fraternity."

"That's too bad," he said. "Which one?"

I told him.

"Beta Theta Pi," he said. I suddenly noticed that behind him stood the vice president for student affairs, who was a Beta here in the 1950s. Dr. Piskor looked me over and said, "Well, son, it's probably just as well."

As winter gave way to the North Country's version of spring, my fellow freshmen formed little groups and had less time for the rest of us. I tuned it out. One afternoon I brought photographs to athletes at Beta. A couple of the juniors intercepted me on the concrete path and politely said the house was not open to outsiders that day.

The pain faded. Maybe I had been spared an experience for which I was not prepared.

My rational side said don't be a fool, rush Phi Kap. But I didn't. In the fall of 1975, junior year, I became a "social brother" at Sigma Pi, meaning I was welcome at closed parties but not pledged or initiated. I rushed there, half-heartedly, and my roommate from sophomore year showed up at my dorm room to tell me the bid was not coming but a social bid was being offered. The seniors who had wanted me were angry that a sophomore denied me a bid, and they wanted me to come to Pledge Saturday after the freshmen said their pledge. So I did, pleased to have some link to the Greek system. The seniors were apologetic but I said it was fine. Later I bought Sigma Pi letters, white letters on a dark blue polo shirt, though I suspected I shouldn't.

As yearbook editor in chief, I brought back team and group pictures, which had been out of vogue the past few years, and printed the book vertically where it had been horizontal. The student funding group tried to cut my budget and I went in to argue for more money. The chair, a sophomore who lived across the hall, was a friend who seemed like a stranger in that meeting. This was my first glimpse of a student's professional side, the side that fraternity members summoned as they discussed and voted upon rushees. I photographed the Greeks for the yearbook, drank at their parties, listened to the fraternity groups cheering at sports. That winter of 1976 a wrestler won our first national championship in that sport, and the men's swimming team pulled off an upset by capturing a national title as well. Quietly, SLU began to add women's sports: swimming and hockey that winter. We had co-ed dorms, though they were co-ed by floor and required parental permission. Women headed four student groups for the first time: newspaper, student government, judicial board, and the organization that scheduled lectures and concerts.

Obviously I needed to learn from all of this, but what? That I needed to hone my social skills far more, and my sales skills, and to downplay what was not cool.

At my 20th reunion, I had a beer with that same wrestler from Beta. This fellow, two years ahead of me, was here because his brother was. Suddenly he said, "You know, you came a lot closer to getting into our house than you realize." I said, "That discussion was 23 years ago and you remember it?" He nodded. I asked another Beta and he said, "Yeah, a lot of guys wanted you. But everything we did had to be unanimous, and some guys went with stereotypes." That must have been some discussion.

✷ ✷ ✷

I left Phi Tau's smoker after a half hour or so, guessing that it would be too difficult for the men to explain who I was. The Phi Taus had their hands full. I sent an e-mail to them, saying I would stay away and wait to hear the results. Rush was not part of whatever I took from being involved with Phi Tau. It never would be.

My presence caused unseen effects in any situation. One evening I saw the men leaving for a trip to the casino. Only two rushees were with them. "That's all?" I said, and Tom warned me to watch what I said since my words carried weight, coming from an older man. I was stunned. In my own family I could barely get a word in let alone have my opinion matter. In my classroom, I was in charge, the expert, and even then plenty of students probably tuned out my words. Now what I said was hurting feelings because my opinion mattered. This would take getting used to.

TEN
Old Words
(Winter 2001)

Anabel Taylor Chapel is one of two non-denominational churches on Cornell's campus. It is all cool stone and high ceilings, with chairs that lock together to form rows, and an altar set up and back under a domed section with three magnificent stained-glass windows. Voices echo softly. This dignified place was where the Phi Tau colony held its second association ceremony, a few days after bids were signed.

I didn't plan to go but LeGrand said it would be excellent research for my book. I think he was hoping I would come to care more about this group I advised. The association session was quasi-public, meaning parents could attend, although none ever did. The men taped sheets of newsprint over the sanctuary door's window.

Train said the guys were pleased to have me there and I should just keep a low profile in back, so I did.

In an association ceremony, prospective members are asked if they will be part of the fraternity, with all that implies, the brothers are asked if they want these men to join them, and both say yes. Whatever doubts either side feels are buried by the old words, at least for now.

I moved to a pew near the front because the room wasn't that big, maybe 100 feet. The ceiling loomed above us, and the stained-glass windows showed the night. The men read too fast, stumbling a little. It would often be that way, as they performed this ceremony only once or twice a year. But in that chapel I felt the fraternity at its most noble as the men calmly let the Phi Tau national's founders speak through them. They focused on the fraternity's soul. They saw each other, in the lights above the altar area, clustered and acting as one. They became the fraternity's essence. The words were so different in diction and combination that they sounded foreign. That this ceremony was performed by men not yet initiated, and a man from another fraternity (LeGrand), became acceptable under the circumstances. The men were thinking as initiated brothers did.

The only actual brother, Vijay, joined in. They had taken a step and I had taken it with them, toward what I didn't know.

✶ ✶ ✶

Jay was now the new member educator (also known as membership orientation officer or MOO) for this first true pledge class. Having been president first, he was descending the order of officers, but he saw this job as his next challenge and a continuation of what he had begun as president. We had two sophomores, Vijay (who agreed to go through pledging again) and Neil, who they later nicknamed MacGyver after he showed his ingenuity in a raft-building exercise, echoing the TV spy played by Richard Dean Anderson. MacGyver had a big smile and kind manner. A physics major from a town just north of Ithaca, he was also a drummer and became part of JB's band. The freshmen included the massive fellow they're recruited in the fall, Bryan, nicknamed Big Daddy. He had come to Cornell to play football, probably linebacker (he'd also started at quarterback at his Long Island high school). He had a round, handsome face and easy confidence. Another burly ex-football player from The Island, named Barry, was nicknamed "Meathead." He was dark, gruff-spoken. The trio of Lou, Ice, and Ken took their bids. The others were Jason, nicknamed J-Mac, and Matt, nicknamed Matty J. The Founders loved nicknames.

The associates began to learn Phi Tau history.

Because Phi Tau was a colony, the men were allowed to keep recruiting after the IFC rush was over, and in April they added five other associates, including a freshman named Rico, a sophomore named Jacob, and a freshman named Mick, a lightweight rower. Jay was talking to Cornell Outdoor Education about using its facilities as a way for the men to bond, a substitute for hazing. He wasn't able to try it that spring, since he really wanted to use COE's high elements course in the woods, with a rope bridge and other apparatus suspended high above the ground. The course was too wet until April, when pledging would be done according to Cornell's new policy that pledging last eight weeks instead of 10 or 12. He settled for giving the new men quizzes about national history. He wanted the next wave of new members to truly understand why this Phi Tau colony had been established in the manner it was, and what its re-founding group expected. A few of Founders suggested customs that their friends in other fraternities talked about: drinking more, and adding a dramatic and tough element, not hazing but something like it. They talked constantly about this thing they'd created, how to change it. They worried that their vision was too squeaky-clean. To the slogans they'd adopted they added another: "Not Soft."

PART II

Admitting Me to Membership
(Or, Old Guy Takes a Risk)

ELEVEN
Brian's Battle
(Winter/Spring 2001)

Tom began to attend Interfraternity Council meetings every week, and there he became friends with the IFC president, a senior named Brian, who belonged to Delta Upsilon. They discovered they had much in common.

Brian required the IFC representatives from each house to wear shirt and tie. That had been the tradition for years. They met in a large, high-ceilinged room at Willard Straight Hall, the student union on Central Campus, where wooden busts adorned the ceiling: Straight's faculty at Cornell, the ones he liked on one side and the ones he didn't on the other, one of them depicted picking his nose. In the evening it was too dark to see the busts in detail.

IFC was like any student government, caught between university and constituents, trying to appease (if not please) both. Here the dance between students and adults became elaborate. Party management was one battleground: since the drinking age's jump to 21, the IFC had carved out territory between the university's wish for strictness and the fraternities' wish to be wild college men. The IFC maneuvered, cajoled, promised. The university said good for you, way to use self-governance. Whatever really happened, only the fraternities knew most of the time. Hazing was another battleground. The IFC judicial board heard cases of parties managed badly and pledging gone awry or simply attracting attention from people who were not fans of Greek life. The panel could suspend a fraternity from having social events for a month, two months, for violating party policy. Hazing was a newer frontier.

A year before Tom tried pledging for five weeks and quit, Brian had endured his own hell.

As a freshman defensive end from Ohio—from one of the stronger high school programs in the nation—Brian had agreed during football preseason to shave his head and roar out school fight songs in the dining

57

hall, to please the veterans and show that he wanted to belong. Five
months later, he felt the same way when he accepted a bid to join DU. The
torment began the day after he pledged. After being welcomed by the
brothers and watching the Super Bowl, the pledges were ordered to the
basement to drink a keg of beer. Brian (who didn't drink much) squirmed
at the idea of being forced to, but did as he was told. After they drank the
keg, the pledges were ordered to reach into the pants of the man next to
them and pull out his underwear—while he was still in it. "We were in
pain, wet, drunk," Brian remembered.

He continued to do as he was told for 10 weeks, through a scavenger
hunt for pornography, being pelted with food at dinner, swallowing goldfish, being screamed at when he failed to correctly answer a question
about the chapter's history, and marching on a back deck. He endured the
infamous "elephant walk," where men line up and grab the private parts
of the men in front of them. He was 18 and thought that getting through
this would make him a man.

Deep down, the teenager suspected he was wrong. He knew after the
first night of hazing that things had to change, after that kill-a-keg night.
He saw 18 freshmen drunk and puking.

Two years later he had quit football (although he hoped to coach
eventually) and was DU's president. He announced that hazing had to go.
The seniors told him to shut up, they ran the show and would do what
they wanted. "So, I was basically a babysitter." Brian had been a leader in
high school, student government president and football captain, but
nothing prepared him for this battle. "I thought about quitting as president every day," he said, "but then it would've been worse."

He turned to the alumni next. Things must change, he said, even
those of you who think the world is too politically correct have to see the
realities. The alumni leaders and university decided to re-structure the
house, not re-colonize it exactly. Hazing was out. Anyone who didn't like
it could move to alumnus status. Many of the seniors did that. But the new
order didn't last. There was no gap between old and new, not like the five
years Phi Tau had been shut down. When the brothers burned a mattress
on a porch in protest, the fraternity's charter was revoked. DU would be
re-colonized in a couple of years.

Despite his anti-hazing stance, Brian was elected IFC president. A
hotel administration major, he stretched out his coursework so he would
stay an extra semester. No longer welcome at DU, he lived in a sorority's
annex, thanks to the president of the Panhellenic Association, the council for the 15 sororities that were not Asian, black, or Latina. There he met

Jay, because Jay was dating a woman who lived there. The next fall Brian would live in an apartment away from campus, with a DU classmate who was doing a one-year engineering master's degree—his only DU friend. He would worry about his car, so he would park it somewhere else. The DU brothers left on campus would wear T-shirts that took his name in vain and said, "DU Forever."

Brian would never waver in his contempt for hazing. Tom and Jay had an ally.

But what would take the place of hazing? Phi Tau had the chance to serve as an example for the entire Greek system, if it wanted that pressure. Closer to home, the men just needed to find a way to pull new members into the fold without tormenting them.

Cornell had decided to fight hazing. The vice president for student affairs, Susan Murphy, had formed a task force to study hazing's reach and effects, with a mix of students, faculty, and staff. She then formed a committee to seek alternatives for hazing (I eventually joined). This committee was headed by the new dean of students, Kent Hubbell, an architecture professor who had belonged to a fraternity at Cornell, and Associate Dean Suzy Nelson, who ran the Greek system.

In IFC and task force meetings, fraternity presidents mostly argued that hazing was a tradition that needed to stay, the university had no right to stop it, and without their tests of toughness fraternity men would feel like sorority women (although hazing existed in sororities too). A few fraternity presidents said they agreed with Brian.

* * *

Everything I knew about hazing came from books and interviews. Looking at fraternities in college and since, I wondered how I would have fared. I had not looked forward to hazing new members, if I became a fraternity member. The high school hockey team's ritual on the bus in 1972 was my only real reference point.

Since college I'd experienced that kind of testing by other men once, and it was brief.

St. Lawrence had announced in the fall of 1994 that its wrestling program, winner of a Division III national team title and nine individual ones, was being dropped to save money and put SLU more in line with other colleges it identified with academically. As their season went on, the wrestlers sued, claiming breach of contract. Their lawyer was a national champion SLU wrestler and All-American football player from the class ahead of mine. A coalition of students who had never gone near a wrestling match rose up to help them. They held rallies and demanded meetings with the administration. Beta Theta Pis filled the front rows at those sessions; Beta became the movement's headquarters. The coach who had transformed the wrestling team into a national contender was a Beta, in fact his dreams of coaching national champions had begun there as he and the brothers hung out and talked. He was not a fan of fraternities now, he told me; as a coach he'd watched fraternities demand so much of an athlete's time and heart that they'd quit their sport. "[His fraternity time] had a beginning and an ending, like my time in the army," he said. But he was pleased to have an ally in Beta. The lawsuit failed, as the judge declined to interfere in the affairs of a private university.

I had supported the team for two decades, as photographer and writer. I decided to photograph as many of its matches as I could. Sometimes I rode in the team van. The coach gave me a locker in the team's locker room as a show of appreciation, and I used it a little but being on their turf seemed strange. At the team's final practice, I took a group picture, then asked to pose with them.

The wrestlers normally harassed their rookies, but the new coach had quashed that, telling the men to behave at their best if they hoped to save their program. Until the wrestlers' last road trip, that is, when the program was lost and he told the men, "C'mon and get me." They pinned him down in the van and shaved "SLU" into his chest hair.

Two, three pictures of me with the team, and then they pounced. It required only two of them to immobilize me and wrap my wrists and ankles in athletic tape. They posed me like a trophy, as someone snapped a picture with my camera. Over my face they taped a mask worn by wrestlers with a broken nose. They set me on a shelf and posed with me.

I laughed the whole time. Fraternity members had emphasized that over the years: Take it like a man, shrug it off. But I was nervous, because wrestlers have a different pain threshold than most of us.

At one point, I broke the tape on my wrists, but a 126-pounder of all people pinned me down and I was tied tighter. It annoyed me that a man so much lighter than I could do that, but he had a vise for a grip and understood, better than in any classroom, how physics worked in this situation.

Struggling wore me out. I was red-faced and panting.

"What else should we do with him?"

"Let's shave his chest. Get a razor."

"Let's shave 'S-L-U' into it."

They pulled back my T-shirt.

"Not enough chest hair."

"Let's just give him a pink belly."

I yelled, "No pink bellies!"

"Shut up."

Each wrestler got to slap my bare stomach. I kept laughing.

"Use our locker room, eh?" Slap.

"Ride in our van, will ya?" Slap.

Finally, the 126-pounder said he'd race me the length of the practice room, with my ankles taped together so I'd bounce while he ran. I won. They pulled off the tape.

"Now you're one of us," a senior captain said.

The hazing had lasted about 20 minutes, just a taste. I had been welcomed in a way I had only heard about. Now I felt included and pleased, maybe because for once I'd done something officially forbidden. I went along because it felt like a quiz on being a guy and I wanted to pass, old as I was, wise as I supposedly was.

✶ ✶ ✶

Hazing endures because American men just don't have much to mark their passage into manhood, I believe. They do adult things at younger ages: sex, working, owning a car, helping to manage a household, seeing their parents' problems, even starting a business. They put off marriage and financial independence. And they do youthful things in adulthood: avoiding responsibility, defying authority, letting their emotions run loose, not being accountable. If men want concrete rites of passage, being hazed by a fraternity, followed by an initiation ceremony, can feel like one—and they will defend it as tradition. They endure torment, try to laugh it off without letting the brothers see this, or they just gut it out because giving up would be a form of defeat and they, as individuals and as a pledge class, will not let the brothers defeat them. The pledges come together, then learn afterward to be part of the whole, when they move into the house and spend time with the brothers, getting to know them as they couldn't before. Over time, if the hazing was strong enough, they retain a sense of the whole brotherhood even as they regain a sense of themselves. Then they follow the same routine with the next batch of pledges.

Sounds good in theory. One problem: for some men the effect is the opposite, as hazing leaves them disliking the men outside their pledge class. Another problem: the men in charge of hazing might be drunk or might decide to up the ante, making a pledge do more than they did. Hazing brought out the bully. As different men put it to me over the years, "He was the biggest pussy when we pledged, and then he became the most hard-core hazing leader."

Hazing belongs to the shadows, and doesn't fare well in the light. Whatever a young man learns about himself by enduring it, about his courage or resolve, evaporates when he has to describe the event to his parents or read about it in a news report.

The stories are endless. Some are awful and some are just kid stuff.

We had to crawl up a hill while the guys pushed us down.

We did pushups with a fellow pledge on our backs.

We lined up and recited our lineage, starting with our pledge father or big brother, then his, and all the way back.

We had a lemonade stand next to the road, nude, or we were tied up and barked like dogs at passersby—nude.

We chugged milk or liquor until we puked (photographs posted on the Web).

We were told to have sex with a woman from Ithaca College, all of us.

We walked on the ledge that goes around the third floor of our fraternity house.

We had to take over the house and take the brothers prisoner (writing assignment turned in by a student).

We had to dress in costumes and not get caught by the RA. (This is not evil, just goofy—and sure to attract the administration's wrath if someone decides to make an issue of it. Which is what happened.)

We had to reach into a toilet and pick up what we were told was feces, then eat it. Turned out to be a piece of banana. (Story from a SUNY Cortland alumnus of the early 1960s.)

We had to be tied to a tree in back and beaten with a garden hose.

We had to be doused with water and then stand in the back yard, in the middle of the night, in the winter.

We had to jog around campus, wearing only gym shorts, coated with grease.

We had to stay in the house for a week and eat nothing but instant noodles.

We had to do calisthenics and run in place non-stop for an hour.

We watched pornography on a TV set for hours, without moving, and if we moved, the guys threw things at us.

This is why hazing sits on the fault line between youthful hijinks, the silly stuff men do in college, and the dangerous, the traumatic, the degrading.

Some older men don't mind telling me their hazing stories many years later, breaking the vow of secrecy. A Cornell alum 20 years my senior matter-of-factly described wearing a burlap sack under his clothes for a week. He laughed about it. A fellow my age said his pledging escalated over several weeks of humiliation and obedience, as the brothers judged pledges had had enough and pulled them to the side, until only one pledge was left in the thick of it. "He was the man," my friend said in admiration. I asked if he ever thought about quitting, during those weeks. "Oh, yeah," he said, "we all did. But your big brother, or pledge father, talked you through it. So did other pledges."

Many of us baby boomers admired the strength it took to get through these trials, even if we would not put ourselves in that situation. Some men had fun with it. Some forgave the men who subjected them to these demands, and some never really did. The men of my generation and the one before ours (and I've spoken to maybe 60) waver between shrugging off hazing as one more silly thing they did in youth and wishing they had not gone through it. "I was 18, and at 18 you do whatever the older guys say, you go along," I heard. "So you'll belong." I understood. You want to be part of this group of men, and you want the satisfaction of knowing you were tested.

A friend about 10 years older than me was less understanding. He had belonged to a jock house, and at the time he bought into their pledging. He showed me scars on his knees, where he'd rested a barbell for hours. "Then, when I was pledge master, I ordered guys to row an imaginary boat until they collapsed from fatigue," he said.

✷ ✷ ✷

How could anyone fight something so deeply rooted in not just fraternity culture, but athletic, military, workplace, and any number of other cultures? Tormenting the new kids has been part of school since the Middle Ages. Even the young men in Aristotle's academies did it.

Hazing as a legal term covers all manner of things that brothers ask of pledges, but Cornell's definition refers mainly to events that cause humiliation or don't pass the Mother Test (would you tell your mother what you did) or the *New York Times* Test (could it be published in the *Times*). Most freshmen didn't know what would be asked of them when they took the oath of fraternity membership. Over the weeks afterward, they found themselves exhausted, bewildered, afraid, if warmed by the support of fellow pledges. They could quit, but many didn't because pledging became a test to be passed, and because after a while they knew the fraternity's secrets; the brothers said if they quit, they'd better transfer because their lives would be hell. Hazing itself could be quite sudden, starting with a phone call or a fraternity member pounding on your door at two in the morning. Summoned to the house, you lined up with the other pledges and faced a quiz about fraternity history, or maybe just some questions you couldn't answer, or you answered correctly but forgot to say "sir." A face inches from yours ordered you to run in place, or chug a beer, or submit to a paddling.

Hazing has vexed university administrators since fraternities grew in number and influence during the 20th century. It could be safely said that hazing happened at most campuses. The legal definition of hazing is so broad that even wearing a pledge pin or meeting as a pledge class is hazing. In the middle of this spectrum of student antics fell scavenger hunts and group projects. At the far end lay the behaviors that concerned people like Dean Hubbell. Though hazing had caused dozens of deaths across the nation in the past century, not to mention injuries and trauma, Cornell had been lucky; its last hazing-related deaths were in the 1800s. But the dean thought it was only a matter of time before disaster struck. "Hazing will be the end of our fraternity system," he said repeatedly, to news media and Greek leaders and alumni. "We must do something about it."

What Cornell did was attack the problem. The dean couldn't run around in the middle of the night and peer through fraternity houses' windows (which are usually curtained or covered with plastic anyway, during rituals and hazing). He didn't plan to drive around on weekend afternoons in the spring, when it's possible to see some hazing in daylight (some events require too much space to be handled indoors). He had to rely on self-reporting, or reporting by other fraternities. Cornell ultimately needed to convince students—and the alumni who influenced them—to turn away from the more brutal and demeaning behaviors, and find alternatives.

It was tough. Too many young men found the allure of power over fellow men intoxicating. Too many pledging events seemed harmless, until they turned ugly when the men in charge were drunk or careless. Too many alumni supported it. So did some freshmen, who thought hazing was part of the fraternity experience.

TWELVE
Muscle Matters
(Spring 2001)

Community service could be a chore, promise or no promise, vision or no. But that spring the philanthropy chair, Joe, found an interesting project: demolishing an old house. The city planned to build a home for a low-income family, on that spot. Joe was joined by Nieraj, Hitman, Paulie the hurdler, Big Daddy, Lou, Magnus, and Pete, the sophomore pledged in the fall. I decided to give up a Saturday and join them.

We were supposed to have power tools but they weren't provided, so we used crowbars and our own muscles. Directed to tear out the floor in the front room, we looked for places to start, finally deciding that the walls and door jambs were the best. Besides two layers of clothing, hat, boots, and work gloves, I wore a mask over my mouth and nostrils. The old guy was being cautious with his lungs.

We dug the forked end of our crowbar into the line where floor met wall. The linoleum came away fairly easily, and then we struck wood. We braced our backs and shoulders, strained and groaned. My arms might as well have been cooked pasta, I was so ineffective at the task before me. How embarrassing. The wood squeaked and protested, but did not give. I paused, tried again. Some wood splintered away, in a big chunk, and I triumphantly pulled it up and carried it outside to the Dumpster. I was not weak, having kept up with the weights steadily.

There were four layers of wood in the floor. After an hour, we were sweating, flushed, and aching, and my back told me that I would pay a price later.

"I'm pacing myself," I told the guys.

"Pacing yourself is for pussies," said Lou.

Practically bending our crowbars, we imagined them snapping back if the floor gave way. Instead, we hung there, our breath feathery in the dimness. We had made a hole in the floor. You could see into the cellar. Big Daddy and Lou were digging up the wood faster than the rest of us and showed no signs of letting up. They ripped through the wood like machines. Both men were jacked. The 6-foot-2, 220-pound Big Daddy awed the sophomores who had recruited him. He also had charisma and was seen as presidential material. Lou was considerably smaller, but his shoulders and back strained against his T-shirt. We later learned that he could bench-press 325 pounds. Like Hitman, who labored nearby, he was an engineer who did not fit the engineer image. We had discovered that Lou was hard-core about drinking, and loved a physical challenge. He pounded away at that floor.

Muscle always matters among men.

We finished in early afternoon. We had done something for someone no matter how we ached. Greek chapters had turned to community service for years as a way to show a campus and a municipality that they were about more than just drinking or choosing whom to admit to their clubs. Some critics dismissed this as apologies of the weakest sort for the hell raised by fraternities in particular, saying one weekend of doing good could not make up for damage done the rest of the year. Most of the Phi Taus genuinely seemed to like doing something for the community just for its own sake.

We stopped for food at Burger King. I got grilled chicken, said the heck with my diet, added a medium order of French fries.

✶ ✶ ✶

The ropes burned everyone's hands. We had not thought to provide gloves. That was the first lesson of Phi Tug, the tug of war competition we staged on the Arts Quad a couple of weeks later. Because there were fewer teams than expected, instead of two divisions each for women and men, we had one. Pizza and soda for sale, little trophies for the top placers, music blasting: we wanted to make a name on campus and raise money for Phi Tau's national philanthropy, the Hole in the Wall Gang camps.

The camps were for chronically and terminally ill children. They had been created by actor Paul Newman, first in Connecticut, then in the Adirondacks of New York, followed by North Carolina and Florida. Camps were planned for California, Ireland, Israel, Great Britain, and France. Newman wanted one in every state. Newman was a Phi Tau, initiated in 1943 at Ohio University, so his cause became ours.

The sun shone on us and we wore maroon T-shirts, made for the occasion, with a yellow diamond that showed a stick figure pulling a black line (later mistaken for a rifle by some hysteric). On the back was a classic misspelling: "Benefitting the Hole in the Wall Gang Camps" (it should have been benefiting, even if that spelling looked wrong). The word "gang" has since been removed from the name. The grunts and yells of men straining on a rope and being dragged over the grass. The groans of betrayal when the team recruited by Andres from the townhouses discovered there was no lightweight division, as Andres had said there might be. The gasps of frustration from the lightweight crew team recruited by Mick as their vaunted rowers' muscle proved no match for Chi Phi, composed of wrestlers. Women screaming at each other to pull harder (sororities brought more than one team, a trend that would continue for years and aid us greatly). Tom manned the microphone to announce winners and brackets.

This was fun, but it was all for children who had little normal about their lives, who lived with HIV or sickle cell anemia or kidney ailments or cancer. At the camps they could hike, ride horses, learn crafts, swim in a heated pool, canoe, fish, play games, stay in a cabin. They could forget about being home-bound, different.

At the end a Phi Tau team challenged the rowers, and the Phi Taus began to pull the rowers toward the center mark. Big Daddy was officiating. Suddenly he jumped to the rowers' side and added his considerable muscle to theirs. So did Dream, who was pretty big himself. The rowers beat the Phi Taus, who laughed and cursed at the traitors.

✶ ✶ ✶

Community service had become part of Greek life before our chapter was re-founded. It was expected. We simply made it a larger component of our chapter.

This was not a part of Greek life until the 1980s, when colleges began to tell their fraternities and sororities to give back to the town they kept awake with their parties: show the world that you are about more than drinking and raising hell and making yourselves happy.

This wasn't the case when I was in college. I asked a St. Lawrence classmate who had been IFC president whether the fraternities were required to do service. He said no, the university wanted it but he argued that "we were not the Boy Scouts, we were social organizations and that wasn't what a fraternity was for." But now campuses expected their Greeks to help the campus and town around them. America itself has gone on a community service movement.

Every chapter meeting we heard the philanthropy chair's report about money raised, how guys were progressing toward their 15 hours of community service each semester, and what events he'd found that week for guys who needed hours. His report came early, after the treasurer starts things off. Usually, as he stood in front of the room, faces remained stoic as if we were about to face a lecture. Service was not as fun to hear about as, say, the social chair's plans for this week's party.

One week the philanthropy chair told us about opportunities for service: reading to kids, playing basketball with kids, working in a soup kitchen, working with Habitat for Humanity for an afternoon to build trusses for a house. He exuded enthusiasm. The chances for service will be fun, he assured the men.

He asked how things had gone last weekend, when guys had played basketball with underprivileged kids at an Ithaca city gymnasium.

"It was fun until the kids started calling us punks and swearing at us," someone said.

"Yeah, it got so aggravating that we finally started beating them."

The chair's smile froze. Then he soldiered on.

"Looking over my charts, I see that 10 guys have got plenty of hours already and are on track, but 12 of you don't have many. A few of you have zero hours." Here he might have wanted to yell at the men. He did not. He just passed the charts around the room, so guys could fill in their new hours.

A few guys never came near 15 hours, but a few went over, so it balanced out. We tried to nicely pressure the ones who weren't meeting their obligation. Alright, maybe not so nicely. I always wanted to say, "Why did you join us, when you knew this was part of Phi Tau?" I said that about other things the men did—to myself, anyway. Of course, I chose to forget how flighty I was in college.

✳ ✳ ✳

Time for our first road trip: Montreal.

Time to get away from Cornell and all the expectations that we would behave as gentlemen.

Well, not "we" this time. I thought about going and then realized that was a mistake. I would see things I should not see.

The men made the five-hour drive and drank in bars where 18 was legal, went to strip clubs, got a little rowdy. Two of them stole an orange cone from a construction site and brought it back. Someone got a speeding ticket on a Queen Elizabeth Way entrance ramp, and felt they'd been targeted because they were young and American. But Phi Tau got to let loose. They laughed for years about who got in trouble with customs for telling an agent they were all brothers, and who puked, and who tried to speak French.

THIRTEEN
Gut Check
(Spring 2001)

Our first real crisis came in April, which somehow would always be a pivotal month for us.

The next meeting after we added the five associate members, the men had to elect a new vice president and treasurer. Hitman, the vice president, was going to spend the fall away from Ithaca, doing an engineering co-op at a large corporation. The treasurer, Tope, was going to Washington, DC.

Tom had moved the meetings to a larger conference room at the student union on North Campus, next to where many of the men lived. Phi Tau was 36 strong now and we filled the room to capacity when we met that Sunday. LeGrand was absent. I looked over the five new men but did not meet them yet. This would turn out to be a special group. One would de-pledge next fall but three of the others would be voted president and the fourth would become treasurer.

The vice president election was supposed to be first, so the losing candidates could drop down and run for treasurer if they wished. Chaz had been nominated but he now said he was dropping out, as he would be Navy ROTC battalion commander and that was enough. One candidate, Vijay, was late. Yes, Vijay was running for office already. We had discovered that beneath his poise he was a comedian who loved to make us squirm with ethnic jokes, like chastising another dark-skinned Phi Tau for sitting in the "white section" at meetings or offering support to one of his "brown-skinned brothers." The guys liked him immensely. Now he was seeking the one-semester term as vice president.

To help Vijay the men decided to hear the treasurer speeches first. One candidate began his speech, while the other three—Joe, Lou, and Ice—went out in the hallway.

The conference room's glass wall vibrated.

Those clowns, I thought. My money was on Lou, a former wrestler, no doubt tossing someone around. The door opened and we saw Lou's blond head. "Someone get out here," he said.

Dream stepped into the hall and then back into the room. "I need help," he said. Tom and I joined him.

Vijay sprawled on the gray carpet, face to one side, felled by a seizure. His eyes rolled, and a moan rattled in his throat.

Two freshmen came out into the hall and squatted next to him: Matty J and Barry. "They have EMT training," Tom said. He calmly pulled out his cell phone—Tom was one of the few Phi Taus who owned one then—and dialed 9-1-1.

I was certain I should do something but had no idea what. I too remained calm, from years as a newspaper writer and photographer, veteran of car accidents, fires, and sobbing athletes who had lost a championship game. I felt nothing, really.

Jay ripped off a brace on his right leg (which he had injured playing pickup basketball) and ran down the hall to find a payphone before we could tell him that Tom had already called an ambulance.

Vijay gasped and mumbled "speech," as in making his speech for VP.

"We should put something in his mouth, to block his tongue," I said.

"No, nobody is putting anything in his mouth," Barry said sternly.

The student first-responder crew and a professional ambulance crew arrived. The medics asked who was in charge. Tom said, "That would be me." I identified myself. The medics ignored me and asked Tom what had happened.

Lou was distraught. Funny, that this tough dude was so upset. Joe said the three of them had laughed when Vijay ran toward them and lurched against the glass, thinking he was clowning. I patted Lou's shoulder but he twisted away, eyes haunted and filled with tears. Another brother, Jeff, was clearly upset too, and I told him things would be fine though I had no idea if that was true.

The medics tried to talk to Vijay. They wanted him to sleep. They strapped him onto a wheeled stretcher. Finally he passed out. Tom, Jay, and a few other guys followed them to the hospital. The medics rolled Vijay to an elevator.

I stepped back into the conference room, where rows of faces looked at me. Most of the men did not seem upset, just numb. I saw the new associates. This was their second meeting, a tough way to start their time in Phi Tau.

"What should we do now?" Jeff asked me.

I answered as if I were a reporter taking notes at a house fire: "We could continue the election."

He stared in astonishment.

"I don't see how we could do that," he said.

Idiot, what are you thinking? What is wrong with you?

"Yes, sorry. We should just call it a night," I said. "Go to your rooms and wait for Tom to report from the hospital. Tom is looking for Vijay's parents. Keep Vijay in your thoughts. Anyone who wants to talk, I'll be around." *As if you've done any good so far, Conroe.*

The men scattered into the night, and I followed. What, I wondered, had happened to me? I knew exactly what. As a newspaper reporter for 17 years, I'd stepped into places, bent customs, slipped what regular people did. I felt compassion only enough to connect with people when I wanted a story from them. No, that's not true—I felt compassion but kept it locked away.

One night in 1983, I heard on the radio that human remains had been found in a marsh, of a girl who had disappeared more than a year earlier. The city where I worked then had never seen anything like this; the city's murders always took place in the maximum security prison. The case had attracted psychics, and developed hundreds of leads that went nowhere, as a family lived in agony and a city speculated about the possible guilt of certain boys. My newspaper was to publish the next day, a special package of stories and case chronology, even a story where I compared a psychic's words to the girl's actual location—an exact match.

"Go to the family," said the managing editor.

"I have to?"

"Yes."

Her father let me in. We had talked a few times as the months dragged on. He had told me ways he was searching for his daughter, convinced she was alive. I sat in their living room with him, his wife, and their son and their son's fiancée. A clock's pendulum marked the time in the quiet. I scribbled notes. *I shouldn't be here,* I thought, *what else can I ask,* and finally excused myself, left them with their sadness. I was shaken and then I made myself numb.

In those years I thought about stories all of the time, stories so interesting because my own life was so ordinary. I pursued stories like quarry, and liked awards. One day I decided enough was enough, and left the news business. But apparently I had not re-connected to that sensitive side of myself, not shown to those I should care about.

At the nearby residence hall where most of the colony lived, I checked on Hitman in his single room and then Rico, one of our new associates, who seemed dazed. I told him to seek out his new fraternity brothers, not to sit around alone. But I decided not to play mother hen.

Out at my car, I pondered whether to go to the hospital. It was not part of my role. The men must struggle on their own to an extent, must learn from failures and triumphs alike. My home lay 25 miles away, and it was 8 p.m., and I must teach tomorrow morning, Monday.

But a feeling like a father's, or at least a big brother's, tugged at me. There was no other word for it. I looked at the stars. Driving to the hospital was the right thing. These men should see that I cared.

In a lounge at the hospital, several Phi Taus munched on pizza as they waited for a doctor to tell them how Vijay was doing. I hung out. Tom was on his cell phone, in search of Vijay's parents. I could not tell if my presence mattered.

A bearded doctor told us that Vijay was suffering from dehydration caused by mononucleosis. Seeing our surprise, he said every student at a college likely gets mono at some point, whether or not they realize it. Vijay would stay there a couple of days.

I remained in town, choosing a hotel over Tom's offer of a couch at his apartment. I did not have a change of clothes, but kept a toothbrush, razor, and shaving gel in my desk. The next day I told LeGrand what had happened.

This was the first time other than association ceremony that something touched us all, let us feel each other as a brotherhood.

Joe was chosen as treasurer the next Sunday. A direct-spoken young man, he had taken a big step. He had become scholarship and philanthropy chair, proving himself a hard worker. Joe was growing into part of the group. The men also liked his style. A business major, he would say during meetings, "Guys, I need your receipts, no damn excuses." Joe had emerged as someone who would call people out, voice the concerns that other men might be reluctant to. In chapter he challenged guys to live up to the standards they had set down as a colony. When Winky came from national headquarters to check our progress, Joe—eye to eye across a table from him—said the men were restless with performing so many duties and wondered when they could start living the real fraternity life. That meant, among other things, moving back into the house, and getting our charter.

Plainly annoyed, Winky said, "You're not having fun?"

Joe said, "I don't even drink and I'm not having fun."

"Keep working," Winky said.

Vijay was elected vice president. His opponents joked that they could not beat the sympathy vote for him.

When Vijay's crisis was discussed at the next chapter meeting, Phi Taus were cited for their contributions. My name was not mentioned, nor should it have been.

That evening represented for me another turning point, this time not the men's so much as mine. For the men it was a scary time shared by everyone, perhaps one of the first real crises in their young lives. There would be times when all of us in the colony, later the chapter, would be touched by something, a tragedy, a situation where a brother needed help.

I resolved to reach out more to them, even when they thought it was not needed. I promised, off in my corner, to listen to Phi Tau's creed when the men recited it, and maybe live by it. I would try to be a friend, and a student of whatever these men might teach me.

FOURTEEN

Cleaning Up

(Spring/Summer 2001)

We gathered at the Memorial Room in Willard Straight Hall, among the stars of the Cornell Greek system. Ten of us, dressed in coat and tie, sat in two rows. It was the weekend in May after classes had ended: time for the annual Greek Awards. Each of the three councils had people managing this program.

First we were honored for having all of our members take part in the alumni phone-a-thon, the fraternity with the most hours. Joe accepted and Jeff, who was taking Joe's place as philanthropy chair now that Joe would be treasurer, stood with him.

Faculty, leaders, new members, and alumni were all presented with plaques. Then came the names of the chapters with the highest GPAs for each council. And for the IFC we heard, "Phi Kappa Tau," and a beaming Tom strode up to receive the plaque. At the end the associate dean listed the outstanding chapter leaders, and now it was Jay's turn to grin and make the trip to the podium. Finally, we were named as one of the outstanding fraternity chapters, despite being just a colony. So Tom got to stand with the presidents of more established houses.

Plaques for the chapter room wall, when we moved back into 106 The Knoll: nice.

Now our name was out there. We basked in the Cornell administration's glow. Unlike the brothers of 20 or 30 years ago, we wanted this.

Awards are a curse and a wonder. They can leave even the most motivated person complacent. We needed to keep them in perspective.

I loved it. I had begun to consider the Phi Taus and some of my students as friends—in the delicate, limited way that someone my age could be friends with someone so much younger. I didn't want to get too attached, since young people are on their way somewhere else. But I accepted from them what I could and was glad for it. I tried to spend more time with the men and set aside my old-guy perspective—abstain from preaching. I began coming to chapter meeting each week. The men began to greet me with questions about how I was and how my life was going.

Phi Tau had swallowed me whole. We hadn't planned this, me least of all. It got so I didn't think it odd if they asked me to go eat with them somewhere (I sometimes did), or said a bunch of them were going to the movies, did I want to go (I didn't but appreciated the invite). I began to worry about them in a way beyond an older brother's—almost like a father's, I thought, until one of my baby boomer friends reminded me that I was not quite there. "You didn't change diapers, wipe tears, see children off to school, or ground them," he said. But I felt it.

* * *

The spring of 2001 ended with the promise that we could move back into 106 The Knoll, no matter when we regained our charter. We looked forward to it. Every fraternity wants a place to call home. For three semesters our colony had existed the way fraternities did back when they started, meeting wherever they could. Many fraternities still did, occupying a rented house or a floor of a residence hall, but now we had the next step in our evolution.

The mansion was a mess. The Newman Room, a handsome room with fireplace and a mirror that covered on wall, was used for storage (it was not named after Paul Newman but after a long-ago brother and benefactor named Floyd Newman). Decrepit desks, dressers, and bed frames gave many rooms a neglected feel. The wood-shingled outside was dirty, weeds clung to the walls, and rocks dotted the yard. We scheduled a cleanup weekend for July. Hitman came from Buffalo. From Long Island came juniors-to-be Paulie, who was the new house manager (elected months earlier, as we began planning to move in); Komo the former vice president, now secretary; and Dream, who brought three friends, a young woman and two brawny football players. Jacob, the sophomore among the five April associates, was in town for the summer. So was Tom, who was teaching sailing. We were joined by Pat Madden, the 1988 alumnus from Boston who had worked hard to start up the fraternity again and who had spoken at the information session during rush 2000. He served on both alumni boards. We divided the tasks and went to work.

The house had potential. The front foyer, the heart of the first floor, opened left into the dining room and right into the Newman Room. The dining room, just a large room with long tables, had a fireplace with a white mantle upon which was painted, in a black rectangle, a looping symbol with

"1902" in it: a Sanskrit symbol for fellowship and the founding year for Bandhu, one of the local fraternities we were rooted in. Ahead lay the Chapter Room. A thick, six-sided wooden table sat near the windows: another Bandhu remnant. Another table had "skull" carved into its top in Greek letters, and men's names were here and there—a relic from Skull.

Inside the front door, to the immediate right was a bedroom and to the immediate left was the mail closet, the stairway to the second floor, a bathroom, and a hallway to the kitchen. The second floor had seven bedrooms (three singles and four doubles, one of which could be a triple) and three bathrooms, each of which had a shower, and we were adding another shower. The showers were all individual, to the men's relief, for they wanted no part of showers for two or three guys at once, which some fraternity houses had. The third floor had a single and two doubles, although the single had another room tucked behind it, used for storage. A lounge formed the center. Two stairwells led to the basement, one from outside. Down there lay a large bedroom with a water bed, the furnace room, and three large rooms for parties, with ping pong table, foosball and billiard tables, and—in the last chamber, which had been used for storage until the 1970s—a bar and stereo system. Traffic signs (presumably stolen) and a Firestone Pegasus sign hung on the walls. A smaller room, once used to hold coal for heating the house, was full of old composite portraits. In the furnace room we found a box of old pledge paddles, some shaped like slide rules or the starship *Enterprise*—a brotherhood of engineers, apparently. "We were a nerdery," one of the men said.

Paulie's job as house manager, one of the more thankless in any fraternity, entailed hiring people to trim our lawn, plow snow, fix plumbing or electrical problems that we couldn't, and clean our carpets; accompanying city fire inspectors as they determined if we met code; and assigning chores for the men to do, such as cleaning the bathrooms or sweeping the foyer. Paulie approached his role with a cheerful demeanor, only rarely letting his frustration loose. He would serve four semesters as house manager, always grinning quietly as the brotherhood stuck him with this role by acclaim.

The colony had also elected a steward, who would work with the cook on meal plans and assign waiter duty, which meant setting up for dinner and then doing the dishes. The role had gone to Garrett, the big Californian who had roomed with Jay and Hitman as a freshman, a sports trivia nut. Both he and Paulie were supposed to punish men who didn't do their chores or waiter duties, although the form of punishment was still being debated. Some fraternities barred men from attending social events, or fined them. Eventually the Phi Taus would decide that cutting off a man's online access in the house would be enough, but when Paulie did that the men sometimes trashed his room. Accountability was a problem here as much as anywhere.

Our cook would be Patty, a middle-aged, direct-spoken woman who had cooked for fraternities before. Tom and the alumni had hired her after interviewing a few people recommended by a company that helped Cornell's Greek societies with accounting and budgeting. The job didn't pay much and the hours were odd—Sunday through Thursday afternoons—but finding a cook who cared about the men enough to provide tasty meals for them at the end of a day of classes was crucial.

The Board of Governors had set room and board costs, and the men had picked rooms. Although he was just a rising junior, Jay, as the founding president, had insisted he go first and had taken a second-floor single on the house's front side. Komo chose another single. Tom, entering his second and last semester as president, picked the only basement room, which had a water bed and was next to a side entrance. He was constantly on the go, so he liked that. Tom was the only one of the six seniors who would live in. Paulie led the rest of the men through the process of determining which rooms would be doubles and who would be roommates. Every fraternity needs to fill its house, for financial reasons, and this can be a struggle since seniors often want to live in apartments. But 106 The Knoll was probably Cornell's smallest fraternity house, and the rising juniors filled it easily, with a few sophomores.

After the first day of cleaning, the men drank a few beers and played Beirut (beer pong) in the foyer. Dream and Hitman took on Dream's buddies from home. Someone's CD player blasted music.

Soon there was a ruckus. Hitman liked to assume a party personality, the tough guy who talks trash. The Phi Taus were used to it but Dream's friends didn't like it. Getting a little excited, Hitman bumped chests with one of them, and suddenly Pat Madden was between them, separating them. The football player, who outweighed Hitman by about 50 pounds, was furious. Dream ran out the front door and walked through the dark, deeply upset that his high school and college friends almost had come to blows. Someone told one of the football players that Hitman didn't mean anything, he just liked to act tough. "He's not tough at all," the fellow answered. "I could break him like a twig." Hitman calmed down but the bigger men didn't, for a while. The football players said they wouldn't help us the next day, when we were going to move things and would need them.

It all blew over. The next day, Dream's buddies pushed old metal desks out of the third floor windows and cheered as the desks fell and broke apart on the lawn. But I made a note: When it came time to have parties in the house, the men would need to be responsible for their guests, especially those who weren't from Cornell.

* * *

Jacob was doing an internship and riding horses as a member of the polo team. He had broken his leg when a horse threw him, so he wore a brace after surgery. He'd been going home a lot to his farm in the Adirondacks. The men noticed that Jacob, who had been fat as recently as Phi Tug in April, had gone on a health kick and lost 60 pounds. Between that and hitting the weights, he looked chiseled.

They also knew his father was ill, although he didn't say how ill. That weekend I said hello and added that I was from Potsdam. I liked meeting North Country people.

Jacob said his dad had a brain tumor. The doctors gave him until September.

I felt sick for him. Now I needed to be ready to counsel. I had encountered death so much. Three of my grandparents were gone, and one of my high school friends, and people I had befriended while covering sports. Cancer, suicide, car accidents—as I grew older I just learned to go on, to cry my tears or feel my sadness, and try to remember these people often.

"How old is he?" I said.

"Forty-seven."

Just over a year older than me. I hated hearing things like this.

"Well, talk to me about it anytime," I said. Jacob thanked me and drove off.

FIFTEEN
Home
(Summer/Fall 2001)

I bought a house, my first in seven years. My teaching job wasn't really stable—I was hired year by year, and veteran faculty had told me not to plan on being there a long time, as the college's dean wanted to trim out lecturers—but I wanted to put down roots anyway. My real estate agent found a century-old Cape Cod on a corner a few blocks from SUNY Cortland, being sold by HUD. I liked it. The neighborhood was quiet in summer, but I noticed student houses around me. Nights would be noisy. Well, I had lived among students before. I bid for the house and got it, bought a refrigerator and curtains, began moving my belongings in slowly.

The men were moving into 106 The Knoll, shifting furniture from room to room, painting, hanging up posters, settling in. Tom tried to appease a mother who didn't think the house was adequate for her son. In the midst of this chaos, I asked a few guys to help me move: Big Daddy, Lou, and a senior named Alfred, three of the strongest Phi Taus. Vijay asked to help too. I drove over to Ithaca and picked them up, and we filled a van with my belongings.

Lou didn't like the color of my living room, which was peach or salmon. "That's pink," he said. I denied it. He also complained that the house was slanted, "all houses in the Northeast are slanted."

I had offered to buy them all lunch, since they wouldn't take any money. Vijay asked what restaurants were special here. I said we had one of the few remaining A&Ws, and they said yes, that's the one. So we ate burgers, fried chicken, and French fries, and I drove them back to Ithaca on a back road where you could see hills stretching toward the Finger Lakes.

* * *

The men were thrilled to have 106 The Knoll again. A house is more than a place to live. It's part of a fraternity's identity, a place to meet and have parties, a home.

The alumni had allowed the men to occupy the mansion because they were displeased with the company hired to manage it during the five years it was rented out. The kitchen did not meet code—the big oven needed to have a metal hood over it, for safety and smoke clearing. Discovering that we'd moved in, the city began to fine us. Our local attorney and the alumni, notably Bob Cundall, began to speak with the city judge about what we planned to do, to bring the kitchen to code. But our area of the city had been designated a historic district, and the city historical commission told us we were limited in what we could do. The building needed to look the same on the outside.

It was an epic battle that dragged on for months. Bob found himself listening to someone from the historical commission one afternoon in court, and wanting to start swearing while our attorney kept a hand on his shoulder and told him to calm down. When the hood was put in, it went up through a closet on the second floor, then through a back storage room on the third floor. It altered the mansion's inside. But the outside was fine.

Many fraternities, including some chapters in our own national, would gladly have taken 106 The Knoll. Like everything else about them, houses had become an issue.

There was the case of Hamilton College, a couple of hours east of Ithaca.

* * *

The fraternity house was the largest in the East, three stories and almost a block long. On this weekend afternoon its lawn was littered with cups, after a huge annual party the night before: the last such party in this house.

It was the spring of 1995. Hamilton College, a small liberal arts college near Utica, was taking away fraternities' houses while leaving the fraternities intact. The seven houses and another occupied by a literary society would be purchased by the college and transformed into residence halls, open to all students. Fraternities could have blocks of rooms in residence halls. Parties would be held in "social spaces" such as dining halls.

So this was a house full of pissed-off men. This house had been theirs for decades, far back, and now it would not be.

A task force of alumni, faculty, and students had studied student life at the college, one of the highest ranked in the East. Once all-male, Hamilton had been co-ed since the late 1970s but sororities didn't have houses. One fraternity house, Alpha Delta Phi, was the mother house for that national fraternity. A Hamilton student named Samuel Eells had started the fraternity in 1832 and then—at a time when fraternities were mostly at Hamilton, Union, and Williams—had made Alpha Delt the first one to establish a chapter to the west, at Miami University in Ohio, where several fraternities were founded after that, one of them us.

Now the Residential Life Plan was here. No students would live off-campus. Hamilton would be a true residential college. The trustees, namely chair Kevin Kennedy, announced the plan on a Friday afternoon in March, at the old gymnasium, as students began a two-week spring break. Gay students and their friends, who thought fraternities were homophobic and elitist and wanted them completely gone, staged a "kiss-in" outside. Fraternity leaders waited, having received hints from people on the task force that change was coming and they wouldn't like it.

The chapter president, who was starting goalie for the hockey team and headed for law school, was in his double room with bathroom. He had spoken against the plan at the trustees' presentation and had met with Kennedy to see how firm the trustees were about implementing it. They were not going to back down, he decided. The task force felt that fraternities were out of control, with the houses occupied mostly by sophomores, and were hurting the college's image, especially with female prospective students.

He said the plan had been written by, of all people, former fraternity members on the Board of Trustees, and had split alumni. Four of the fraternities were suing the college in federal court, claiming violation of the Sherman Anti-Trust Act—creation of a residential monopoly. The men were disgusted and bitter. I saw pledges painting and cleaning this building they would never be able to live in, looking happy but bedraggled, meaning they were in the last week before initiation. The pledges had talked about quitting, and the president had dissuaded them, saying the fraternity would still be worth belonging to. The men hoped their alumni could save the day, but doubted it. "Other people are going to be living here who did not earn it the way I did," a junior told me. As a protest they had allowed food and dirty plates to pile up in the kitchen. Plates and silverware sat on a porch roof. When they moved out in May, they left some of their rooms intact, with clothes in the closets and books on the desks, as if they were going to return. Students rallied for the fraternities one afternoon and marched around campus, cornering the college president as he worked out on a Stairmaster.

Anger was the main theme whenever I was around college-aged men. I heard "Damn college. I'm glad I'm leaving soon!" "This place has changed too much." I was hearing that at St. Lawrence too. Rage poured forth when men drank, rage at the political correctness movement that told everyone a new way of talking and thinking. One Hamilton fraternity member who was a student government officer and resident advisor—respected, in other words—told me that he tried to explain to students and faculty who hated fraternities that he gained so much, had learned so much about himself, from being part of this. People barely listened.

With the anger came frustration over how to express it. Vandalism was one way; at Hamilton, someone used a truck to tip over a statue and someone defaced an antique bronze map of campus. Defiance was another way. The fraternities took their pledging activities into nearby woods.

Fraternities could be their own worst enemies. There was the junior who complained that when his house was no longer available for him and his brothers to live in, he could no longer smash beer bottles against the back wall when he came home at night. Down the hall, another Psi U said to me, "Anyone talk to you about the way fraternities encourage addictions?" I said yes, sort of, did he mean booze? He said no and showed me his Gamblers Anonymous card. The men often drove to a casino 10 miles away, and did not know why he wouldn't go with them anymore.

The trustees chair, Kennedy, was a managing partner at Goldman Sachs. I met with him at his corner office in Manhattan, as pieces of a hurricane threw rain on Wall Street. The trustee who had written the residential plan, Barrett Seaman, special projects director at *Time,* joined us. Both men had belonged to fraternities at Hamilton, which had been male-only in their time; Kennedy was Alpha Delt and Seaman was DKE. Both men said the fraternities had to change, and did not care if this made the two of them unwelcome at their former houses. They were incredulous that some men placed so much importance on fraternities, when this was not the center of college life. Change had been necessary. Then the federal lawsuit, dismissed in 1996, was revived.

I visited the fraternity again in February 1998. One of the 1995 pledges, now a senior, gave me a tour. It depressed me: the mansion's floors were unswept and littered, the cavernous main hall smelling like a dank cellar, the water pipes having burst from the cold. The walls were stained. The fraternity's members were split between residence halls and apartments. Without many parties on campus, Hamilton students said they drove to bars and piled up drunk driving tickets. I did go to one party, in a dining hall, and the fraternity members asked me how it compared to the old days when they had their house. I said it looked like fun to me. In the dark room, a party was a party.

A smoke alarm at the empty house dangled from a wall, ripped out of the wall and hanging by its wires. "Oh, that," the senior said. "Well, we weren't supposed to use the house for fraternity rituals, but we snuck in one night, for a pre-initiation event. Our cigars set off the alarm, and we ripped it off the wall but the cops came. We ran out the back while they came in the front."

The federal lawsuit was eventually dropped, and the fraternity houses are now residence halls.

SIXTEEN
The Booze Question
(Fall 2001)

"I say, roll out the kegs and party the way a fraternity is supposed to."
For a moment everyone was silent, surprised—not that Lou would be a rebel but that he would say it so bluntly. Lou had established himself as a party animal. A chorus of men said no, we can't have kegs, the legal risk is too high, and "anyway, that's not what we're about." Someone said, "We're a fraternity, not a frat." The rebels who sided with Lou rolled their eyes while everyone else nodded.

Phi Tau had gathered on a Friday night to talk party policy: a retreat, for what would turn out to be six hours. We had chosen the War Memorial Room on West Campus, a large stone chamber decorated with odes to the heroism of war. The whole brotherhood sat packed together, mostly on the floor, while Chaz—now a senior—stood at the front to chair our discussion of what role partying would play in the chapter, and how to manage parties while reducing legal risk. Tom had not wanted me to chair it, fearing the fallout from the men's irritation over rules would hurt my standing with them.

Lou spoke and there it was again: Ideals and principles collided with a 19-year-old's craving for fun, manly excitement, and control. Were we the kids who always pleased the principal and teachers, or the kids who flaunted the rules? Or maybe it was more like the straight-A student deciding to goof off, even cheat, because students who do that seem to enjoy life more.

So we hashed out yet again what our Phi Tau chapter was about. The question of whether to drink seemed moot. The great irony of college life was that drinking, illegal for more than half of the student body at Cornell, continued as if 1986 (the year the drinking age became 21) had never happened. It might even be worse. Freshmen lectured me about mixed drinks and beers. Most college administrations considered the law against under-21 drinking as unenforceable, and concentrated on education and

84

prevention. Cornell's attitude was that if students drank, they should at least be responsible for each other and for keeping the university out of legal trouble.

Tom suggested we "go dry" as DRI had. The room exploded with "no."

"We're going to drink, guys. It's a question of whether parties fit us," someone said. "I mean, can we really compete with the bigger houses that are famous for their parties?"

"No, we don't have a big enough facility."

"We need to make our mark in other ways."

"We don't have the money that those houses do."

I sat in a chair that the men had reserved for me. Every time I thought of something to say, one of the men would say it first—usually Jay or Joe.

"We should define what a party is, as opposed to a gathering with friends."

"Yeah, a gathering doesn't require being registered with the university."

"But does a gathering mean we still need sober monitors?"

"No, dipshit, sober monitors are just for parties."

I pointed out that with friends, someone still needed to keep control, especially when brothers mixed with friends from home who attend other colleges. Dream nodded. The confrontation between his friends and Hitman, brief as it had been, was still in our thoughts. Dream said, "Yep, everyone be responsible for your friends."

Lou was stubborn. He wasn't the only party animal in the room, but he had decided to be the voice of anarchy. "I still say we have kegs," he said. "The hell with the law."

"C'mon, Lou, you know we need to do this right."

Another rebel chimed in, maybe JB or Andres: "But we're still a fraternity. We don't want to be lame."

"Let's talk about sober monitors," Chaz said. "How many, and what are their duties?"

The men agreed that several sober monitors would be best, to watch the front door, patrol the party for problems (people acting like idiots, people too drunk), and keep people on the first floor. One problem: sober monitors who drink and therefore defeat the purpose of having them. The risk manager periodically weighed in with his opinions. He was an appointed officer, not part of the exec board but carrying power. Often someone who was thinking about going to law school, he advised the social chair and president about potential risks, and he could shut down a party if he thought it presented too much liability.

This issue of who we were—reflected today in this debate about parties, reflected in other ways all the time—never really ended.

$\ast$ $\ast$ $\ast$

Now, that was the group process, and it did not cover random drinking at the house and rules for Beirut.

In teams of two, the men stood at either end of a table—either a dining table or a board specially made and painted for this game. They put seven cups of beer at each end, in diamond formation, and one at a time a team tried to throw ping pong balls into the cups. If a ball landed in a cup, one man from the pair at that end had to drink the beer in it and set the cup aside. When the cups at one end were gone, that team had lost. When one cup was left, the winner had to sink that last shot, naturally, and if both members of a team sank their shots in that cup, both losers had to drink.

On weekends—at least in the early hours (before 11 a.m., student time)—the Beirut tables were covered with cups filled to different levels with beer, water cups for washing off the balls between shots, beer stains, and beer cans empty or partly full or even unopened. The floor was sticky, the air from a brewery. In other words, a classic scene.

One night a spirited debate erupted when somehow a ball came to rest among three cups in the formation. Dream and Vijay argued what to do, and finally called Big Daddy for a ruling. He said someone from the pair at that end had to drink all three—Vijay, in this case. And he did.

SEVENTEEN
Shattered Day
(Fall 2001)

One of the days when I truly felt like a Phi Tau was the same day the world changed, a Tuesday morning in September.

I was mowing my lawn for the first time at my new house. That fall I didn't teach on Tuesdays. I waited for the grass to dry, and watched a movie on HBO where Sandra Bullock is in a rehab clinic. You see her driving toward a city, and when you see the twin towers, you know it's Manhattan. If I had clicked to other channels, I would have seen that those towers were no more.

A SUNY Cortland student I knew was walking past as I finished mowing. He said he was on his way to his girlfriend's house, since class had been canceled. Hadn't I heard? Our nation was under attack.

I went inside, turned on the TV again, and stared at the images: a cloud covering Manhattan, jet aircraft plunging at full speed into each tower, balls of flame exploding orange into the blue sky, floors of offices collapsing as people fled.

My friend and administrative assistant Lynn Alve said I wasn't needed and she was OK. I drove straight to 106 The Knoll, numb and almost tearful. What would I say to the men? I remembered two other times when I had felt this way: the 1986 *Challenger* explosion, when I was interviewing someone for a story over lunch and thought I had misheard CBS news anchor Dan Rather, and President Kennedy's shooting in 1963, when I was in third grade and barely understood what was going on, unnerved by the sight of my teachers crying.

Because the men had just moved into the mansion and didn't have the television cable hooked up, they didn't know everything I did. Paulie had heard a rumor that a plane had crashed into the Pentagon, and someone else said a plane had hit the Capitol. I said I wasn't sure, let's not listen to every rumor. The Long Islanders at the house that morning—Paulie, Jeff, Big Daddy, Dream—couldn't get through on the phone to their families.

Dream said let's go to the apartment where Lou, Ken, and Ice lived and at least watch this on TV.

My words would not come. Finally I told them I felt awful, that this event was as big as those others engraved on my mind that they had only read about. America would be fine, I said.

At the apartment we saw the cloud settled over Manhattan. Glum faces, some almost crying. Lou lay on a couch, sick. The Long Islanders reached their families and felt better.

At a campus prayer service on the Arts Quad that evening, surrounded by hundreds of people, I stood with Nieraj, the Founder of Indian descent from Rochester, and our new chapter advisor, Mike Hayes, and took comfort. Dusk darkened the world. A choir sang from the terrace of Olin Library. The next afternoon, thousands gathered on that same quad to hear the university president, Hunter Rawlings III, and clergy from different religions speak about our nation's strength and the battle ahead against terrorism.

We tried to resume life. I was teaching science journalism and used the news coverage in lectures and labs, but my science writing students were not so objective and wanted no part of what was being called 9-11. Tom worried about being pulled out of college in December, given a general studies diploma, and shipped into a war. It didn't happen but the ROTC students were suddenly much grimmer and busier.

EIGHTEEN
Goal Attained
(Fall 2001)

We got our charter back two weeks later. By now I thought of Phi Tau not as me and them but as "we," which was fine if not technically true.

That week a tree in our front yard came down and took off a corner of the house. Paulie had to scramble to get a tree service in. All our many guests saw was a pile of wood.

National staff and alumni initiated the men on a Friday, half at the house and half at the War Memorial Room where we had met for our alcohol retreat. I was careful to stay away. I was not a Phi Tau.

Vijay's old chapter at Rutgers University came to town. So did some guys' parents. I met Jay's father the town councilman. I met immigrant parents who weren't sure what a fraternity might be. I assured two sophomores that it wasn't embarrassing that their parents came.

We gathered Saturday in a campus auditorium where two copies of the charter were signed, followed by a banquet in a dining hall, the same one where Tom had invited me to speak to the colony more than a year earlier. Jacob chaired the event, showing a mastery of detail and managing people. He had told only a couple of the men how seriously ill his father was—his roommate Vijay, Tom, MacGyver, Jay, Adam—and poured his grief for his ill father into everything he could: his studies (he would achieve straight A's), recovering from his broken leg and making the polo team, and helping Phi Tau. I merely asked if he was talking to someone in the house and he said yes, chiefly Adam, the quiet, athletic business major who had grown up in Cortland. Usually pleasant, today Jacob showed an edge as he asked guys to do things.

The newly-initiated brothers sat together in the front rows of the auditorium. The parents, alumni, men from Rutgers, and university administrators spread out behind them. The men from national headquarters—the president, Todd Napier, from the University of Evansville; the CEO, Joel Rudy, former dean of students at Ohio University; the longtime staff member and heart of the fraternity Bill "Mr. Bill" Jenkins (who as usual joked about his resemblance to the actor Wilford Brimley), and the two young staff members who had launched the colony, Gabe and Winky—chose seats off to the side. I sat even further to the side than they did. The men from Ohio introduced themselves to me and one said, "We have big plans for you." I felt complimented without knowing what he meant. LeGrand, who had left Cornell, was back and seated above me.

On the stage Napier and Rudy signed the backs of both charters. I heard my name called. Blushing, I walked up onto the stage and slowly wrote my name. LeGrand was next. The men signed the front, in two columns down each side. One charter would be framed and hung in our chapter room, the other would go to national headquarters. We took a group photo of the chapter's initiated brothers, then a photo of the chapter with alumni, national staff, and the Rutgers men. I stayed up in the seats and felt my first pang of being an outsider again. I dismissed it.

At the banquet, speeches greeted the new era for the chapter, and the men's accomplishments in getting their colony off the ground and earning their right to be a chapter. We had only two disappointments: a senior was quitting because his father's business was failing and he couldn't afford the dues; and an associate member had backed out of being initiated the night before the ceremony because his chemical engineering major and varsity sport were enough to fill his time.

The national staff presented LeGrand with their Bridge Builder Award for his efforts in behalf of a fraternity not his own.

Tom and Jay shared the limelight. Tom gave the introduction to the evening. He and Jay both spoke about people who had played key roles in the colony's growth. Then Jay gave the acceptance speech after the national president and the national CEO officially presented us with the charter.

✳ ✳ ✳

Tom had become president without holding an executive board position. Most presidents I'd seen or known had served first as rush chair, treasurer, or vice president, learning to work with other officers. But the colony was too new. Only one of our chapter's first six presidents did hold office prior to becoming the top man (such a thing would be unlikely now).

Tom had not been president of anything before. In high school, he'd been co-captain of the football team. His father, an attorney and former Navy captain, had told him to be like the captain of a ship, holding the men at arm's length while listening to their concerns. Tom had his vice president (Hitman and later Vijay) run the chapter meetings as well as the exec board meetings.

Though not a Founder, Tom needed the Founders' help to get anything done. Within the core group Jay, Hitman, Train, Dream, and Joe were the most vocal. When the Founders weren't happy about something, such as one of Tom's decisions, they would retreat to Jay's room and loudly complain to each other. They also gathered when they split among themselves over issues such as drinking, where a couple of the Founders wanted traditional fraternity fun and the rest said no.

Tom was compassionate and big-hearted, but he was not a hand-holder. He left the settling of squabbles and gauging of the brotherhood's mood to his VP and Jay. Tom would hear the guys complain, confide doubts to him, seek his support, and his face would say suck it up, deal with it. Tom felt that he needed to focus his energies outside the brotherhood, meeting with the Office of Fraternity and Sorority Affairs staff to make sure Phi Tau was in their good graces, talking on the phone with alumni. Many of the guys didn't care about this sort of thing and were glad to let him do it. A few chafed against what adults wanted. "Screw national, screw OFSA," I heard sometimes at meetings.

"No, we need them," Tom always said. "Our chances of growing as a chapter depend on them. They can be a great ally. Plus it's wise to build good will for when you get in trouble."

The men would quiet, knowing that the colony had to appease Cornell and the national staff if it wanted its charter back. I think they felt a bit less so once they got the charter.

Then there were the alumni, starting with the Board of Governors that advised the men and the Board of Directors that oversaw the physical house and property. A fraternity consists not just of the students within its ranks, but the men who came before them—a complicated body of people. The culture of a chapter changes almost every year, but especially every few years, the mix of men in different stages of life and with different memories of what Phi Tau had been, making for a sometimes cacophonous whole. Alumni are great allies for a reborn chapter but also great nemeses, slowly and steadily pushing the fraternity to be what it was. If a fraternity stops hazing pledges, the alumni will probably push the men to start doing it again. Young men like to please older men, for respect but also for their money. I have met alumni who agreed that fraternities should change to fit society more, or be gone, but they were fewer.

Tom was comfortable around older adults, always had been according to his family, and he became a buffer between the colony and these external entities. He argued with alumni about rent and fees, their expectations and hopes, their wish that the current men know more about chapter history, such as the names for each room: Presidential Suite, Tailor Shop, Gandhi's Room, Crow's Nest. One Saturday morning in the BoG meeting, he fought a spirited battle over the senior whose father had gone bankrupt and who wanted to be excused from his annual dues. Tom said yes, only to be overruled by the alumni, which left him fuming. "As president, I have to make some decisions, and I have to be a man of my word," he told them.

Tom said little to the men about his dealings with adults, only what he thought they should know. I heard him reduce an hour's argument with an alumnus into a five-minute, almost casual report. He said just as little about Cornell's administration, other than to tell the room that OFSA loved Phi Tau and this was important.

By his second semester as president, Tom wanted to accomplish things by building consensus, since the chapter president's actual power was limited. "The president's job is mostly smoke and mirrors," he said. "I have as much power as the guys give me. I have all of the responsibility but none of the power." He suffered his share of setbacks, but Tom possessed another quality: quick recovery from any disappointment.

Joining the anti-hazing movement as it got started, Tom listened as fraternity presidents argued that hazing was a traditional, legitimate way to test a pledge's commitment. Then he stood to say hazing was illegal, a public relations and legal risk, and totally unnecessary. The other fraternity presidents quickly came to know who Tom was. He spoke his mind, as some fraternity leaders glared and the dean looked on approvingly. He was joined by his friend Shane, now the president of the fraternity Tom and Chaz had de-pledged from, who was trying to eliminate hazing but encountering resistance among his men. He had gotten rid of Night of Porn, which was a start. Choosing a less confrontational method than Brian had with DU, he managed to convince the brothers that their fraternity would be caught and shut down if they persisted. "I think some hazing will be transformed into socially acceptable forms," Shane said. "Fraternities need a rite of passage, and alumni don't want hazing totally gone, just the stuff that causes us to lose kids," he said.

Tom's style hurt his relations with the men. He rarely ate dinner with them, preferring to eat at about 8 p.m. He was always on the run, cell phone pressed to his ear, with ROTC, campus tours, serving as teaching assistant to public speaking courses, visiting administrators. This irritated the men at times, since they thought he was off on his own orbit—too distant. That fall, Tom asked the men to make Brian the IFC president into part of Phi Tau. Brian's own fraternity had disowned him and he was not feeling part of them anyway. Tom thought it would be a great thing if Brian quit Delta Upsilon and became one of us, since he identified with our vision. But the chapter did not go for it and Tom thought it was because he had proposed it.

He did enjoy a large social life. Tom loved taking people to dinner, including me, putting it on his credit card to an extent that alarmed me, since I tried to use my credit card as little as possible. His parents gave him a red Porsche late in his senior year and he loved it. He savored settling back with a good cigar and glass of wine or mug of beer. He taught himself to judge a bottle of wine at dinner, using the senses, but he also liked a barbecue joint out in the hills that Brian showed him. One day he cruised up there in his Porsche with me. It was pretty rustic. Diners sat at wooden picnic tables. I protested that I was trying to get away from fried food. He elbowed me and said, "C'mon, buddy, a little grease won't kill you. Eh? Eh?" I had French fries, corn on the cob, and barbequed ribs, and it was good.

A witty storyteller, Tom called upon a unique vocabulary, with words he'd absorbed from administrators ("paradigm," his "model" for running Phi Tau) and the business world ("like herding cats"). I told him to turn off that way of speaking since the men did not relate to it.

I avoided the subject of alcohol. Tom, who once had wanted to party every weekend, had done a 180-degree turn. When we moved back into Phi Tau's house at the start of his second semester as president, Tom began to hate parties; he stayed in his room in the basement, available if anything happened but really anxious about the potential impact upon us and him. He thought it was insane that we would risk everything we'd worked so hard to establish with our chapter, just because we wanted to have parties at the house.

One thing Tom was not busy with: school. He did enough to get by. Bright as he clearly was, he had always disliked school. He complained to me that he saw no connection between his courses and what awaited him in the real world.

He and Jay maintained a mutual respect. One of my favorite moments was in August 2000, when Tom hooked up a TV set on his front porch and the two watched the final episode of this new reality show called *Survivor*. Richard outlasted the former Navy SEAL, Rudy, to win $1 million. Jay and Tom drank it in.

Jay and Tom started a trend: our president was always the man we needed at that time. Jay was decisive and dynamic, re-founding a fraternity chapter as a freshman—in effect, starting a pledge class that operated as a fraternity. Tom was also dynamic but more of a PR man who schmoozed with the outside entities we had to accommodate or work with. He also added energy to our first rush. The presidents who came after them all fit Phi Tau's personality or group dynamic in their year, bringing something to their role that the chapter could use.

✳ ✳ ✳

Now they were truly Phi Taus. At first I promised to stay on the first floor of the house when I visited, to give the men privacy, and they had said I was welcome everywhere. But I had been studying this fraternity thing for nine years, so I sensed that a line between us would be more concrete.

Yet I had become a Phi Tau. The men wanted me at their Sunday evening chapter meetings, wanted me to go eat with them sometimes, liked talking to me. I let them see a little of my middle-aged world, but only what they could relate to. And what was that? I didn't mention the precariousness of my job situation, or the process of finding and buying a house, or any number of other grown-up things. Yet they knew that people my age worried about work and career. The men set up a chapter list serve and asked if I wanted to be on it. I said no, imagining messages every day about sexual escapades, jokes, pranks (I joined a couple of years later, to be more informed).

We had a party at the house after our Chartering Weekend banquet, and jaws dropped as I drank a shot in an upstairs hallway. The men had never seen me do that.

Vijay followed me to the front door. He asked if I was OK to drive. I assured him that I was. Behind him I saw Lou.

"We're initiating him, right?" Lou said. Vijay shushed him. I pretended that I had not heard anything. Talk like that had always led to a dead end. But still I would do it if the chance came.

PART III

The Obligation to Others

(Or, Learn to be Part of Something)

NINETEEN
Up in the Air
(Fall 2001)

Fingers gripped my head—Jacob's. "Hands on," Jacob said, and down the length of my body, I was gripped in the shoulders, butt, calves, and feet. My eyes were closed. I lay on grass.

"Waist," said Jacob. As the man at my head, he was in charge of our 10-man team. I heard the same command not far away: a different group. The men raised me from the grass to waist height, then shoulder height when he said "Shoulders," and finally over their heads. A breeze caressed me. I remained still, trusting them.

Jacob repeated the words in reverse order, and I lay on the grass again. We all smiled at each other as I got up.

The Phi Taus were gathered in a half-awake cluster in a field next to a forest, on a hill several miles from campus. We were doing team-building exercises while the facilitators for Cornell Outdoor Education decided if we could progress into whatever lay among the trees.

As we looked toward January rush, the question remained: What could replace hazing? For Jay as our new member educator, and for other Founders, outdoor education appeared to be one answer. We would work together in a positive way instead of humiliating someone or questioning their manhood. Jay and Tom had trained as student facilitators. This Saturday morning in October, we were trying it out. So were the staff here, for not every fraternity could do this to their satisfaction; some goofed off or harassed each other. We had broken into teams for this exercise. Next, we turned a man head over heels as he held a cup of water and tried not to spill any.

The facilitators—two men and a blonde woman—told us to head into the forest and split into two teams of about 14 each. They led us to webs of elastic cords strung between two trees, with different-size triangular or rectangular spaces. "You must pass each man through a gap, deciding who will go first, how to get yourselves from one side to the other, and what rules you will follow," the bearded young man with our team said. We decreed that if anyone touched a cord on the way through, we'd start over. After four men, someone brushed against a cord and it vibrated faintly. We started over and it happened again. We dropped that rule.

To get through a gap, we needed to hold our arms straight against our sides, point our feet, pull in pants or loose T-shirts that might touch. A sophomore engineering major, J-Mac, figured out the best way to use the different gaps, picking the order for which of the stronger guys would go first and be there to help others through. It was J-Mac's first moment as a leader in the fraternity. We learned later that the other team, in another part of the woods, had stripped to their underwear in a couple of cases as they struggled to pass men through the narrower gaps.

Next our fraternity split between a rope bridge and a log suspended between poles, both 25 feet in the air. My group was chosen for the log. The idea was for two men to climb up, one on each end of the log, and walk to the middle and somehow pass each other. We were belayed from below, strapped into vests with cords held by several men on the ground. I couldn't strap on my vest and one of the brothers helped me. Someone called for him and he said, "I'm over here in the 'special ed' section."

I could not believe I was going to go up there until I did it. I hated heights. "Yeah, Conroe!" voices called as I gripped the cold metal rungs on the pole and then, reaching the spot where the log was attached to the pole, maneuvered around onto it. I stood, feeling that I was balancing on this log when in reality I couldn't go anywhere or do much without telling my belay team to give me slack. Across the clearing, the other team threw sponge footballs to each other on the rope bridge. I stared up at the tree tops. Clouds had covered the sun but it could still be felt. I looked down at my slightly stained white sneakers against the log's cracked but smooth brown surface. Below that I saw the clearing's floor of wood chips and the men's upturned faces.

"Ready, Scott?" Vijay stood at the other end, unafraid. I inched my way along, reaching up to grip the rope that the belay rope played into. Someone yelled for me not to do that. I wanted to just stroll down the log—Vijay was already at the middle, waiting—but couldn't do it. He kept saying, "C'mon, Scott, almost there." Finally, I was, and we decided that I should crouch on all fours while he crawled over me. My team let out my rope and I slowly dropped. My hands settled against the wood, and Vijay gripped my shoulders and climbed over me. When we reached the other ends, we had the option of climbing back down the rungs or jumping off, with our belay team catching us. I thought that I'd have to jump out far enough not to swing back and hit my head. I'd also heard Big Daddy complain about the shock to his groin earlier. I climbed down while Vijay jumped.

Instantly I regretted taking the easy path. "You could've jumped," Jay said disapprovingly.

A couple of the men had a more difficult time than I did. A sophomore who was slow to leave the tree, Barry, would go back later and conquer his fear, becoming a student facilitator. Another brother, paired with Lou on the log, could barely move. Lou coaxed him to the center and then climbed off the log, hanging by his hands while his partner crossed the center. Then his partner had to turn and pull Lou back onto the log, overcoming his fear. We applauded.

Nearby stood a huge tower modeled after the iconic bell tower on Cornell's Arts Quad. On one side, cables stretched down into the forest from 45 feet up: zip lines. I climbed a ladder to the tower's top, strapped myself in, was paired with Jacob, and knew I had to launch myself without thinking—a lesson from jumping cliffs. I whizzed down, trees passing in a blur, and felt a surge of joy. I looked over and saw that Jacob, without saying anything, was excited for me. He obviously had done this before.

We were there, in that meadow and then in that forest, because it was crucial to try this. Nobody made fun of other guys' mistakes or fears. While some of us clambered around the log and rope bridge easily, others (me for one) settled for pride that we had done anything. We shared this day.

In the stories I've heard about hazing, this sense takes a different form: men together in adversity, welded by the will to prove their toughness. Especially in the final week of pledging, when pledges sometimes stayed at the house, kept awake for days, the new men shared misery, the resolve to show their mettle. Exhausted, maybe terrified or angry, they were then welcomed.

Outdoor education was about more than braving the air or showing your guts and muscles. The COE facilitators gauged our reactions to challenges and our willingness to look for deeper lessons. Aching, after it was over I slumped on a log. A staff leader took us back through the day. He prodded us into saying you could discover things about yourself without being humiliated. I felt that I'd accomplished something, but I couldn't tell what the Phi Taus felt. Had the problem posed by the web of cords satisfied them? Could they transmute overcoming fear and encouraging someone, rather than jeering, into feelings for each other and, ultimately, the fraternity?

I didn't know enough about this side of Cornell students. What caused them to feel they had truly earned their way? Could a generation handed so much by their parents work for something as intangible as brotherhood?

We left the answers in the forest, on the windy hill.

TWENTY
Ambition
(Fall 2001)

November meant elections for the coming year. Hitman was a logical choice to succeed Tom as president, since he'd served as vice president. Jacob and sophomore Ken were nominated as well.

The night before the vote, Hitman asked me to rate his chances. I promptly proved that I was not the fraternity's greatest political pundit. I had stayed late for some reason and was standing at the end of our driveway, watching a nearby party break into chaos. A fight had erupted. I looked up to see Hitman next to me. He said the combatants were high school kids who had gotten into the party. I couldn't tell.

"So, what do you think?" Hitman said. He had been nominated two weeks earlier, which is how Phi Tau's officer election process went: the candidates were named, they accepted or declined a week later, then the chapter voted a week after that. President and vice president came first, followed by seven other year-long positions and three semester positions. This was the first time we'd had more than one candidate for president.

"I have to give you the edge," I said. "You're one of the Founders, you were vice president, you really love the house, you get guys fired up. Jacob is so new and Kenny is so young." Hitman was living a few hours away for the fall, doing an engineering co-op. He'd returned to the house on a couple of weekends. I wasn't sure if his absence would matter. I respected Jacob enormously, from his work ethic from growing up on a farm, to his skill at planning and executing Chartering Weekend, to his handling of his family situation. But he had just joined Phi Tau in April, I thought (forgetting that Vijay had won the vice presidency after only four months in the house). Ken was a campus leader but unproven. Hitman's only knock was that, having just turned 20, he was young for a junior. But he was most likely our next public face and leader.

I should've asked around.

Ambition takes so many forms at a place like Cornell, beyond just the hunger for that Ivy League degree and whatever doors it might open. In

100

Phi Tau alone, we had former high school sports captains, class and student government presidents, valedictorians, club officers. We also had guys who had never held an office but thought this might be the time.

Nominations for office, offered during chapter meeting, followed the pattern I'd experienced in high school and times in the workplace when I had pondered other jobs, promotions, new challenges. A candidate could have a brother call out his name. He had decided to go for it, to just see what he was capable of or do better than the brother who held that office. Other candidates were surprised to hear their names called out, and thought it over, consulted people they respected, then the next week accepted or declined. You could drop down and run for a lower office.

Guys talked about you.

"I don't know. He's been pretty tough to deal with whenever I've wanted help with something on my committee."

"He might grow into the position."

"He'd be a good addition to exec."

A man wrote his speech. Soon he found himself standing before the chapter, dressed in at least business casual, telling them why he should receive their votes. He answered questions, and even guys who didn't want him to win were polite. He retired to a room upstairs to await their verdict.

Speculation about the next president started as the new one settled into office, and maybe that's when Hitman began to think about his run. He knew success. At his suburban Buffalo high school, he'd been a top student, musician, basketball and track athlete. He more than survived as an engineering major, carving out a decent GPA and showing what many engineering students lacked: social skills. Mostly he was intense about whatever he was doing, and kept everything separate, school and drinking games and intramurals. He also came armed with a sharp wit.

Jacob, on the other hand, was already 21 and quite poised. He was not shy about asking questions. He listened, and thought carefully about what people told him. He had already decided to trust me, a stranger at the time, with the secret of his father's illness. He too knew success, as class and student government president at his high school. The question was, could he lead the fraternity and function in the larger world of Cornell, for his high school was one of the smallest in New York State: only 15 in a graduating class, half the size of my homeroom. He'd almost quit Cornell after his freshman year, unhappy with the courses in his animal science major and lost in the university's sheer size. Having grown up on a farm, he loved animals, especially horses—last year he had lived at the university's Equine Research Center—but that wasn't enough to love the major. Yet Jacob had stayed and found Phi Tau at the end of the year. He'd begun to take business courses and liked that better. He'd decided over the summer to run for president. He needed to plunge into life, to shake his sadness over his father.

Ken had served as president of his residence hall council as a freshman. He shared an apartment with Lou and Ice, the party animals, but wasn't a heavy drinker himself. He had joined an entrepreneur club and had already run for vice president of Phi Tau as a freshman last spring. His role as scholarship chair wasn't much of a challenge; our house was No. 1 among Cornell fraternities in overall GPA, so he really didn't need to encourage improvement (the same quandary I faced as faculty advisor). Other fraternities had tried having a sophomore as president, but I doubted we would.

I had noticed that Jacob sat with someone different every night at dinner, without suspecting why. He had been smart to keep his politicking low-key, because the men resented maneuvering that was too overt. During elections they remembered every slight, the times when a guy had failed to perform, times when he had not expressed himself well in public, long-windedness when they wanted brevity. With elections, if the men were in the right mood and the moderator (vice president Vijay, in this case) let the discussion go long enough, the candidates—and debates between their supporters—could be dissected more than they ever imagined.

Tom backed Hitman, out of loyalty to his first vice president and out of a belief that Hitman would mature with the challenge of being president. Jay backed Jacob, to the surprise of his fellow Founders, for Hitman was his buddy. But Jay saw Jacob as a more mature, articulate person, skilled at talking to men. Ken had backing mostly from his fellow sophomores.

That Sunday evening Ken spoke first, as the candidate with the first letter alphabetically among their last names (later we went by order of nomination). He reminded everyone of his hall council position, and his intense interest in the fraternity, his wish to lead. Upstairs, waiting for their turn in someone's room, Jacob and Hitman compared ambitions and found that neither of them planned to run for vice president if he lost.

The sergeant at arms escorted Ken upstairs and fetched Jacob, who had dressed in coat and tie. Jacob read a statement reminding everyone of his management skills in pulling off Chartering Weekend, of his ease with older people, of his high school offices.

Hitman, dressed more casually and talking without notes, gave a rousing promise to lead the house to greatness and win the Maxwell Award as top chapter in the national Phi Tau.

Each was asked if he could be tough—that is, could he say no to the men when several of them were advocating something inappropriate for us, which sometimes happened. Each said yes. With Jacob, I thought, *you guys have no idea what is going on in his life.* Hitman could be pretty forceful as well.

Each was asked to list his weaknesses and why he felt the presidency should be his. JB, the rock musician who majored in business, drew a laugh with a question from job interviews: "What kind of flower would you be?"

In absentia, the three men were critiqued for about a half hour. I said nothing; I never said much in elections, not wanting to take sides. Supporters of each candidate offered something, then critics, and finally each man could talk before the vote. The chapter weighed everything: fit for the position by temperament and motivation, vision for the house, speaking abilities, work ethic. Ken was a comer but could wait. Hitman wasn't poised enough to handle dealings with the university or alumni, someone said, and someone said yes he was. "Besides, you heard his speech—he was fired up, while Jacob's was just ordinary." Jacob had been a president in high school, but his school was so tiny, could he translate any of that into a fraternity of more than 40 men?

Round and round the room, guys asserted their support for one candidate, questioned another's strength. The discussion never strayed into the petty, as some could. No grudges surfaced. Finally Tom said, "Look, guys, the president has as much power as you give him. There's not much real power. A lot of what I do is smoke and mirrors." Jay didn't disagree. Their experiences as president had differed. The next president would lead the chapter into its next phase. While the president was indeed a PR man, he needed to be respected by most of the house, a man the house would like to see at the front of the room, who could quiet the chapter when a discussion broke apart into joking and side conversations. He needed to speak to gatherings of other Greeks, and to face the surprise of alumni who stopped by unannounced.

The men voted by secret ballot. The secretary, Komo, reviewed the voting procedure. Some things were done by secret ballot, some by hand. Elections were done with ballot, always. Komo was meticulous and would not yield when someone wanted to deviate from procedure. He tore up sheets of paper, everyone got a slip, pens were passed around, and Tom said to vote for a name or abstain. We had another option called trust my brother, which meant that ballot would go to the majority vote. Komo passed around a baseball cap (we use a brass cup now) to collect the ballots, and he, Tom, and Vijay counted the votes.

The three candidates were brought down. They looked subdued.

"Gentlemen," said Vijay, "please welcome our next president—Jacob."

We applauded. Ken said he'd run for vice president. Jacob sat, stunned, smiling slightly. Hitman, showing no emotion, said goodbye; he had to be at work the next morning and faced a three-hour drive. He headed out the door. "I'll be right back," Tom said, following him. "I want to make sure he doesn't jump in the gorge."

My own days of seeking elected office came back to me then: the giddiness of victory, how losses made me feel so humble, wondering what flaws other people saw that I didn't. I didn't envy Hitman his long drive in the night.

＊ ＊ ＊

The vice president's race that night followed the same pattern, with five candidates and, maybe because it was getting late, a bit less discussion. The nominees for vice president included Joe the treasurer, another junior, and sophomores Ken, Big Daddy, and Barry. Big Daddy was witty and charismatic, close to the Founders. He had been assistant to the social chair, Train. Barry was gruff and direct, sometimes brilliant and sometimes off-target. He was a man of contrasts. He could be found most days in the Newman Room, sprawled on a couch, watching TV—yet he planned to go to medical school and become a pediatrician, and had the grades. He was physical and intense—as anybody found out who tried to wrestle with him—yet compassionate. He told the men in his speech that every summer he coordinated first aid and medical help for children at a large summer camp.

Joe won. His critics said he was blunt-spoken but his supporters defended that as a fine skill that he had already used as treasurer—you faced his wrath if you were late with dues or overspent your budget. He was quick to remind men of our principles at times when they were going to stray. The vice president, working within the house to solve squabbles or motivate men, should be forceful.

The next week, Hitman put aside his shock at losing and dropped down to run for new member educator. He made his pitch via speaker phone. Barry and Big Daddy were chosen alumni relations and social chairs, respectively. Ken ran for treasurer and lost. Some of his fellow sophomores grumbled that they had been encouraged to seek leadership roles, yet were denied by the Founders, who controlled the house. Ken remained upbeat, though, continuing to faithfully attend chapter meetings and serve on committees while some of the others lost interest, and the next year he would be elected social chair.

* * *

Jay ran for IFC president to succeed Brian of DU. Among the assembled presidents, some so poised and confident, he could sense jealousy. Phi Tau had been held up by the administration as a model fraternity. Some of these houses had been leading the IFC for decades and disdained this newcomer. Jay's anti-hazing stance might hurt him as well. Brian had been elected IFC president despite his passionate attacks on hazing because he was a commanding presence, a listener and a speaker, from a house long established in the Greek community. Phi Tau was new.

In his speech Jay was frank about his wish that fraternities replace hazing. His opponent, who was from a fraternity that had dinged Jay as a freshman, was less philosophical. He promised to end the long-standing tradition of wearing shirt and tie to IFC meetings, so guys could dress in T-shirts and backward baseball caps. They could meet in a bar or restaurant sometimes, not just in this room.

Chapter presidents spoke for both. Tom, Big Daddy, and Jacob (taking Tom's place on IFC sometimes) spoke for Jay. Others stood to insist that the opponent was best. Nobody criticized either candidate, only spoke for their man.

Jay and I had become friends. Because he didn't seem to need me, as president or new member educator, and I thought I could help him, I probably worked harder to actually contribute something to Phi Tau. We developed a gruff way of needling each other. I wanted Jay to get this, for us and for him.

He didn't. Presidents who had promised Jay their support made deals and voted against him. He lost, narrowly, and went into a funk for two weeks. He did very little in the Greek community after that. In time, he decided that his loss was just as well; IFC wasn't worth his time. I always thought IFC was an odd organization, where students tried to please Cornell and the legal system and society it represented while trying to please their fellow students. It was a complicated act.

We did get our first IFC officer, probably the first IFC officer in our chapter's history since 1930. Train—our social chair, an Asian-American brother from Southern California—won the election for vice president in charge of finance. He beat a young man who had taken a semester off to join the cast of a reality show, MTV's *Road Rules* (MTV liked Cornell—a former DRI brother had been in *Real World: New Orleans*).

Jay gradually faded from formal leadership in the fraternity, although he held the office of steward in his final semester. He focused on other things. The men liked to remind Jay that he wasn't king all the time and was one of them, yet they did as he said—because his reasoning was so clear and mature. Candidates for office that he backed usually won. Whatever he said was heard.

OFSA created a new award for citizenship, and I nominated Jay. At the luncheon that concluded the annual leadership conference for Greeks, he was named the winner. The IFC president and vice president looked unhappy as he walked, beaming, to the dais to accept. We Phi Taus stood at our table to applaud him, chuckling as the presenter described Jay as a leader, with his non-hazing pledge program, and called him approachable, when lately he had kept to himself more. Being president of Phi Tau so young had taken something out of Jay, I thought. It was a lesson to remember.

That luncheon was memorable for another reason: keynote speaker Cornell's President Hunter Rawlings III, widely viewed by the Greeks as an enemy because they thought he had dismantled the Greek system at the University of Iowa when he was president there. (Erroneously—Iowa's system was still there.) Rawlings said that freshmen, who were split between North and West, all would be housed soon on North Campus while West Campus would be transformed into a place for upperclassmen. Residence halls built in the 1960s would be torn down and replaced by living-learning centers that would compete with the Greeks. To survive, the Greek chapters would need to strongly define who they were and what they could offer. The fraternity system might shrink to half of its current size. The speech scared Tom. I said we'd endure if we stuck to our guns.

✶　✶　✶

Jay might be a good citizen, but he had his hard-edged side. Playing goalie for our intramural soccer team one night because nobody else wanted to, he spotted an IFC rival on the opponent team. "A case of beer to whoever takes him out," Jay said. A brother named Mick sent the guy limping out of the game. Jay's enemy later went to the IFC meeting and told Train, "Man, you guys play hard."

I asked Mick how playing dirty matched our values. He said he had to back a brother.

Jay never did give him the case.

TWENTY-ONE
Late Bid
(Fall/Winter 2001)

A Sunday evening that same November brought me face to face with what I wanted.

It was our monthly formal chapter meeting, so we wore coat and tie. As was our custom every day, one of the waiters rang the chimes in our foyer to summon us for dinner—"First Call," the tune that a bugler plays to herald horse races. As per custom for Sunday dinner before chapter, we did not eat until everyone had food or until the chaplain, in this case our athletic, slightly wild Magnus, said words of inspiration. Magnus liked to quote Tolkien or Teddy Roosevelt. I don't recall what he said that evening but I'm sure we chuckled.

Sitting across the table from me, Tom looked preoccupied. I set my plate of chicken and beans near his, and filled a glass with "red juice" from a pitcher. "Scott," Tom said casually, "I need to tell you something. Tonight we're going to do ritual for the first time, to begin and end the chapter meeting, so you'll have to leave the meeting and come back. Just for a few minutes."

Exiled? Seeing my face, he added, "You can go down to my room or up to the second floor, to Jay's room, your choice. You just have to be where you can't hear anything."

Exiled. The group that had gradually made me feel at home the past 15 months was reminding me that I was not officially one of them. Well, this was old territory and it was fine.

No, it's not.

Yes, it is. I was not a Phi Tau. I had known this moment was coming since I met the men in their colony stage.

Being upset would be ridiculous, even disturbing, but I was. Upset, that is. Being with Phi Tau spoke to some need I barely recognized and could not name.

And I was not a Phi Tau, never belonged to any fraternity in college.

I was quite capable of gracefully exiting a roomful of people and then coming back, with aplomb. I understood my place.

But I was so pissed off, no denying it. There it was, a duller version of that gut-wrenching despair from my teenage years, when I looked for a bid from a fraternity and found none.

Stop, Conroe. Save the drama. Just grow up.

"OK," I told Tom, "but I think the third floor is better. I can hear too much from the second floor." I would ascend above the men, not descend. An English lit major in college, I knew symbolism.

So the meeting began with the guys seated in the foyer outside the Chapter Room, waiting to do ritual with Magnus, the man in charge of such things. Tom signaled for JB, the sergeant at arms, to escort me upstairs. As I climbed the staircase, I glanced down at the rows of men. None looked at me.

I was indignant and embarrassed—why? As a newspaper writer and photographer, I'd often waited outside closed doors. Even when I'd attached myself to sports teams to a point where I felt like part of them, a moment always arrived when I would return to my life. Once, in the tradition of George Plimpton, I skated with the Clarkson University hockey team during a practice, then warm-ups for a game. I learned from my "teammates" how to put on the gear. I did the skating and shooting drills, albeit slowly. For the game, I wore a gold uniform and looked through the glass at the fans as I waited to shoot on the goalie, in the arena where I had watched my hockey heroes. I pictured standing on the blue line for the national anthem, but the coach said he could have only so many players on the ice. The referees had let me get this far but that was it. I could stand on the team bench in street clothes. In the locker room I pulled off the layers of padding and wet cloth while the anthem played from beyond the wall. It was a welcome return to reality, but it was also sad. I felt that way now.

A gavel struck wood. Men's voices said something in unison. I did not try to catch more, not wanting to sacrifice trust by snooping. Damn, I felt defeated.

What is wrong with you, Conroe? Do you want your youth back? Don't we all.

A knock on the door: Big Daddy, his boyish face turned into a man's by his solemnity. He walked down with me, fulfilling his duty as the new sergeant at arms, and I truly felt like an outsider in a way I hadn't before. The men had moved into the Chapter Room. I quietly took my seat.

Before the meeting ended, I had to leave again, briefly. I offered to just depart the house but Tom said no, just go upstairs and come back. Afterward I could not control my anger, and I corralled Tom in his room and told him, "I hated that." He answered coolly, "Well, the alumni told me they wanted us to start doing ritual, and we need to be doing it. I didn't enjoy making you leave, but the fact of the matter is, we need to start acting like a fraternity."

He was right, of course. My indignation made no sense, and I said I would get over it.

What Tom wanted to tell me, but could not, was that I really was part of Phi Tau. The time was not yet ripe to ask me how official I truly wanted to make it.

✳ ✳ ✳

One day the next week, I walked into the house without noticing that the windows were covered. Magnus said, "No, Scott, get out, you can't be here." They were setting up to initiate a brother who'd missed the September ceremonies because he was on a road trip with the soccer team. As he ushered me out through the kitchen, Magnus added, "You'll know what this is about soon enough."

I'd passed through a form of rush. I had been discussed. The vote was in on Conroe.

Jacob the president-elect said the men wanted to take me to dinner on my birthday. I'd be a guest at a dinner with a sorority. Then he called to say change of plan, we'd go to an expensive steakhouse in the hills above Ithaca. Dress formally, he said, and bring an overnight bag. Maybe they planned to get me drunk. It would be a Thursday, the night before the last day of classes for fall semester. Instead of a final lecture, my writing students had a project due, so I did not have to prepare as much.

✳ ✳ ✳

A slice of especially thick chocolate cake had been placed in front of me, and I would eat it, no matter that my middle-aged gut squeezed against my belt, a slight belly that no workout regimen had yet conquered. What the hell, it was my birthday—well, the next day was, December 7. I would turn 46. Eat up.

Around the table from my left to my right were alumnus Bob Cundall, Vijay the vice president, president-elect Jacob, and president Tom.

"We have another present for you," Tom said, against the sounds of other diners. He slid a small white envelope across the dark green placemat.

Money? No, I saw what this was, and my heart lurched. I'd received hints in the past few months, and ignored them, refusing to be disappointed again. But now the envelope was here, almost 28 years after I first yearned for it, and I pried it open and read the white card inside.

The brothers of Phi Kappa Tau fraternity's Alpha Tau chapter requested the honor of my becoming one of them. Actually, the language was not quite that fancy, but in my sense of wonder I did not really see the actual wording so much as feel its meaning.

I said nothing, just let thoughts spill through me as the men watched and waited. I squirmed in my blue jacket, white shirt, ornately decorated necktie, and tan khakis. I looked at the card again. A few dozen men young enough to be my sons wanted me to be one of them. So did the alumni. Not just the guy who offered an occasional comment at their weekly meetings, wrote recommendation letters, asked how school was going—but more.

A bid from a fraternity. Unbelievable. How I'd longed for this when I was 18, back when President Nixon was fighting for his job and then was gone, and I was fighting to show that I could be one of the boys. Alumni initiate—that was the name for what I was about to do. A man's undergraduate days are done, but he can go through pledging or be initiated without it. I'd known men who did it, but my own chances seemed remote.

I could imagine the talk at my next St. Lawrence reunion, my 25th.

"What's new, Conroe?"

"I've joined a fraternity."

"You what?"

"I'm advisor to a fraternity at Cornell, and I became part of it."

"Ah. Well. You mean you get wasted with them?"

"No, no, it's not like doing what the guys do. But I help with initiation and I go to their meetings. It's changed my life."

"Right. Well, I see Fuzak over there. Catch you later."

Thoughts shuffled like a deck of cards. The men waited.

I was here because I sensed a juncture in my life, days coming where I would be tested as to who I really was and—no getting around it—what kind of man. It had happened as Phi Tau accepted me. The little card in my hand, I didn't so much decide as soak in the elation, and the wonder and yes, a powerful sense of "yes, take that" to all those fraternity guys who said no to me in college.

Be objective, Conroe. Should an advisor do this? Should a faculty member? But my teaching job could blow away in the next stiff curricular wind. I was a one-semester temp who had hung on, and I taught journalism, which my department wanted to shed like an old snake skin. I lived in denial about this because I wanted to stay put.

I had understood fraternities the same way I wrote about sports I'd never played, which is to say in my brain and not my heart. That had changed. I could always hang out with some men, and be loyal to them, but not to a whole herd of them. That too had changed. I could be tough and be part of something without losing myself in it. I was confident that being connected to these guys did not harm me or my reputation.

What was beginning here, tonight? What was I getting myself into? I would have to keep secrets, a novelty for a lifelong journalist.

The men watched.

Warmth rose within me.

A door had opened. It might not stay open.

"Of course I accept," I said.

They sighed with relief.

"This was a unanimous vote of the chapter," Tom said. I was stunned. He said the men lobbied national headquarters in Ohio for the right to initiate me into full brotherhood.

"I even wrote a letter, and I hate to write anything," said Jacob.

"We were afraid you'd say no," said Vijay. Bob just nodded. Vijay retreated to a hallway to call the house on his cell phone: "Conroe said yes, set up for initiation." This was why we'd dressed up, and why I was told to bring an overnight bag. And this restaurant was a better setting than a sorority dinner if I had said no.

I ate the cake.

In an odd coincidence, across the room Brian the IFC president and his roommate, who had been my student in science writing, were having dinner. While Tom took care of the check, I showed them the bid and watched them absorb the idea of bidding an older guy. I would not have told any professors, if I had seen them in the restaurant.

How to explain this? I'd need to learn, facing sneers and silences.

I had said yes.

I had accepted my bid as a freshman would, knowing more about what a fraternity is than I did as a freshman but still unaware of what lay ahead. A freshman sees a little of what a fraternity is, from visiting them during rush, and maybe from his father or older brother, but he has not yet become part of it. He must prove himself, learn fraternity history, do something in its service—a project, say—and be initiated if he doesn't depledge or get blackballed. Then, in a year or so, he'll make a niche for himself in his brotherhood's web of relationships, and the niche will change as he ages. As a senior, he'll exit. But on the day he accepts his bid, he has only the beginning. For all of my interviews, hanging out, talking, I was almost as ignorant as an 18-year-old. As with accepting a job offer, I waited to see what the situation really will be.

Most likely I would take an oath of some kind, my first in the three decades since Boy Scouts and National Honor Society, a promise to be somebody well-rounded and loyal. Something would mark my rebirth, the way my Jewish friends' Bar Mitzvahs did for them, but rooted in Christianity, since most national fraternities were created by WASPs. Yet maybe my ceremony would be altered to fit this new world. No doubt I'd be guided, and surprised, on a quest or journey. I suspected that if you looked at all of the initiation ceremonies for national fraternities, even the ones founded by Jewish men when other fraternities wouldn't accept them, you would see such a thing.

I rode with Tom in his Jeep Cherokee, down into Ithaca and then up a steep hill and around West Campus, where a cobbled street led past one of my favorite taverns (decorated with fraternity composite portraits and sports pictures), and past the towers of Cornell's oldest residence halls, stone castles that rose in the moonlight to our left. To the right, Libe Slope stretched up to the campus's original stone 19th century academic buildings, built where Ezra Cornell could look down on Cayuga Lake. I was nervous.

We headed up through the streets and across a rattling old metal bridge above 150-foot-deep Fall Creek Gorge. Turning right, we followed the lip of the gorge then hung a left onto a short street in a quiet residential neighborhood a few blocks from North Campus. Cornell did not have a "fraternity row" but a few clusters of houses, then a scattering of the rest through the side streets, mixed in with student houses and year-round residents. Our house loomed in the dark on The Knoll. The front door and first-floor windows were covered with something black, probably just sheets of plastic.

* * *

Now it was my turn to wait, in the yellow light of the basement, next to the billiards table. The floor above me creaked with the weight of men and shook as furniture was moved. Barry appeared, looking solemn. Nothing would happen to me, he said. I would be taking an oath. I was fine with the Christian slant to what was coming. I had even been thinking of returning to church on a regular basis.

Barry escorted me upstairs.

* * *

A drop of sweat slid down my side, born of heat or nervousness, and vanished into the fabric of my shirt. Why was I sweating? *There you go again, Conroe: afraid of risk, as always. Relax.* Whatever was coming, it wouldn't be too brutal, just a little pushing the new guy from his comfort zone.

I passed through stages of a ceremony forged a century ago. The details do not matter, and I cannot reveal them anyway, so I will stick with how it felt. Men long turned to bones and dust—given voice tonight by 19- and 20-year-olds—asked in poetic and stately words what kind of man I was, what kind of brother. The young men around the room challenged me by their solemn presence. Walking as people walk around me—how odd. In front of me, a Phi Tau read the old words in a tenor voice, asking in essence if I would be strong, humble, a loyal friend, a good man—a Phi Kappa Tau man. So many times I had asked such questions of myself even when it seemed, well, corny. I mean, how many men ask themselves such questions? Tonight I did not doubt the answer. I said yes. My bid invited me to become a Phi Tau. Looking at it, I had made a decision, but really I'd made it long before tonight.

I would turn 46 the next day.

The men saw—at least on my outside—a man like many of their parents' generation, restless, switching careers, afraid of change and yet willing to drop what he had and grasp at something new. He worried about the Vietnam War in high school and fantasized about running to Canada, 20 miles from home, if President Nixon didn't stop sending us over to Asia (what I would've done in Canada is anyone's guess). He got bifocals not long ago. Gray sprinkled his hair, which was still plentiful on his head and, unfortunately, in his ears but not (and never was) on his chest.

My mind wandered, as always. I wanted to tell everyone about the gift I had received tonight. How, I was not sure. Some friends from college might like my new status as a Greek, others—their sensibilities hardened by What Is Proper—might not. Professors might excuse my taking this step, as Phi Tau's faculty advisor, or, they might turn upon me that special academic's brand of scorn. Family and friends would say either that Scott was once again off on some adventure, another baby boomer on a journey, or he had lost it. Personal growth, or a need to grow up: Scott has never done anything normal.

I was to be re-born as a Phi Tau.

Transformed, yes. In recent years I certainly had loved solitude a bit too much and let too many friends slip away. Tonight marked the first day of something more.

Re-born on the day of my birth, I realized that I was not sure what hour I entered the world in 1955. My mother would tell me that it was about 2 p.m. My parents lived in a tiny apartment in Regensburg, Germany (West Germany then). My father was a private in the U.S. Army, assigned to patrol the Czech border. Mom had traveled across the ocean to be with him when I was born. Twenty-four and pregnant, on a ship from New York City. She chuckled now at how foolish youth can be. But they had been friends since kindergarten, when they walked to school together and my dad said he had met the girl he was going to marry. Together through high school and college, they would be together again.

My arrival was the second big event of December 7. The German family that owned the house had sent a hog to be butchered at 6:30 a.m.

A year later, on the boat trip home, Mom had tried to keep me in a cradle but the ship rolled and she finally put me in bed with her.

* * *

Secrets were not my forte, as a writer, but I promised to keep Phi Tau's. I was already keeping private facts about the fraternity, facts that few of the guys knew.

Someone snickered behind me and I wanted to tell the comedian to stop goofing around, this was my moment. But I knew young men felt silly reading old words.

I must live up to this night, this gift. Transformation: I needed, this past year, to regain more of my humanity. May I continue to learn from these men. May they continue to drag me, so skilled in avoiding responsibility, into life's messes. I absorbed their affirmation, their welcome. Never married, arraigned in court, or sworn to public office, I could not think of another moment when I was asked publicly to promise something, or to say who I was.

I dismissed the name we hold for young people, "the kids." Age meant nothing in this room tonight, which was partly my doing—I allowed it. Doubt whispered that I had gone native.

Fraternities could be drinking clubs, or places where future leaders practice persuasion and command. Men could grow within a fraternity, learn about themselves in ways they would not if they lived in a single residence hall room or an apartment. They might not like all that they learn, but such is life.

Maybe this man could grow.

The ceremony wound down and I emerged a brother of Phi Tau. Someone asked the men in the room if they truly wanted me. Yes, they boomed in unison, and warmth surged through me. Grateful at sharing this, I wondered how so many men could be so casual about being chosen by a fraternity, as if it were their due. We locked arms around each other's shoulders and sang of brotherhood. I was wedged between two big bodies: Magnus and Big Daddy. I was initiate No. 79,827 in national Phi Tau since 1906.

It was 1 a.m. Exhausted, I decided to stay at Phi Tau. In the third floor lounge I pulled a mattress from a stack, tossed down my sleeping bag, chucked my blazer onto a chair, and lay there. Heating pipes rattled, a floor creaked.

A fraternity man—unbelievable. This could not be a total gift, of course—I would not always be so giddy. Who knew what lay ahead for us all? Wise elder? I was lucky if I could balance my checkbook or stay current with technology.

Sleep.

I must do well by them. No, by us.

What I could not see was that, while this night was indeed a threshold, it was still just part of the beginning.

TWENTY-TWO
How Rush Imitates Life
(Fall/Winter 2001)

Two days were chopped off the rush period. Our men's second real rush would go more than a week, to the third day of classes. Interfraternity Council had experimented with different lengths and no matter what happened someone was unhappy; houses complained that with more days they might have swayed someone, but other houses said the period was long enough.

The men cleaned the house and then gathered in the Newman Room to formulate their game plan. We always struggled to define our fraternity in 10 words or less. We were diverse ethnically and racially, we ranked on top academically, our community service requirement was high, we didn't subject pledges to hazing, and we wanted campus leaders (as did most fraternities). We had a few jocks, a few ROTC men, a few top students and a few slackers, a mix of personalities. This made us strong and exciting, but it needed to be condensed as something to say when rushee, parents, even alumni asked who we were. Our slogans, like "A Cut Above," sounded too noble.

This was the first year that all 3,000 or so freshmen were housed on North Campus, after decades of being divided evenly between the two. The West Campus fraternities worried that they would be at a disadvantage, even if some of them were so established that they attracted more freshmen than they could handle. Each night, freshmen were to be in their rooms from 8 to 10 p.m. for contacts. After that, without classes to worry about yet, everyone had all night for other kinds of fun.

So who were we looking for? A few athletes would help us in intramural sports. A few good-looking men, to attract women to our parties and serve as our public face. Solid men, not frat boys. Andres was serving his second stint as the recruitment chair. Another Founder, Dream, was chair-elect, meaning he was supposed to serve as an apprentice and actually do the job next year. They urged each man to find someone like himself—Mock Trial, Concert Commission, the track or soccer teams, any group where our men belonged. Dream had lists of guys interested during the fall, and soon he would add new names. As usual, no matter what everyone had in mind as an ideal candidate, they would be ready for guys who didn't fit that mold but caught the chapter's fancy with personality or some quality they couldn't quite define (I say "they" because I was nowhere around for rush).

The campus at large had two images of Phi Tau, both inaccurate: that we were a dry house or service house. Either image could attract men with the wrong impression and turn off men we might want. To make matters worse, at least for those brothers who really resented the dry image, we were determined to have a dry rush, to follow IFC policy. IFC wanted rush to be without alcohol, to show rushees there was more to being Greek than drinking. Our adherence was a risky move, as most fraternities might have dry smokers, but at night they had wet events, thinking it was crucial to see what prospects were like when drunk. We had decided not to follow the pack because we had our vision, didn't want to project the false idea that we were a party house, and were still on shaky ground as a new chapter. But several brothers argued for wet rush, saying we wouldn't attract high numbers because freshmen wanted to drink, and we did drink so no point in pretending for a week that we didn't. But they were outnumbered. They agreed to support the majority.

Our vision had to be stated well and without arrogance, for we knew we weren't perfect. A few guys made jackasses of themselves on weekends or didn't do all of their service hours. The men needed, Dream stressed, to push our chapter without bashing other fraternities.

The fact that we didn't use hazing on pledges created a different dynamic, for we still demanded that new men learn our ways and history, and we didn't want them to think they could just sign up. They still needed to earn the letters.

The men didn't say so, exactly, but they agreed on the point men for this sales process. More eccentric or awkward brothers would stay in the background or be coached on what to say.

I watched from the sidelines. One day I could feel the men's anxiety and other days their elation. I heard the debates about what kind of guy a rushee seemed to be, and caught the discussions about how to spin our high GPA so that we didn't sound like a bunch of geeks.

* * *

Quality guys. Don't scrape the bottom of the barrel. Face guy. Ding squad. A good fit, or not. Loser. Cool dude. The language of seeking of new members, of a process dramatic and painful and, yes, occasionally fun, made me cringe a little. A fraternity needs a certain amount of fresh blood each year, to not just survive but thrive, even if these newcomers bring different agendas. Freshmen (and a few sophomores) come to the houses, hear about us, spend time with us, and decide—even as they themselves are assessed and chosen. Both sides win and lose, day by day.

It's like trying out for a team where you're picked not by a couple of coaches but by 50, not on physical abilities but on who you are or who you show yourself to be.

It's like interviewing for a job along with all of the other candidates.

It's like making friends but over days instead of weeks or months.

The goal of finding men who fit meets the wish for diversity (or not) meets the need for just plain bodies. The guy who slides in with little effort rushes alongside the guy who requires debate. The freshman who acts neutral, like a card player holding his hand, contrasts with one who doesn't hide his eagerness.

In the Northeast most campuses hold rush for freshmen at the beginning of the spring semester, so freshmen have a semester to adjust to college. The South and Midwest are more hard-core, as freshmen can pledge in the first weeks of college at most campuses. Fall rush at Cornell University is small and less structured for those houses that choose to do it at all. The main push comes in January.

While knots of men walk from fraternity to fraternity, groups of 40 well-dressed girls tour the sororities. They have to visit every house, per national rules, then slowly they are invited to specific houses and given bids based on how their top choices match the sororities that want them. Fraternities have far more options, with meeting freshmen in the fall and being able to rush any house. They make their choices against a backdrop of smokers (gatherings where brothers and rushees meet each other over chips, soda, and maybe finger food), contacts (teams of brothers who visit candidates in their rooms at night), and off-campus events such as paintball, go-karts, road trips, dinner. That's where rushees and brothers really spend time together and really talk.

It all leads to discussions and votes on who will receive bids, the formal acceptance of bids, and the ceremony that marks the beginning of pledging.

Two girls greeted the freshmen inside our front door—Phi Tau was experimenting with the hostess idea, calling upon girls who were friends with brothers—and signed them in, the top few spaces of the sheet already filled in with fake names or brothers' names so nobody would feel like the first to arrive. Name, campus address, e-mail. Next the freshmen had their pictures taken with a digital camera, so the brothers could put a face with a name during discussions. The pictures showed the rushees blinking, grinning, stoic, self-conscious. Then the rushees drifted into the room, where brothers would be waiting to speak with them.

"Where you from?"

"What's your major?"

"What music do you like? Go to any concerts over break? Movies?"

The brothers started with the smallest of talk, and some freshmen stayed the whole two hours, toured the house, maybe played pool in the basement. They asked about Phi Tau as a fraternity, what set us apart, our values. They may have known something about fraternities before they got to Cornell, from fathers, grandfathers, older brothers, and older friends. They saw movies like *Animal House* (brilliant, layered with truth beneath the comedy), *PCU,* and *Revenge of the Nerds.* Maybe they read or heard news stories about awful things happening at fraternities—death, injury, controversy. Maybe their parents weren't sure about letting them pledge anywhere, or maybe their parents had been Greek themselves, which could go either way.

Some brothers quickly grew weary of this small talk while others gamely did it day after day. Some guys genuinely liked meeting the kids and telling them why Phi Tau was special, and explaining that that we weren't as well known as other houses because we were new. Everyone was judged on wit, handshake, eye contact, manner, physique, appearance. It was a lot to absorb on both sides, a blur of conversation and faces being filed away. From the freshmen's point of view, it meant mulling over the president from the mountains, the big man who could recite sports trivia, the comedian of Indian descent, the broad-shouldered fellow with the easy charisma—and comparing them to guys in other fraternities. It meant being greeted again and again.

Some of them traveled in groups, friends from a hall, hoping they would all find a home at one fraternity. A package deal, it's called, if the freshmen insist on staying together. Sometimes it works, as a fraternity accepts four men when it really wants only three but will take a chance on the fourth.

After two hours the freshmen went on their way, and Dream studied the list. A prospect who had not shown up for the smoker would be called or e-mailed to find out why, was he looking at another house or sick or just taking a day off. The men ate dinner, looked at potential course schedules, relaxed, then divided into contact teams.

I checked on the second day and could feel the men's anxiety, as only a few rushees had stopped by. The next day the men were pleased with the turnout. Sticking with dry rush, they had a casino night, with brothers dealing, and it was OK but not great. I waited.

* * *

The word "rush" has described the courtship between Greeks and would-be Greeks for at least a century, but it used to have another connotation on college campuses. It meant a battle between freshmen, who were "rushing" the campus, and the sophomores who wanted to keep them off campus. This happened every day at some campuses, or more infrequently at others, where the rush was treated as symbolic competition. Up until a few years before I went to college in 1973, campuses kept other traditions that separated freshmen from everyone else, such as wearing beanies for the first two weeks and collecting signatures from seniors.

In his 1898 collection *Cornell Stories,* James Gardner Sanderson offers the story of a small, physically challenged freshman outcast who desperately wants to help his class when it rushes the campus from the city streets below. The rush entails having a flag on the edge of campus, with three sophomores and three freshmen laying hands on the flagpole and trying to claim it, while mobs of their classmates fight around them. Class pride. The historian Helen Lefkowitz Horowitz says in her book *Campus Life* that at some Northeast campuses such as Princeton, freshmen had to prove their right to be on campus every day, rushing the gates as the sophomores greeted them with snowballs and fists.

All lost in time now, but some other things remained true. Sanderson also wrote a story about an incoming freshman who is courted by three fraternities, each of whom has a different idea of what he is like. The freshman is dazzled if a bit puzzled by one fraternity that thinks he's ultra-religious. Sanderson describes the way freshmen were wooed and then, after they'd signed their bids, shocked at how everything changed and they were suddenly slaves for a while. I have heard this repeatedly—a fraternity projects a false image during rush and then, a few days or a week after pledges are in hand, shows its real nature or what will actually be asked of them. This had happened to Brian the IFC president, in a sense, and to Tom at his original fraternity. It wasn't always the hazing that stunned the pledges but the callousness, and how shallow their fraternity really was. I believed, I hoped, that kids didn't feel this about us.

Nobody speaks of this much, but in sorting through the fraternities and their different cultures and attitudes, a freshman or sophomore asks himself what kind of man he is. He may not even know he's doing this; he's just picking men to associate with, whom he respects or likes or admires. He's selecting a place to live and a set of opportunities.

He's drawn to the wealth, confidence, sense of ruling the world, of mattering.

He's drawn to men who look as if they walked out of a clothing catalog.

He's drawn to men who laugh at anyone who would get too serious about this fraternity thing.

He's drawn to athletes like himself, powerful and quick and aggressive, always wanting to win.

He finds a house that talks a good game about how much its men care for each other and about being good men. But he thinks after a while that it's just a line, senses this even before he hears rumors about drug use and date rape. Some fraternities suck out your morals and leave you at graduation time with no sense of how to behave or treat people. Sensing this, the freshman goes back to another fraternity and hopes there's still an opportunity. The freshman hates being judged this way, but this is the path into a fraternity.

∗ ∗ ∗

I heard the Phi Taus mention a freshman who was absent from our Casino Night, a non-alcoholic event, and the brothers had called him to find out what was up. He had chosen to go to Rochester that night with another fraternity to play paintball, and he had come away thinking those guys were jerks. I heard that one rushee from the South might be bigoted, but was this really true or were we, mostly from the North, imagining something?

I donated $500 to be used toward rush. The men bought a basketball hoop instead and installed it on the driveway's edge. I disliked basketball—as a sports writer in Syracuse I had grown tired of hearing about it—but the hoop made the Phi Taus happy, so fine.

∗ ∗ ∗

At night Dream divided the men into contact groups and they wandered among the residence halls, lists in hand, assigned to specific rushees.

Contact teams were designed for different purposes: to sway a freshman to accept a bid, to gauge where he stood if he was being pursued by more than one house, to touch base if he was a lock, or to give someone a chance to meet him in a less chaotic environment than the smoker. The contact team would not include his close friends in the house, for there was no need. It would have to be someone he could relate to, though, ethnically or in terms of interests or home region. If there was to be a real sales pitch, a brother with strong verbal skills and sincere manner might be on the team.

This too was something I could not take part in, but I drifted around campus, seeing who was dressed in coat and tie for this and who was just in business casual. I could look through a window and see a kid sitting on his bed, facing four or five men. I could hear conversations:

"I still don't think I can vote for him."

"Just talk to him some more before you write him off."

Or, "That kid was smooth. He had no idea who we were but he acted as if he did."

"I thought you were supposed to offer contact teams something to drink."

"Where did you hear that bullshit? What did you offer anyone during rush—orange juice?"

One year, before I met Phi Tau, I hung out in the lounge of a hall where I knew the resident advisor, a junior who had been rushed but never pledged a house. I had written him a recommendation letter for Cornell when he was in high school. Several of us watched *The Simpsons* on the lounge TV while contact teams appeared and knocked on doors and then went their way. They would ask one of the occupants of a room to excuse himself, then go in. Another team would come along, knock on the same door, and wait in the hall until the other team was done. They might even greet each other. My friend the RA asked one fraternity brother to get rid of the beer bottle in his hand, nodded to fraternity members he knew, and told me that he was concerned because one freshman badly wanted a house that was not going to give him a bid (the rush chair must have tipped off the RA). A freshman sitting next to me got up to follow a contact team that appeared and indicated that he was to speak with them—not a pledge yet but taking orders already. Another told me that he was happy to know he had a bid locked, as he would hate to not get a bid anywhere.

The ding squad took different forms. There was the one with the rush chair himself, unwilling to let anyone else do this, wanting the rejection to be clean and cool. There was the group that included men who had voted the kid out, sent to his room so they could see the impact of their opposition; maybe they would gain some compassion or humility. Then there was the same kind of group, where the men who had voted the kid out went to his room because they disliked him and got a kick out of watching his face as they conveyed the news.

One rush chair told me about the "soft ding," where a freshman was told that not enough guys knew him but that he might have a shot if he tried again in the fall or next spring. We did not seem inclined to let men rush again unless we agreed with them that they weren't ready. Once we dinged someone, that was it. I didn't like it. I had known men at St. Lawrence and Cornell who had rushed a second time and gotten bids. They changed, or sold themselves better, or just fixed bad feelings. But somehow we did not allow that.

Barry became our first ding squad. He just calmly told the kids how it was. He liked the job and did it for three years, which some of us found odd. At least, he savored telling kids the brothers didn't like that they were not getting a bid from us, although he was dead-pan as he delivered the news.

* * *

A senior in an upper-crust house was nicknamed Iceman. I asked why. He just smiled.

"Because," said one of his brothers, "when there's a kid at one of our smokers who we can see obviously won't make the cut, Iceman asks him to take a walk in the library to look at some nice paintings. There's a door in the library, and he shows the kid out. He does it so professionally that we call him Iceman."

I thought the story was heartless until I mentioned it to one of the Phi Taus. He said he wished we did that; it would save us some ding squad missions.

* * *

One of the seminars that year at Cornell's annual conference for Greek leaders focused on how to improve your house's rush. A sophomore from one of the fraternities known for looks and attitude told his group that he wanted to learn how to avoid attracting nerds.

"You could argue that everyone at Cornell is a nerd," said the young woman leading the group. She meant that most Cornell students worry about grades.

"I don't think so," the young man said. "In high school I got nerds to do my work for me. I do the same thing here. I drive a nice car. My parents went here, and they got me in here. No, I'm sure I'm not a nerd."

✳ ✳ ✳

A short meeting at Phi Tau turned ugly. As we chose seats in the Newman Room, Barry told me, "There's going to be trouble. A few of the guys brought recruits to a party at Lou's apartment last night." So much for dry rush.

Jacob wasn't there so Joe the new vice president took charge. He announced that before we talked about the day's rush event we needed to deal with what had happened. Behind him, Big Daddy's face was red and he loomed over us. He said, "I can't believe some of you went against our position as a house." He stared at two of the juniors. "Sorry you guys don't like some things about Phi Tau. Sorry we can't be like your friends' houses. Maybe you should've joined another house."

"OK, that's enough," said Joe. Big Daddy ignored him. He kept ranting that the guys in question were lame and didn't believe in our values.

They stared back at him, not looking especially guilty. Finally Joe got everyone to quiet down, said we'd deal with this later, and moved on. I sensed something I had before, that guys didn't like being scolded. Big Daddy's show of anger may have cost him someone's respect.

✳ ✳ ✳

I joined the guys for a longer bid meeting. This time we filled the Newman Room, lounging in chairs and sprawling on the floor. Dream inserted a compact disc into our big TV set and began to show us faces. It was Saturday, the fifth day, time to talk less about rushees and start voting. In my era the men would have looked at the photographs in the freshman guide, or at Polaroid prints, or maybe just used verbal descriptions. Now technology had delivered the CD.

Dream went through 30 images, supplying a name for each. For some the verdict was fast: never came back, not interested, definitely going somewhere else. Others inspired discussion, even debate. A few freshmen were choosing between us and other fraternities, well-established houses that we had never competed with before—a good sign for where we stood. Or freshmen wanted only us, but did we want them?

"Comments?" Dream said each time, and they came.

"He's annoying."

"He'd add a lot our house."

"He didn't do anything for me, when I met him."

Tabled. Next guy, voted a bid. Next guy, quickly given a bid, no discussion. Then:

"This guy's a dork. Look at that shirt, and that hair."

I winced. I understood that physical appearance played a role in rush, as it does in so much of life, but I hated to hear us sounding like a frat. More mature minds prevailed.

"What else besides his appearance?" Dream said.

"I didn't like some of his comments about our house. I thought it was out of line."

"He's a nerd. We need more good-looking guys. We need more guys who can bring in the ladies."

"Yeah, and athletes."

"Just cool guys in general."

"But," someone piped up, "this guy has potential. He could really benefit from being part of us."

"Is that our function, though? To teach social skills?"

"Yes. Besides, we've always prided ourselves on having a wide range of men."

"Yeah, we don't want to be a pretty-boy house."

"I don't think there's much danger of that." They talked about face men. Someone said we want quality and what's the point of having a face guy who doesn't contribute anything else to the house? Sighs, eyes rolling, looks of disgust from the small faction who wanted to really emphasize, if not looks, then personality this rush season.

I'd seen it before: A fraternity looked for new men who would raise its level of coolness. What the men forgot sometimes is that when they offered a bid to such a man, he might bring more like him to the chapter, and by the time they were seniors, the less cool men would be outsiders in their own brotherhood.

One big fellow who could instantly memorize maps, sports trivia, and facts about anyone got a bid because the men felt he had something. He made Hitman laugh, had a great heart, filled the room with his wit and raw emotion. He was in. He would be nicknamed Rainman.

One fellow possessed a sarcastic wit but he too struck a chord in the brotherhood. To keep track of him in their discussions, some of the juniors decided that he resembled Ice, so he became Ice II or Dice. He was in.

One fellow was too quiet but had come to everything since last fall. He didn't get a bid, but Barry whispered to me that he'd revive the debate in a couple of days (the rushee got a bid).

A poised sophomore who sounded like the actor Nicolas Cage—deep but faintly nasal—got in. He'd be nicknamed Cage.

A tall, muscular sophomore who looked like a model got a bid. He'd pledged somewhere last year and de-pledged because he hated being hazed.

They chose another hilarious freshman who rarely attended class but would end up going to Harvard Law School—another character.

I thought about one fraternity that attracted about 200 rushees every year and winnowed them down to 18 bids. Their final bid meeting usually stretched from 6 p.m. until 4 a.m., with guys too worn down to vote no on someone, or crying because a freshman they badly wanted got dinged. Our decisions were not as painful or as long.

I could sit there and not get upset with what I heard. Unfairness was part of life, and learning lessons about how to try for a goal, and how to anticipate and counter what people might think about me from looking at me, hearing my vocabulary, and seeing my resume.

Whatever people think of fraternities, we are all going through rush all of the time.

In the end the men voted bids to 15 rushees and turned down only two. They presented the bids at a dinner, a custom at other fraternities that they thought they would try. Brothers presented each recruit with his bid, accompanied by a usually humorous speech that extolled his best qualities. It kind of put the recruits on the spot. Two were absent: the Southerner, and a Navy ROTC midshipman whom we really wanted. Dream promised to find out where they were, but we guessed they either didn't want to face the pressure of this dinner or they were at other houses.

The next day, Tuesday, fraternities weren't allowed to speak with rushees. On Wednesday, between classes and lunch, rushees sauntered to a table in the Memorial Room to sign bids and then sign an agreement that they would not endure hazing. Most would indeed get hazed, but at that moment they didn't know how much.

Some guys looked in the door, at the waiting IFC representatives, and decided to think about this some more. One freshman thought out loud about the guys he would pledge with, whom he didn't like much, and about how he would tell his parents that he had done this, when they might not approve. He worried that the money for national dues and pledge dues might be too much. Then he signed. Friends compared choices and congratulated each other on becoming fraternity men.

The signing period stretched from 10 a.m. until 5 p.m., shorter than a decade earlier, when it would last for 12 hours while rush chairs waited anxiously. Phi Tau got 13 of the 15 who had received bids. The Southerner picked another house. So did the Navy ROTC midshipman, but not without a struggle. I saw him sitting off to the side, in a row of plush chairs, staring at the carpeted floor. In each hand he held a bid, one from us and one from the fraternity where Tom's buddy Shane was president. He looked almost ill. I went downstairs to eat lunch, and when I walked past the room again an hour later he still sat there, deep in thought. Later I heard that he had settled upon the other house, and my brothers shrugged and said maybe he'd be happier there.

I met the new men a few days later, when they came to our house for the association ceremony. Most of them didn't know I existed, and were surprised to find this older guy in their midst. I just said that I was the faculty advisor, and a brother, and I attended meetings and ate dinner at the house a few times a week. Whatever else I was, to the fraternity and to them, they could wait to discover.

TWENTY-THREE
Generations
(Spring 2002)

I punched the knobs on the lock and swung open the heavy oak door to 106 The Knoll. Ah, here I was again, in a place that was sometimes like my second home and sometimes an outpost in a foreign country where I did not quite grasp the conversations around me, the cultural references, the customs.

I crossed the foyer to the Newman Room, collapsed on a couch, and watched *Pardon the Interruption,* a sports talk show, with Dream, Barry, and Hitman. The coffee table was covered with plates, cups, beer bottles, even a bowl with milk and a spoon in it. Not unusual—sometimes milk sat there for two days. Disgusted, I picked up a few of the dishes and took them to the dish room between the kitchen and dining room. I started to say something but remembered how cluttered my kitchen was. "Conroe, let the waiters do that," said Dream.

From the dish room I could hear water being blasted onto plates: the two brothers assigned to waiter duty rinsed the dishes that had piled up since yesterday. Both waiters—assigned by the steward—were there, a plus; they had not forgotten their turn. They pulled pans of food from the oven (left there by Patty the cook) and carried them to the foyer, where a longer table and the hexagonal Bandhu table had been set together. One of them tapped a knife against the chimes hanging on a wall, signaling dinner with "First Call," the tune that a bugler uses to start a day at the racetrack.

We formed two lines. The waiters brought the other trays and pans of hot food, then the bowls of salad and rolls, and the trays of silverware, and the stacks of plates. They set pitchers of iced tea and red juice on the tables (we also had a water dispenser), and rang the chimes, and we got our dinner. Since this was a weekday, not Sunday, the chaplain did not offer words of wisdom, nor did we wait for everyone to have food before digging in.

I chose a seat at the end of a table, so I could get up if I needed to instead of being trapped between long legs and reaching arms. Waves of conversation rose and fell around the room, shifting quickly. A guy was needled about his grade on a test, another about a girl he'd hooked up with.

A current movie sucked or, "you're crazy," rocked.

What should President Bush do about Iraq? He might invade someday.

A sorority was analyzed for likelihood of having a mixer with us. I asked how hot this one was, this not being my area of expertise. "Hot, as always," I was told, "but their pledge class isn't." Mixer possibilities? "Not yet. Maybe down the road." Around me, like explosions going off, I heard bits about women they knew, who seemed to be divided into categories of availability, bitchiness, coolness, wildness, and other kinds of ness (as the women no doubt assessed fraternity men).

Who was the hairiest in the room? "Nice sweater, dude." Who could grow a beard faster? Some days I managed to join in, other days I just let it all swirl around me. The noise could reach such a din that I could get a headache. I ate here about twice a week. At dinner, amidst the laughter and loud talk, I listened for movements, trends, topics that did not go away but lived from week to week.

Someone bitched about how much money the alumni set aside in our budget for future problems, equity that we called the Rainy Day Fund. The men thought they should have access to the fund, and that it was too big, why did it have to be $20,000? The idea was to have money saved up that would keep the house afloat for one year, if anything awful happened to it. But the guys thought about what they could do with the money, and for some reason (maybe all the corporate scandals going on) a couple of them wondered out loud if the alumni misused it. I questioned their concept of saving; they were the credit card generation, and they had not made a living yet. I could tell them that I should have more money saved than I did. I had used it on graduate school and travel and any number of other things.

Bitching about the alumni was a favorite pastime here, followed closely by complaining about the food. Some meals were not quite up to par, and the men urged the steward to work with Patty on what to buy and how to cook it. I never joined in since I was not paying dues or meal plan, and seldom took second helpings. And I'd grown up in a household of four kids and my mother was not only a good cook, she did not accept comments. If you didn't like a dish you didn't eat much of it. These guys, it seemed, were accustomed to Mom making whatever they wanted, probably because families were smaller now. They could be quite finicky.

"Hey, we should get a house dog," someone said, and guys said great idea, a lot of fraternities have a dog, it's awesome. And other guys said who will take care of it, with the alumni allow it (the alumni were the landlords).

I said, "Lots of fraternities have dogs, but it's usually a brother's own dog. It can be a problem." Like the Rottweiler that confronted a brother at Chi Phi as he walked down a hallway. Then I said, "If it's a dog for the whole house and it stays here year after year, who trains it and takes care of it?" Sigma Chi had had a string of Saint Bernards, managed by the Delta Beta (Dog Boy). "It can work if you're consistent about commands and where the dog can be," I said. "Like not in the kitchen or dining area." I guessed the chances of that were slim. That week two brothers went to the SPCA, but the staff did not give dogs and cats to college students, who were considered too unreliable (every college town was full of animals set free by departing students). Tom suggested a Vietnamese pot-bellied pig—disaster, from what I'd heard. The pet talk stopped, for now.

There might be talk about guys who didn't pull their weight in the fraternity, who came to parties and maybe meetings but didn't serve on committees or help with cleanup. The talk faded because when a fraternity kicked out brothers, it was usually for something that endangered the house, like drug dealing, and the better solution was for the president to convince the man to change.

Every time I heard talk that made me angry, I left the room and cooled off, reminding myself that these were bright, critical men who naturally would challenge the status quo.

A junior told someone that his girlfriend was annoying and she'd get flushed down the toilet if she wasn't careful (she was about 4-foot-9).

A sophomore who—like many students—spoke hip hop said, "Conroe, if you tried you could be more gangsta." A big white guy from Westchester County was telling me this. I answered, "Dat is wack, yo," and guys around me laughed. Always entertaining to see Conroe, or any old guy, try to act young. But I did not play videogames and didn't notice when new movies were based on videogames. I did not do instant messaging (IM), although I heard the guys wished I did. I was not up on new music and bands, had given up on that, and the men were sometimes jealous that in high school and college I had music they revered: Beatles, Doors, Creedence Clearwater Revival, older Stones, Alice Cooper, Led Zeppelin, Eagles. I bought those records new, heard those songs fresh on the radio. The men enjoyed their own music but really loved those classics of my youth.

We would sprawl in the Newman Room, switching channels, and the guys would offer comments on which actress was hot, or which old show brought back memories. That last got me, for the show might be from my boyhood. The men had watched it on some nostalgia channel. Our boyhoods, separated by 30 years, connected through these shows. Or the men said they danced to a song in high school that I danced to. It was so odd that I gave up thinking about it.

Sports was a different matter. If I tried to brag in a weak moment about athletes and teams I had written about or photographed, I either got blank looks or knowing nods from trivia buffs. The 1989 U.S. Open in golf? Nice. Baseball stars Cecil Fielder, Kenny Lofton, Steve Finley? Yawn. Pete Rose? Yeah, the guy everyone argued about for the Hall of Fame. Hockey players like Dave Taylor from Clarkson? Never heard of him. Joe Nieuwendyk from Cornell, NHL star: yes, they recognized his name—or the hockey fans did. In the end, the only one I could really talk about was John Elway, and I'd interviewed him when he was in college, playing minor league baseball, not in the National Football League yet. I was better off looking for other ways to bond with the men besides reminiscing about a vanished career.

I stepped into the kitchen to check on dessert. A pan of brownies looked inviting, but I decided to skip that, grabbed a bowl off a dish shelf, and headed for the cereal dispensers instead—a childhood custom my parents encouraged and that the men found odd. I put milk on it from the milk dispenser's hose and stepped back into the dining room, to see that someone had sat in my place. This happened a lot. The men were always switching seats, moving to another table to talk to someone else. I'd sit down with three and then look up in a while and find one had relocated across the room. Or it might be a latecomer. "That's my seat," I snapped. "Can't I get up for one minute?" The brother offered to give me back my seat, but then I felt silly. I said, "No, stay there" and found an empty seat.

Afterward we took our plates and silverware to the dish room to rinse them. The waiters put everything in the steam cleaner that we had instead of a dishwasher. If a waiter didn't have a partner I might offer to help, but they always said no, this was not part of my job. The dishes and pans tended to really pile up on weekends, when there was no assigned waiter duty until Sunday evening. One Sunday morning I came to the house for a meeting, but I was early and when I saw the pile—it was huge—I couldn't help myself and started in. For a half hour I rinsed and scrubbed, and I liked it. Then Tom came up from his basement room, for the same meeting, and said I shouldn't ever do dishes, I certainly contributed enough to the house without that.

I was glad that the men talked as if I wasn't there, complete with profanity, as if I were one of them. It was nice to step away from my older person's world for a while. But it was temporary, and doing it too much was not healthy.

*   *   *

One day I ate at another fraternity at the invitation of a student—the world of Shuck, another elder fraternity member. Except that Shuck's story was different: he had pledged in 1993 and never graduated. Pushing 30, he still lived in the fraternity house.

Shuck was bright, personable, and good-looking in a bookish way. He lived off stocks and investments. He had dabbled in various departments at Cornell but never finished a degree. He thought about moving out but kept his room in the fraternity's basement, next to the weight room. The fraternity loved having him around, as an older brother type. I once saw him de-fuse a potential fight between two brothers, one drunk and feeling he had to defend his honor as a man, by suggesting they take their disagreement to a parking lot up the hill where nobody could see who won. They did, but instead of fighting they talked it out.

"I love this life but I have to remind the guys sometimes that I really am not one of them," Shuck said.

"We're glad he's part of us," one of the brothers told me, "but we wish he would move on. We want him to move out sometime and get on with his life."

My respect for Shuck was enormous. He was a live-in advisor of sorts, at home in the complicated everyday life of the fraternity. The men listened to him. He was wise in the ways of young men. But I could not be him. I certainly could never have lived at 106 The Knoll. The topic came up once when Jacob wrote in an e-mail "I wish you could live here so you could get the whole experience of being our brother." I thanked him for the sentiment but a guy pushing 50 would not be happy in a house full of dozens of college men, who were up until all hours, drinking every Thursday and Friday and Saturday night. I wondered how anyone had privacy in a fraternity house, and got my answer when I found a brother reading in a corner of the pantry or a corner of the Chapter Room, with the doors closed so he could actually have a thought to himself.

*   *   *

Don't get me wrong, some days I was just not in the mood. I had my own life and didn't want to get sucked into some drama, or I was just overloaded on students after a day of teaching and grading and everything that went with it. I did not want a world where everyone was cool or un-cool.

I was old and it couldn't be helped, even if the men might sometimes wish I were younger.

Staying overnight one time, I told Mick that I would need to get shaving gel and razor from my office. I did not like being unshaven. "Oh, Scott," he said. "That's a fashion statement for some men." I said yeah, men under 30. College men shaved every few days, from what I could tell, and I doubted it was just a fashion statement.

With Phi Tau I lived in a bubble of blissful ignorance. We might be a model fraternity in many ways but we were also red-blooded men. I caught snatches of talk about what went on when I wasn't around, alcohol-related or not, and I was sure that plenty else stayed out of my hearing (and I liked it that way). The universe remained in harmony.

✳   ✳   ✳

The question of who we were never went away. That became obvious when the men made another early-spring road trip to Montreal and one of the seniors was upset with the turnout. Too many men had stayed on campus to work on school—the chapter's 3.66 GPA. The chapter was planning a bar tab, so he wrote a two-page e-mail trying to get the men fired up.

He said he recalled joining a social fraternity—not a dry house, not a service house, but a house that actually drank alcohol.

"Guys, I gotta tell you, when I graduate Cornell in a whopping 90 days I'm gonna remember a few things. I'm gonna remember being thrown in the trunk of Jay's car and being taken home after hitting on every girl at the '80s party. I'm gonna remember being drunk out of my mind with Chaz in Montreal (yeah fat chicks). . . . I'm gonna remember getting trashed at the white trash winery on the wine tour last semester. I'm gonna remember vomiting in my formal glass last year." He said he'd remember making valentines with a sorority, Phi Tug, and the philanthropy events. But he would truly remember the parties. "These are the stories YOU will tell—these are the stories I want to tell. Guys, face it—alcohol is part of the college experience. Alcohol is part of fraternity life. I joined Phi Kappa Tau for fun . . . a house that would be different, and we ARE. We stress philanthropy and non-alcoholic events. However, I also joined a house that was open-minded and realized that **alcohol was part of the social scene at Cornell—and would not turn its shoulder totally at it.**"

We are risk takers, he said. We started a different kind of fraternity. Now we should take the risk of having this bar tab.

"Brothers, we're not Philanthropy Kappa Tau. We are not Dry Kappa Tau. We are not Cornell's Bitches Kappa Tau. We are PHI KAPPA TAU. A SOCIAL FRATERNITY. Let's get social already.

"My 2 cents."

TWENTY-FOUR
Commitment
(Spring 2002)

The Founders turned again to their new member program and tweaked it. As chapter advisor, LeGrand had discouraged scavenger hunts and brother interviews because either could be used as hazing tools, and scavenger hunts could cause pledges to steal. But LeGrand was gone. He had taken a job in Colorado. Things could be different for this, our Beta pledge class.

The new members were told about the chapter gradually, meeting once a week and stopping by on their own. The brothers wanted to impress. Pledging is almost an extension of rush, because until a man is initiated you can lose him, if he decides this is too much of a time commitment, or thinks the organization is not what he thought. Every year we attracted a few men who had sworn they would never join a fraternity, and that could be a challenge, for such men might not give part of themselves to the whole. We wanted them to become part of us. At the same time, we had to teach them to respect our ways, which they had glimpsed during rush.

Hitman and his committee introduced two new elements: an associate class project (improving some part of 106 The Knoll itself) and histories of the chapter's re-founding, done in teams and based on interviews with brothers. The best history would get some sort of prize. The associates decided their project would be painting the far basement room, where the bar was, in Phi Tau red and gold.

The histories from interviews were mostly accurate and mostly humorous. One basically mocked the whole idea and Hitman chose that one as the winner. One pair did their paper about me and how I'd become part of Phi Tau, which was flattering. The seniors and juniors got a kick out of becoming trivia, making associates learn where they'd met as a colony and which sorority had joined them for their first mixer.

* * *

Late in the pledge process, we saw why fraternities had hazing, and why some houses said we would have it eventually too.

That Sunday we brought chairs into the Chapter Room and set them up in rows, as always. We put rows of four chairs in the foyer outside the room, where the associates sat because, not being brothers yet, they were not in the Chapter Room yet. The associates' class president, Cage, could come into the room to give his report, if the brothers said he could.

We sent the associate members upstairs while we did ritual to open the meeting. Then, before the associate members came back and we recited the creed, Hitman usually offered a short assessment of how they were doing. Today he said, "Guys, stop telling the new men how great they were. They're making too many excuses to miss events. They have an attitude."

First, several of the new men had told Hitman they would be late for an event for different reasons. He wrote a profanity-laced e-mail to them saying they had better be on time. Only one guy, Rainman, had a legitimate excuse because his car had caught fire at the house (some electrical problem) and he was trying to figure out what to do.

But the clincher—according to my best speculation later—came when Jay said he was concerned the associate members weren't on target for their required community service hours. The class's vice president wrote an e-mail back to him, saying they were aware of the requirement—Cage had even gone beyond it—and had every intention of reaching it. Several members, he said, planned to attend Phi Tug.

Hitman's reply was short: "You insolent jackass. 1. Everybody participates in Phi Tug, it is not optional. 2. You do not have 10 hours. Cage does. You don't. Stop swinging off his nuts. 3. Didn't we tell you to go away??????"

"This is where I understand why houses have hazing," Hitman told me. "It keeps guys in line."

The brothers needed to bring the new men back on mission some other way. They finally reminded the new men, point blank, that nobody was guaranteed initiation—the brothers would be voting on it. Hitman would evaluate each associate member at points during the process and warn the ones who weren't making progress. We stressed that our program would demand their time and energy, and they needed to prove themselves to us.

Someone asked me at dinner if that kind of threat was hazing. I said maybe, technically, but really we had to do it. "People make a commitment and they have to be held to it," I said. "What happens in the real world if you are hired or you say you'll do something, then you don't? You can get fired."

Critics of fraternities say that pledging itself, not just the hazing piece of it, is foolish. I don't agree. When so much of American life demands times when you show who you are and what you will contribute to a group or organization, it's difficult to tell fraternities that they can't do the same. This isn't a club that anyone can join. A man can't wear the fraternity's letters or know its secrets until he better understands what he has joined. I used to doubt this, as a college student and then as a young adult—in the case of fraternities, that is. As I explored the fraternity landscape and became part of Phi Tau, I saw the value of believing in an organization and agreeing to make it strong, before you are really part of it. So I recognized the fit of pledge class meetings, wearing of pins over the heart, history lessons, scavenger hunts, and exclusion from matters only brothers should know about. I grasped the power of being summoned to the house at 1 a.m. to stand in a line and recite fraternity lore or be told to work harder, and the challenge of servitude, like doing errands for brothers.

After that, sliding along the scale of what hazing can entail, by legal definition, my sympathy weakened. Call me a wimp, but most hazing events I heard about didn't speak to me of brotherhood.

Pledging is a time when the fraternity and the men who would join it study each other and see if their gamble paid off. I go back to those pledges who discover this fraternity they plan to call home is not what they thought it would be. As the weeks go on, sometimes pledges realize they've made a mistake. Sometimes it's the brothers who realize that. It's true of any relationship. The job search is an example: both sides learn about the other after the person has been hired. Rush lasted only eight weeks at Cornell then, 10 weeks at other campuses, and even if a fraternity and a freshman have encountered each other, they have a lot to learn about each other. The learning comes during pledging and after it. Maybe it's nothing awful, just a freshman deciding he is disappointed or sensing something new within himself. Maybe he resolves to change something about the house as the weeks pass. Brian and Shane took aim at hazing. I heard a couple of our associates were thinking about making us a more poised, better-looking house.

Not everyone is a good pledge, making it to meetings and learning history and getting the prescribed number of brother interviews. Guys think it's silly. This gives rise to the question, is a lousy pledge going to make a lousy brother? Not always. Guys change, just as brothers who aren't very active might still become active alumni.

＊ ＊ ＊

Men at Cornell said they had no patience with touchy-feely activities that made everybody feel warm and fuzzy. We'll be like sororities, they said. "I try to get the guys to do some of this stuff you want," said a president, "and I'll get beaten up." This was why Phi Tau tried Cornell Outdoor Education, bonding under the duress and thrill of maneuvering in the air. Problem was, the high-elements course was not available until probably late April, if then, and by then pledging would be done.

But COE was about other things than the high element course, things that were deeper philosophically and not as likely to thrill. This turned out to be unfortunate.

Hitman and the brothers tried a raft-building exercise. Two teams of men met in a swimming pool at one of the recreation facilities and were made to work together to build rafts. This was where MacGyver got his nickname—he proved the most adept at assembling a raft.

The other event that spring was a storytelling hike through a snowy forest. COE used this method to get groups of people in touch with each other—in this case, in touch with our chapter's history. We climbed through the forest and found stations where first brothers and then two alumni described key moments in chapter history. One of the alumni was Pat Madden, who had become both Board of Governors chair and Board of Directors president. The associate members were polite but a couple of the sophomores clearly felt the whole thing was a bit goofy. They began to plan ways to make this fraternity they'd joined a bit cooler, and found allies in a couple of Founders.

We were glad we did not have hazing, but that spring the issue came up again, in different form. I think of it as one of the first crises to test our young chapter. As initiation approached, the associates said in evaluation forms about Hitman's program that they wanted to be surprised, wanted excitement and drama. Most of their events had been pretty dull. At the same time, Jacob's situation was becoming grim.

TWENTY-FIVE
The Tough Man
(Spring 2002)

For months I had watched Jacob grapple with his father's illness. I tried to make sure he was sharing his pain with somebody, if not me, and learned that he sometimes talked to MacGyver or Adam, late at night. I saw past his clench-jawed stoicism, his quick assurances that he was doing well. I kept my eye on him and at times he seemed annoyed by this.

Jacob fought his pain that fall semester by pouring himself into life. He achieved all A's. Though his leg ached, he climbed back onto a horse and proved himself worthy of the polo team's three-man starting lineup. He eagerly took over as president, unafraid of the legal risks attached to the job, reveling in the many duties. Jacob tried a leadership style that kept the men at a professional distance but showed compassion. He wanted to have fun at parties while watching over everything, aware of but not cowed by the reality that the president is arrested and sued when things go wrong. He ditched Tom's policy of having the vice president run the chapter meetings. Jacob's baritone was the only voice besides mine that could quiet the room. He drove himself so hard to master every level of the fraternity that I finally said he needed to delegate more, particularly to Joe, the vice president, who found himself without a role. So I suggested he find Joe a role. Jacob was annoyed with me but listened, and he and Joe became an effective team. It was the only spat of sorts that Jacob and I had.

I sensed that Jacob had played a major part in my receiving Phi Tau's bid and being initiated, but I did not ask for details. Now I needed to be simply a good friend. I had not always been such a friend to people. I could be peevish and hypersensitive. When is friendship to be taken seriously? That's an eternal question among men, who let friends go like leaves in the wind. But now I thought about it, plenty.

I wondered what Jacob's father was like. He was a bit older than me, so he could have graduated high school when I did (1973) or the year before. We had grown up at roughly the same time, 90 minutes apart. While

I daydreamed about Pulitzer Prizes in writing, he dreamed about the Olympics as a bobsledder. I worried about Vietnam but only a little, convinced that President Nixon would end the war or that my college deferment would be enough—and he enlisted in the military. While I went off to a rich, elite college and then wrote newspaper stories, he married a local girl and became a farmer. I imagined a cool gaze like Jacob's.

We set up an independent study in business writing for Jacob that second semester of his junior year because I thought it would make his recovery easier, when his life was disrupted, dealing with one less professor. I was pleased to have done something for him. Our weekly meetings also let us discuss the fraternity, and when I remember that time, I remember him drinking in my words as if they were truly wise.

What could I do to ease Phi Tau through this? The men knew Jacob's father was ill, but Jacob would not tell the whole fraternity how serious it was. He did not want pity. I could not do much but wait, thinking again about the dozens of people I had said goodbye to.

I kept the secret, and that too was a new skill. All my life I had been a gossip and then a journalist, someone who finds stories in gossip. Now I needed to be an advisor. As a friend, I left Jacob alone when he wanted to be and did not pry. He would tell me when the time came. Surprisingly, while we did not talk much in person, we spoke eloquently through electronic mail and handwritten notes, where he said he was grateful to have a friend like me and I said it was not a problem. For once I did not look for somebody else to take over for me in a crisis, somebody stronger. I was strong.

✷ ✷ ✷

When the end was near, around Easter, Jacob went home at mid-week to be with his family. He planned to return Friday for the initiation ceremony, then head home again. I thought he should be with his family. That Monday he was to attend a breakfast honoring Cornell athletes with 4.0 averages, with me as his faculty guest. I did not think he would make it.

The fraternity needed to know and I had to do my duty. I dreaded this, but shook it off and summoned everything I knew about what people did in the face of death. I checked online for a florist near Jacob's hamlet. I thought about how this would go. I was no professional counselor, but anybody in his forties had lost friends and family, and missed them.

Word filtered through the brotherhood about why Jacob had gone home. The other officers gathered in the third-floor lounge while Hitman and I met with the associate class in the Chapter Room. I let Hitman explain what was happening. His voice shook and I wondered if I had done the right thing. The associate members were stunned. They said they would not be initiated without Jacob. I told the officers and they voted to postpone for a week. Jacob was supposed to call Joe later, and Joe didn't want to tell him, thinking Jacob would veto it. He asked me to tell him, so when Jacob called at about 11 p.m., Joe had him call me and I told him how it was. Jacob just laughed and said fine.

Joe asked me to write an e-mail to the whole chapter, since not everyone knew, so I spent half an hour choosing my words and then sent it. I offered facts about the situation, that Jacob had known since July and was now waiting, and would tell us details of the funeral service. He knows we're thinking of him and behind him, I wrote, and will draw strength from us.

It was one of those rare moments when a whole fraternity feels each other and is glad to.

* * *

But unbeknownst to me, the men wanted something to mark the end of association. Of all people, a few of the Founders came up with an idea: a mock hazing.

Next thing the associates knew, they were lined up in our basement while a couple of juniors, one of them brandishing a baseball bat, told them how unworthy they were. They were told that they couldn't leave the basement until they finished the pledge project. It was all straight out of what their friends in other fraternities did.

Some of the associate members thought the mock hazing was funny and got right into the spirit of it. The event wasn't too intimidating. But two associates were infuriated. One of the two talked to me about it, saying he wanted to de-pledge. I was angry and disappointed that only a couple of years after the chapter's re-founding, we already had strayed from our vision.

I feared that once the men tried hazing, they might like it too much and would try it more. I said nothing, because they sometimes became quite indignant when I did, but the thought lingered. Fraternities that had gotten rid of their worst hazing practices reported that it was difficult to keep the men from bringing it back.

Or was I over-reacting? Weren't we different?

A few of the guys used to wonder if we should try some hazing events, because we were still a fraternity after all. This faction of the house was restless to move us away from the utopian image of the perfect (and boring) fraternity toward something more appealing to guys. This faction said we could try hazing and then, if it didn't seem to fit us, abandon it.

But nobody knew how to conduct hazing. The pro-hazing supporters were met with comments along the lines of "You guys would never have joined us if we had hazing, and you would never have put up with it, yet now you want to try it? Bullshit."

✳ ✳ ✳

That weekend Jacob called to say his father was gone, peacefully. I said nothing about the mock lineup; he didn't need to know yet. I attended the athletes' breakfast Monday, aware of how pleased he would have been to join the others. On Tuesday, I drove five hours north to the funeral, with three Phi Taus in my car: Jay, Adam, and Train. MacGyver drove separately with a young woman who was a close friend of Jacob's. I wished more Phi Taus had made the trip, but MacGyver and the three in my car were his closest fraternity brothers, so it seemed adequate. Later I found Jacob had said he didn't want a lot of the guys to come up and overwhelm his family.

During the five-hour drive the trio of Founders didn't talk about the mock lineup directly, probably assuming I didn't know, but they mentioned one of the associates who had complained to me and how disappointed they were in him. He wasn't tough. I wanted to scream at them, "You shitheads, you turned your back on everything we've accomplished in the past two years! You hypocrites!"

But I remained silent. Jacob and the other officers could figure out how to handle this. And just what he needed right now, a crisis.

✳ ✳ ✳

The tiny Catholic church sat off to one side of the little four corners of Jacob's hometown. We stood back in the crowd as he arrived with his family and MacGyver, who nodded to us that we were to go in. Of course Jacob had planned the service, down to the music and who would speak. He had reserved a pew for us while about 40 people had to wait outside because the church was too small. When he stood at the pulpit to talk about his father, I looked up at this young fellow who had left these mountains for the Ivy League and come back so poised and articulate. He wore an earring and, though I could not see it, a tongue stud. Some of the people around us were not even dressed formally, secure in jeans and flannel. How did they view Jacob?

Only at the end did the tears come, as he walked up the aisle with his father's ashes, and we watched in awe, gripping the pew's smooth wood. Jacob trod a path I had not yet, my own father fine at 71. The three Phi Taus and I kept silent on the drive to the cemetery, and as we walked partly up the hill, stopping when we could see the white tarp under which the family sat, next to a headstone, our shoes rustled against the grass. Men in uniform raised rifles and fired off a military salute, the gunshots echoing off the mountains.

We drove to his family's farm, a couple of miles up a winding road, finding a six-mile spread ringed by peaks. "Jacob used to ride up and down this mountain on his bike, to school," someone said. I repeated a story that he'd told me: after the Blizzard of 1993 dumped several feet of snow on upstate New York, he took care of a cow that had become trapped to her neck in a hollow. Now his cattle and horses were sold off and the fields without crops; the farm was being divided up. He showed us around, quiet and withdrawn, and I felt like hugging him but he did not seem willing so I patted his shoulder.

The only bar in the hamlet opened that day, early, having been mostly shut down between ski season and the coming summer. I knew these people of Jacob's valley, heard in their voices the rural twang, crushing of vowels ("life" into "loif"), and the faintly Canadian ring that comes from living near the border. I said little, even my years of dealing with death not enough to grant me words. Jacob was friendly but also remote, and tough, so tough.

✻ ✻ ✻

On the five-hour ride back to Ithaca, we passed Saratoga Springs, where my parents had lived since 1986. Jay and Adam rode with me; Train had gone home with MacGyver. We didn't have much time, but I had in recent years been trying to spend more time with family, and value them more, so I didn't like the idea of not visiting my parents. My youngest brother lived farther south, but he would understand if I didn't stop.

My parents greeted Jay and Adam warmly. They didn't know much about my involvement with Phi Tau at the time—fraternities were not a subject that interested my father, since his own fraternity had disappointed him deeply in the 1970s, when one of its pledges had died. But they understood that this group of men had become special to me. (Four years later, they came to Parents Weekend.) We spent about an hour talking, and they fed us dessert, one of my mother's pies or cakes. I kept thinking about getting back on the road, with four hours still ahead, but my dad looked anxious for me to stay. "Conroe's father looks and talks exactly like him," Jay reported at the next chapter meeting.

When we finally did leave, I said I would be back soon, and I tried not to remember that I had both parents and other people did not, that my parents were in their seventies and I had no idea how much longer they would be around (they kind of scoffed and said they'd be around another 20 years). They were such good people, married almost 50 years. They lived in Saratoga partly because it was close to where my father's parents had lived. Grandpa Conroe was gone but Grandma was approaching 100 and still sharp. Dad looked after her, visiting at least once a week. I could see myself moving to be near them, when the time came.

For so many years, I had taken them for granted, and now I did not, as if aging were a form of waking up.

* * *

Fortunately, the mock lineup was the extent of the experiment with hazing. I told Tom about it and he promised to look into what had happened. I informed Jacob about it when he returned from home. He scowled.

I heard the men had one hell of a discussion.

We tried ways to make association more dramatic, but we stuck with our vision. The staged lineup in the basement was never discussed in chapter. It faded away.

There was no manual for being a fraternity advisor. Cornell liked hands-off, but national seemed to want more. How close should I be to the men? How much should I weigh long-term issues against short-term problems? When should I speak out? The men hated to be preached at. MacGyver complained in chapter about tasteless and rough comments the men made on the chapter list serve. He believed that e-mail users needed to adhere to standards. The guys nicknamed him Flanders, after the goody-goody neighbor on *The Simpsons*.

I had to let them learn. My approach was more educational than being the hammer that some advisors were. But it could be frustrating. I marveled at people who advised Greek chapters for 20 years. Probably they had more sense than to care so much and get so emotional.

TWENTY-SIX
Trophies
(Spring 2002)

Outside the Statler Hotel on Cornell's campus, a thirty-something man in a U.S. Marine's dark blue dress uniform saluted Tom, then Chaz. The two saluted back, their dress whites shining in the sun. This was the gunnery sergeant who had trained them the past four years and now, as commissioned Navy lieutenants, they out-ranked him. Each handed him a silver dollar, a military tradition, and he said, "Thank you, sir."

Both had been commissioned by their fathers, who had served in the Navy. Tom and Chaz were to graduate the next day, the last Sunday in May. Both were headed for the nuclear sub program (although Tom would later switch to communications officer on a ship). I had to be there. These men that I had met as sophomores were serving my country, mere months after 9/11.

This spring semester had been a trial for Tom especially. First he wasn't sure if he would finish his degree or be pulled out of Cornell and sent to some war, after the towers fell. Girls broke up with him. No longer chapter president, he was the target of pranks by the men. They had joked about electing him steward so his last semester would be miserable. They pulled off his Porsche's cover and parked in his spot. He tried to hang out with them more. Finally, Tom's dislike for school bubbled up. He blew off assignments. He did an independent study with me, comparing communication strategies within a fraternity and a military unit, but didn't turn in the paper until the day before final grades for seniors were due. I threatened to flunk him, I didn't care who he was. I doubt I would have. On the plus side, the *Cornell Daily Sun* had named him one of the 25 most influential students at the university.

Phi Tau's five seniors had passed through the national graduate ceremony. The Board of Directors had given Tom its Skull Award for a senior who helps the quality of life in the house. The brothers had voted him the Meritorious Service Award, given to one or more seniors. Chaz, who had taken over an assortment of projects for the house, including the scheduling of photos for our first composite portrait, was recognized as Vice President for Miscellaneous Affairs.

Cornell doesn't have a commencement speaker other than the university president. There is a Convocation gathering the day before, and someone speaks at that. The actor Danny Glover got the nod that year, to the indignation of many seniors. Former President Bill Clinton had cost too much (although he would be the speaker two years later). On graduation day—the last Sunday in May—the seniors gather at the Arts Quad, school by school, and march around a library, past an old fieldhouse, to Schoellkopf Stadium, where 40,000 people await. The ceremony lasts an hour (there are no honorary degrees either), then everyone goes to their own department or school ceremony to receive diplomas.

After the ceremonies, Chaz's mother commandeered 106 The Knoll for a reception honoring Navy ROTC's graduates. She had once owned a catering business, and she transformed our dining room into a place of white tablecloths and fancy pastries.

Tom's mother was from a town 30 miles away, and his family had a party for him at a restaurant overlooking the city. Tom looked annoyed as his parents showed slides of him as a boy. I asked his mother about his lack of connection to school. "Well, I was summoned to meet with his teacher once," she said, "because he didn't know his shapes and colors."

The Porsche was like a jet aircraft on wheels. Tom took me to dinner that week and thanked me profusely. We'd been good for each other.

* * *

More plaques hung on the Chapter Room walls.

We liked awards, as a measuring stick and proof that we were making progress. Alumni, parents, even recruits the men talked to during rush, wanted to hear about awards and honors. I approved, I would take any award someone wanted to give me, but at the same time it was weak to tie your life and career to them too much. I'd known news photographers who chose assignments based on awards potential.

Six Phi Taus plus myself, Pat Madden, and our chapter advisor Mike Hayes had attended the annual Greek Awards. Before the program I said hello to the IFC president, the guy who had defeated Jay. I knew plenty of Greek leaders and had nothing against him. Andres, Hitman, and Adam glared at me: traitor. I glanced at Train, our brother who was IFC financial vice president, who worked with the president. I supposed he took some crap for it.

We received the phone-a-thon award as the fraternity with 100 percent of the brothers taking part, an award we would get for several years. Tom was chosen one of the outstanding chapter leaders, as Jay had been the year before. Sitting next to Jacob on the end of the row, I had just told him, "The best honors are the ones you don't expect" when I heard my name called as outstanding faculty advisor, a chapter award actually. Grinning like a fool, I went to the front of the room for my plaque.

Phi Tau was named one of the outstanding fraternity chapters, but we did not receive the IFC outstanding new member education award, and Hitman was disappointed. We wanted this nod from the administration for our anti-hazing path. We grumbled that the winner probably had hazing but lied and described a wonderful-sounding program.

Back at the house we were having the final chapter meeting of the academic year. Hitman walked in somberly and told the men we had not won any awards. Then he said, "Suckers" and we brought in the plaques.

* * *

Brian of Delta Upsilon had graduated in January but had come back to walk through the stadium, with the Class of 2002. He had joined the Peace Corps and was being sent to Romania to teach English. I had lunch with him and his roommate at Collegetown Bagels the day before graduation, on the patio, each of us digging into a bagel.

The DU brothers would walk together without him. Brian was walking with his close friend the Panhellenic Association president, whose sorority had let him rent a room in its annex the year before.

"To see Delta Upsilon brothers on campus and have them ignore me is very painful," Brian said, "but I'm glad I fought hazing." He thought for a minute. "The elephant walk—yeah, that really made me want to be a guy's brother, after having my hand on his scrotum," he said sarcastically.

I asked if he felt that the most awful forms of hazing could ever be eliminated.

"Nothing is impossible," he said. "That was my stance. People told me to give up, but I wanted to plant a seed for future classes to build on what I did. I think I succeeded."

TWENTY-SEVEN
Men from the Past
(Summer 2002)

A voice cut through our blurry reunion talk and the reggae band's beat, right out of a fraternity party 25 years ago.

"Did you hear this bullshit?" my classmate bellowed. "We can't bring beer to those open houses at the fraternities and sororities. No alcohol allowed, it says. At our age!"

Stretched on the grass of St. Lawrence University's central quadrangle, bottles of Labatt's in hand, we blinked up at him. It was June in Northern New York, warm but with a cool breeze. We'd gotten past fumbling to remember the kids behind the grayer heads and thicker bodies. We'd exhausted the basic questions about what people did now, which sounded so much like our shy stories of hometowns during freshman Orientation in the fall of 1973. We'd settled into a comfort zone of talk about sons grown tall, businesses taken over from fathers, divorces—and, of course, the university we knew versus what we saw around us and had heard through official channels.

My classmate was referring to this afternoon's unlocking of the university-owned Greek society houses and the three residence halls that used to be fraternity houses, the fraternities having either moved or gotten the boot. The Greeks among us could sit in these houses and remember the parties, the laughter, the midnight discussions about all that puzzled them about life—but they couldn't bring beer, which was funny considering how we drowned ourselves in it back then. "We used to have a keg in every corner," my classmate snarled.

"That's the way this place is now," said a classmate who visited campus often. "They worry about everything. They want to keep a grip on anything like that."

We knew this, of course, as veterans of the past two decades, when certain career paths shook as we trod them, as if from an earthquake, causing some of us to choose other paths while others simply looked for better footing. We also understood that the legal drinking age now was 21, that law-suits awaited everyone seemingly at every turn, and that we needed to learn new language and ways of thinking. Some of us had adjusted better than others. We wobbled between lamenting what was gone and marveling at what was impressive, like the sunken soccer field named after our late class-mate, a huge new fieldhouse with a climbing wall attached to the fieldhouse that in our time was a showpiece, and an all-weather track around a freshly-installed football field. We'd learned to temper our anger with resignation, even acceptance.

The group around me split among two fraternities, SAE and Beta Theta Pi, and a sorority, Kappa Kappa Gamma. We still tagged each other with those Greek letters as we had back in college. One SAE, the football player who had been my high school friend's roommate fresh-man year, was so trim and strong he could still be out there on the field in pads. He laughed about losing his bid for chapter president—chuckled with a dash of chagrin. He remembered long-ago meetings. "People always talked about those meetings like they were so big and se-cret," he said. "Hell, there wasn't anything to them." I remembered differ-ently, as one of those outsiders. SAE had been gone from St. Lawrence for a few years now. The Betas clustered about 15 feet away, keeping to themselves as they did in college. These men were now business execu-tives, company presidents, lawyers. At least their fraternity still existed here. Three of the seven from my time were gone, and another was about to go. St. Lawrence's Greek system was fading. Where about 50 percent of the 2,000 students joined in my time, fraternities and sororities claimed only 20 percent now, of 1,800 students. Rush and pledging had been shrunk to much shorter time spans. Now the current university presi-dent had decided to let rush extend to the spring as well. SLU's adminis-tration, like the ones before it, said Greeks still held a valued place in campus culture but needed to prove their worth and show more connec-tion to the community at large.

My classmates balanced dismay and anger—that something they loved so much, and had invested with so much effort, was threatened—against the feeling that maybe Greek societies had outlived their time. Around me at the reunion, there was no mistaking the fondness shared by men who lived together in a fraternity and fought the battles of grow-ing up. Arms around shoulders, buying each other beers, exploding into laughter at old stories, the men carried something forged long ago, even when their chapters might be gone or different in personality—one long-haired counterculture house was now an athlete house.

Relaxing on the lawn, I heard the indignation.

"Damn university says it wants Greeks to stay, but I think the administration really would be happy if we just disappeared."

"Don't they know that Greeks are the most active alumni and give the most money? Doesn't that count for something?"

"They can just wait for us to get older and be replaced by alumni who never belonged to a Greek society and never knew any differently."

A couple of women called "Going to the house?" to the ones sitting next to me, one of whom had served as their president. She said no, she was content right there and didn't need to see an empty house. I asked her if women in our class ever expected to become bankers, like her, or company CEOs, like our classmate who headed AT&T Consumer, or college presidents and athletic directors. She said her classmates were thinking about it during college, sensing that perhaps women would soon have the chance at a man's career. Other classmates agreed. A fair number of women, however, were looking for a husband, usually in the fraternities.

We didn't see gendered imagery in everything back then. Fraternity members worked in sororities as houseboys, cleaning dishes and helping with dinner. A few of the independent women belonged to fraternity "little sister" organizations, now defunct. When one fraternity, Sigma Chi, staged Derby Day in the fall, teams of women wrote the fraternity's Greek letters on their shirts and jeans in white tape. They competed at drinking and things like the limbo stick and breaking water balloons inside their T-shirts by bumping together. We shrugged off the ridiculousness of it. This was college.

The university had changed and we could be angry about it, but bitterness took too much energy. Better to remember what was.

"Well, something interesting happened to me this year," I said to the former sorority president, as I had said to several classmates since the reunion began. "I joined a fraternity."

"You what?"

"I became advisor to a fraternity at Cornell, and they initiated me in December."

"How cool," she said. "You can do that?"

I explained it briefly.

"Hey," I said, "I know it sounds weird, but it's been a pretty nice thing for me."

I had told the SAE brothers about my adventures a little. "That's a switch," said one. "Good to hear someone believes in being Greek."

The story became just one more for them to absorb this weekend where past and present broke against each other. Maybe it was just that

Conroe was always different back then too, that kid with the camera. Maybe it was just another mid-life journey, like yoga, adopting a child, riding a bicycle across the West, or retiring early and creating a charity.

We moved on to other topics, the former Greeks whose system was fading and the newly-minted fraternity man. I did not kid myself that I was really one of them. I was something else.

* * *

Cornell held its own Reunion Weekend, and I shifted from alumnus to host. I welcomed alumni as one part of the Phi Tau that lay beyond the chapter's day to day existence, when they cared enough to stop by or send money or just write to us. (The other part of Phi Tau out there was the national.) We made sure to be at the house for the times, both scheduled and not, when these men from the past would walk through the front door, usually with wives in tow. I guided several men through 106 The Knoll. They were from 1942 and 1952, their hair white, faces creased, voices strong but crumbling around the edges. Men stepped into their foyer with their wives, staring almost like freshmen during rush at the staircase, the chandelier, the Chapter Room ahead.

A handful of our guys were around, and they stuck out their hands and said, "Welcome back." We grinned at each other and waited for a place to begin, but mostly the older men just plunged into this. They glanced at every room, the way people do in a house they used to live in. They paused to ask each other about their lives, then they went on. One fellow was so overcome with memories that he chose a couch in the Newman Room and just gazed into space for a while. In the Chapter Room we had set out yearbooks from our collection, and the alumni had brought a few photographs as well, and they pointed to each other in group pictures of brothers with dates at Spring Weekend, happy and young.

In the basement I showed them walls and ceilings painted by the spring of 2002 associate member class. I pointed out wooden seats sanded down and re-finished, and brighter lights. The men said our party room had been a root cellar in their time, beyond the basement. They recalled a coal storage area in one corner, now just a storage spot for us. "We had one guy who'd been in the war," said one man, "and when he got drunk, he'd get a little crazy. We didn't know what to do. He'd be down here, imagining he was sticking his bayonet into Japs." I glanced around but luckily none of the Asian American brothers was nearby.

Another man gazed at me as if to gauge whether I wanted more stories. I did.

"We used to argue about how many parties to have, and how big to have them," he said. "We called it the Lily Whites and Dirty Blacks." I flinched inside at those names, and said that Phi Tau still discussed such matters. It turned out that he was talking about war veterans, older men at college on the GI Bill but not as dedicated to school, against more studious younger brothers. The current brothers just listened, asked questions, looked bemused.

The layout of the house had been altered somewhat in these men's eyes. They noticed the impact from tougher insurance rules: metal doors that split hallways in case of fire, smoke alarms, and the hood above the stove that provided fire protection. Another difference: some of the rooms that we used as singles had been doubles. The final difference lay in the house's condition, which we had improved from a year ago but was still a bit shabby. We were beginning to tackle this problem by asking for alumni donations attached to a wish list, and through the pledge class project.

The older men's culture may have been different—they couldn't fathom wearing a baseball cap to class at all, let alone one set backwards on the head, and I didn't dare ask about the clash in musical tastes—but they could remember the little moments.

A smaller man clapping a bigger man on the shoulder, in a gesture between respect and impudence.

A man's stunned pleasure as he hears that he was elected to office and, a few feet away, his opponents' silent absorption of defeat.

The wisecrack so cutting yet on target that everyone says "ooh" and the victim can only accept it.

The insult—and the apology.

The inside joke for the brotherhood. The inside joke for some part of the brotherhood but not the rest.

The slight smile of fondness for a fraternity brother, quickly hidden when you're 20, not hidden years later.

The confession to a room filled with brothers, of weak performance in office, or non-brotherly behavior, with a promise to do better.

Men who defy chapter rules—won't wear coat and tie, like to push for forbidden parties, skip house chores—and discussion about how to handle them.

The funny and interesting things to share with current brothers, like the labor relations major who got into Cornell with a recommendation letter from Jimmy Hoffa, and the former Green Berets who would climb into a large tree in our side yard and drop from it as if in combat.

∗ ∗ ∗

The chapter belonged to the current brothers, but the alumni watched, said their piece, approved or stopped what they needed to. Few students groups besides Greeks had an alumni body to answer to or listen to; Student Assembly didn't hear from previous assemblies. Alumni mattered but they could be annoying, could tempt brothers to reject any higher standards, could revert to their goofy college selves. I watched the generations feel out each other, each raised differently from the others, each believing they had the answers. I could only flow with it and try to be an interpreter. At other fraternities I heard about alumni complaining that the house was a mess, not clean and neat as it was in their time, when in fact it was no different back then. But ours didn't do that—the house looked clean today—and were pretty happy to see us back after five years' banishment, and glad for our awards.

The white-haired men always paused in the dining room to study our composite portrait, to see our faces. I imagined they were absorbing the different shades of skin and the exotic names. Until the early 1960s, national fraternities were all-white, mostly WASP. "An Italian would've made us diverse," one 1950s alumnus cracked to the men once at dinner.

I was in college myself when I first discovered that fraternities excluded Jews and non-whites by national policy. I learned this when I heard that St. Lawrence's most famous alumnus, the actor Kirk Douglas, had been deserted during rush once fraternities discovered he was Jewish. Back then, in the 1930s, he was Isadore Demsky (and he'd been born Issur Danielovich), a star wrestler. The fraternities wanted nothing to do with him, Douglas wrote in his autobiography *The Ragman's Son*, and he never forgot the hurt, even as he went on to become student government president and then a Hollywood superstar.

Then there was the story of Joseph Bruchac, Native American writer and educator, who joined a fraternity at Cornell in 1962. Bruchac writes in his memoir *At the End of Ridge Road* that while dozens of houses courted his roommate, Bruchac heard from only two. He went to a smoker at one and was "shunted into a side room along with a bemused young man from Thailand. It was exactly like the scene in *Animal House*, with the rejects herded out of sight of the serious pledges." The other house was a jock house that took him because he was a wrestler. He discovered that the fraternities had learned of his non-white heritage in the fall when his Native American grandfather and a black high school friend stayed at his dorm for a weekend. Racism aside, Bruchac joined because "I was only 19 years old and wanted to be accepted. Because I was lonely. Because they asked me."

Fraternities I'd visited in the South were mostly all white, but I was a guest and didn't ask about it. The one time I did, the chapter president said they tried to recruit black men but none wanted to be the only black man among 100, and they usually chose black fraternities or black student groups. I'd heard this at Cornell too: black and Indian students faced pressure to stick with their own organizations. Most fraternities here were somewhat diverse. Cornell had so many ethnicities, it was difficult not to be.

The alumni never said much to us about what they felt. They lived in this complicated world too. Maybe they were even glad. I never mentioned that at Passover, Barry and Rainman held a Seder in the Chapter Room, with 10 guys seated around the Skull table. Barry made matzo balls.

* * *

The first mention of Skull came in the 1905 *Cornellian,* where each fraternity got three pages: its national coat of arms, a list of its members, and a picture of its house. The books back then contained few pictures, mostly of campus. Skull was listed at 16 members living at 105 Catherine St., established in February 1905 (it was actually 1901). The men were divided between arts and engineering, the only colleges in the university at the time. They were from Ohio, Pennsylvania, and the Ithaca region. One of them was Eugene Montillon, architecture major from Buffalo, who became an architecture professor and remained active with the fraternity for his entire life. Bandhu appeared in the fraternity section the following year. Skull had 13 members, eight with German names.

The yearbooks' faculty sections listed not just each faculty member's name but their alma maters and—unimaginable now—their Greek affiliation. They were named again with each fraternity's roster: "Faculty in Fultate," it was called. Since "fultus" means supporter in Latin, I am unsure if these men were initiated into the fraternity or just advisors. By 1917 Skull had 19 members, Bandhu had 21 (one from the Territory of Hawaii), and Bandhu now occupied 106 The Knoll. They belonged to choral groups, drama clubs, and engineering societies.

After the two merged to form Phi Delta Sigma, the names were all former Bandhu except for Professor Montillon's. With their hometowns, majors, and activities, male seniors had phrases like "Three and a half

years at Cornell" and "four and a half years at Cornell" below their portraits. Small black stars appeared next to some names, as well as some faculty names. A war was on, across the world, and these men were serving
in it. Phi Delta Sigma remains the name of the alumni corporation that
owns the house and property.

Fraternities have been criticized and eyed suspiciously at Cornell
practically since they arrived in 1868. Morris Bishop's *History of Cornell*
says the university's first president, Andrew Dickson White, had belonged
to fraternities at Hobart College and Yale, and approved of them. His successors did not feel quite as warm. One of them believed that fraternities
offered rich boys a haven where they could be lazy and exclusive. Other
university presidents reached the same conclusion as fraternities grew in
the 19th century, but soon the men from those fraternities were trustees,
faculty, and involved alumni, carrying clout. The fraternities also offered
a place where students could live, something previously available only in
rooming houses. When colleges began to build dormitories—known as
residence halls since the holistic student development movement began
in the 1970s—they didn't need fraternities quite as much.

Phi Tau was healthy in membership over the decades and had a
strong social calendar. The 1950s produced two of our prominent alumni,
Philip Searle, chair of Sun Bank, and Don Snyder Sr., chief financial officer of Eastman Kodak. One of our first orders of business as a colony
turning into a chapter, and winning awards, was to re-connect with Don,
who lived just over an hour away in Rochester. Both of his sons had belonged to our chapter. He became a champion for us and an annual presence at Reunion Weekend, telling the men stories about chapter traditions
and parties back in his time.

Those faces in group photos and composites watched us from a past
that was more distant because of how quickly the chapter's membership
turned over and how fast anything could be forgotten, people especially.
A batch of men left every year and another batch arrived. The Founders
joked that future pledges would have to know their names. We were just
starting the custom of assigning a "big brother" to each associate, a
brother whose duties were vague but could include encouraging and
teaching the associate. They established a "lineage" that would have, besides a chain of names, a special drink and maybe more. A few brothers
never had littles, but most did.

One of the reasons our Phi Tau chapter was doing well was Pat Madden,
the alumnus who had now become chair of both alumni boards. An engineer
and computer consultant, he tried hard to know the men as I did but found

it more difficult, because he lived in Boston and, while he remembered what it was like to be in college, was not as attuned to the current brothers. He set up our house list serve, worked with the men on budget management, and tried to handle crises that either didn't fall under my role or that the men preferred to consult him about. He had tremendous compassion and a wish for the chapter to keep growing and improving. Yet he could be the hammer that punished, in his position as Board of Governors chair.

Pat and I tried to speak regularly and work together, especially after chapter advisor Mike Hayes became unable to work with us as much, because his own fraternity asked him to help with its struggling Cornell chapter. I began to take on more of the chapter advisor's job, though not as much, since the Founders were good about reminding the chapter about its central vision and calling out anyone who was out of line.

We had other 1980s alumni who were there for us. Our concern was that they had served on the boards almost 20 years already and were ready to hand over the reins soon—and there was no one because of that five-year gap. The current brothers would not be ready for several years. The 1970s alumni didn't even stop by much let alone serve on boards.

✶ ✶ ✶

Our risk management chair was floating around the first floor, and I asked him to speak to alumni about his role, which was to patrol parties for behavior that put the fraternity—both our chapter and the national—at legal risk. He cheerfully told them that two-thirds of undergrads were now unable to drink legally, so life had changed. The older men and their wives gaped at the idea of having a brother who could shut down a party if he felt the risk of lawsuits was too great.

Lou's girlfriend popped through the front door and headed upstairs. Lou was staying at the house briefly. One of the 40th reunion men asked what a woman was doing in the house. Luckily I knew how to answer this one, because several alumni had told me that in the 1950s and 1960s, women were allowed in a fraternity house only on a couple of weekends each year. Even then, the men's doors were supposed to be open, and a chaperone might be nearby.

"She's visiting her boyfriend," I said. "Women come and go at will these days."

"But she's here all the time?"

I said yes, women stayed here sometimes and were here at all hours. It had been that way since maybe the late 1960s.

The alumnus couldn't quite absorb it.

"You allow women in the house every day?"

"Yes, sir."

I was glad that he had asked me, since the men wouldn't have comprehended what he was talking about.

The language was different too. One alumnus asked if the men still had "bull sessions," discussions late at night about anything that concerned them. I said yes. Another talked about a fellow who had "busted out"—flunked out.

Hearing that he was an electrical engineering major, an alumnus cornered Lou against a wall to tell him the bachelor's degree in engineering was five years in his time. He was indignant about it. Lou just smiled and listened. The older men spent a couple of hours looking over the house and us, talking to the undergraduates, remembering, then went on their way to the beer tents on the Arts Quad.

TWENTY-EIGHT
Meet the Cousins
(Summer 2002)

He looked dapper, as always, in his suit.

Andres stepped to the microphone and stared out at a few hundred faces on the convention floor. Almost every Phi Tau chapter was represented by two or more men, arrayed in order of founding from Miami University, Ohio University, and Ohio State into the far corner.

Andres focused his dark gaze. His brilliant smile was not to be seen. His wavy black hair and thin, handsome face gave him a certain sober look. Twelve men were running for three undergraduate seats on National Council, and his speech fell in the middle. The room was dead.

"My name Andres Ricardo," he said in a thick, fabricated Hispanic accent, "and I need job."

The room erupted in laughter. Andres grinned. He, MacGyver, and Jacob had been circulating through the men from across the nation here in New Orleans, showing them an Ivy League man could talk to anyone. Born in Colombia, he had grown up in Westchester County. Now he told the assembly that he would represent their interests among the older men.

Andres won on the first ballot. The other two seats required a couple of runoff votes.

This was about as fun as it got at our chapter's first foray to national convention, which alternated years with Leadership Academy. The rest of the handful of days was about listening to debates about national policy and voting on motions, and electing the council and a new vice president, who would become president in two years. Several men had made the trip for our chapter. They tried to meet brothers from other chapters, instead of sticking together as some chapters did, and on a riverboat dinner cruise Jacob fell into conversation with the University of Georgia chapter president. They found that they had much in common.

This too was Phi Tau beyond our little chapter's border, a level that encompassed our alumni yet was apart from them. We were certain our chapter had not spent time at national events over the decades, other than 1950s alumnus Don Snyder Sr., who had served on National Council and as the fraternity's financial advisor. Most of our men really were not interested even now. But a few were, and last summer we had sent several guys to academy, a week at Miami University where men discussed the creed and chapter management issues, trying to gain ideas to take back to their chapters. We had received the award for top colony.

The other excitement was Georgia alumnus Bill Crane's nomination from the floor to run for vice president, and his subsequent victory over the two men who had come to the convention as candidates. Crane was a baritone-voiced former TV news anchor in his late thirties who was vice president of an Atlanta communications company. The new president was Jay McCann, a Pittsburgh insurance executive who was mid-forties, from a now defunct chapter in Alabama. Jay was a wiseguy who took pride in being average-looking and bespectacled, hardly the stereotypical frat boy.

Our chapter had encountered other chapters at the spring regional conference in Maryland, but national events brought Phi Taus from all different regions, types of campus and Greek system. Southern accents and Midwestern twangs filled the air. To me—I didn't go to New Orleans but later attended two conventions and two academies—it was like getting acquainted with cousins I had only heard about—we shared something but weren't sure how deep it went. It also reminded me of going to conferences and coming away with new friends I planned to keep in touch with but didn't. We could compare notes and see in each other's eyes what we shared. It was different for the undergraduates from our chapter. They made friends and had fun hearing about problems that other chapters faced, but usually they came away feeling how different we were; our grades were higher, we were more diverse ethnically, we had a house where some chapters had a residence hall wing or just a meeting place and mail box in the student union, and we did not have hazing. We were Northerners in a gathering where most guys seemed to be from the South and Midwest, other than those Latinos from California chapters, or those rowdy men from Oklahoma State.

We had decided not to apply for the Maxwell Award as outstanding chapter; it was a lot of work at the end of the spring semester, and we had not been around long enough to have a shot. But we received something else: the Monroe Moosnick Trophy, a big brass cup on a wooden base that weighed about 20 pounds and meant we had the highest grade point average among all chapters (we had around an A-). That was a chore to bring home on the plane, the summer after 9/11, but the guys got it to Ithaca and put it on a bookcase in our Chapter Room.

Every national event closed with a Candlelight Ceremony, led by "Mr. Bill" Jenkins, who had been a staff member for national for decades. The Phi Taus lined up along the walls. Guests who were not Phi Taus remained seated at their tables. Each brother received a small white candle. In the dark, Mr. Bill's deep voice invoked the magnificence of Phi Tau, the four men who had founded us at Miami, the men who had joined since and passed on to Chapter Eternal. He was quite proud that he had known the last of our four founders, William Shideler, who had died in 1977. Mr. Bill's love for the fraternity—he had attended more than 20 conventions—always moved everyone to silence.

Mr. Bill always designated four men to represent the Founders and carry their candles to the far corners of the room, to light everyone else's candles. Then he read a wish for everyone to feel the power of this fraternity that had given them membership, and wished us good travels.

＊ ＊ ＊

The road to Oxford, Ohio, from Ithaca leads straight through New York's Southern Tier and Pennsylvania to Cleveland, south to Columbus, west almost to the Indiana border. My Pontiac Grand Am always seemed to be squeezed between 18-wheelers and construction barriers. Then I turned south and crossed through small towns and farmland. North of Cincinnati, I turned west through hills, until a small city of quaint streets appeared. Off to one side I saw a university that seemed an endless expanse of red brick. A white tower, the Beta Carillon Tower, stood sentinel. Beta's headquarters was just outside town, in an alumnus's former mansion, with a spyglass always trained on that tower. Beta was founded here along with the other two Miami Triad fraternities, Sigma Chi and Phi Delta Theta, in the mid-19th century. We came along almost 70 years later.

This was America's western frontier back then.

Like our chapter, Phi Tau itself began as something else. What follows is courtesy of the 1996 book *From Old Main to a New Century,* the history of Phi Tau written by Charles Ball, a Miami graduate elected national president for 2006 to 2008.

The national fraternity that the Cornell men joined already had 40 chapters, established over 24 years after being born as an anti-fraternity, an association for men who were not part of the fraternity system at Miami University that dominated student life.

Miami, named after the Miami Valley (itself named for a Native American tribe), was a frontier university. In 1792, Congress passed an act requiring the man who owned an enormous tract of what became Ohio to set aside a township that would be home to the first western university. Six miles from what was then the western boundary of the nation (and is now the Indiana-Ohio border), this university's trustees chose land in 1809 and settlers built a community named Oxford, after the English university town. Miami opened its doors in November 1824 and, as eastern colleges did, formed two literary societies for students. Fraternities arrived from the east 11 years later, in the form of Alpha Delta Phi, brought from Hamilton College. Alpha Delt's founder Samuel Eells worked in a Cincinnati law office and initiated a co-worker, who initiated two friends at Miami. Students feared this new secret society. The U.S. was going through a movement against the Masons and secret societies, led by John Quincy Adams. An especially vocal opponent of Alpha Delt, who was president of a literary society, noticed that some men he admired were joining this fraternity. He liked the idea and in 1839 formed Beta Theta Pi with seven other men. Their idea was to adopt what they liked about Alpha Delt and avoid what they saw as bad qualities.

This became a theme of the fraternity movement: if you don't like certain aspects of fraternities, create your own, even if you must break away from a fraternity you belong to.

Reinvention.

By the early 20th century Beta and two other fraternities, Sigma Chi and Delta Kappa Epsilon, ruled student life at Miami. They determined who was elected to student offices and even who was on sports teams. The men who formed what would become Phi Kappa Tau were inspired to defy "the ring," as they called it, first by defeat in a campus indoor track meet in March 1905. Freshmen William Shideler and Clinton Boyd, distance runners for the varsity track team, and junior Dwight Douglass took part with a team of non-fraternity men. The non-fraternity team lost to a DKE team, which was aided in jockeying for position during races by a team of Sigma Chis. Boyd and Shideler vowed to fight the ring any way they could. They disagreed years later as to how much this track meet had to do with their partnership, but it seemed to spur them to fight the fraternities.

The next academic year, two political groups arose that were not affiliated with fraternities. Shideler and Boyd led one, Douglass and a sophomore named Taylor Borradaile the other. They decided to work together and to form an alliance with two other fraternities, Phi Delta Theta and a local. They got their candidates elected sophomore class president and vice president (Boyd), then they defeated the ring in a track meet in February 1906.

One night the next month, as winter vacation came to an end, Shideler returned to campus a day early and met up with Douglass, his roommate. The two decided to continue a discussion they'd held before vacation with Borradaile and Boyd: the creation of something they called the Non-Fraternity Association. Because the heat was turned off in their dorm they found their way to Old Main Building, a massive brick classroom building, and found the dean's office unlocked. Douglass, a football lineman who was 6-foot-2 and 200 pounds (supposedly the largest man among Miami's 202 students), sat in the dean's swivel chair and found in his desk a couple of cigars. The two men lit up. Of course the dean walked into the office and "it was difficult to say who was the more surprised," Shideler said. After hearing their explanation the dean, close to 80 years old and able to take life in stride, smiled and told them to carry on. Such meetings, he said, were how his fraternity, Beta Theta Pi, was founded.

The four men's new association met on March 17 with 21 members, in the same hall where Beta Theta Pi had met for the first time so many years before. Borradaile and Boyd spoke of "the urgent need for a permanent nonfraternity organization built on the principles of democracy, square dealing, and equality." Borradaile was chosen as president. The next school year, this upstart group ended the fraternities' dominance of campus politics.

Three of these men were from Ohio and one, Douglass, from Illinois. Douglass became a mining engineer. Shideler was a campus leader and outstanding speaker at a time when oratory skills were highly prized and political debates were huge entertainment. He became a paleontologist, with several fossil species and a mountain in Antarctica named after him, and convinced Miami to establish a geology department, which he chaired for 36 years. He served as Phi Tau's national president in 1913–14 and held other offices with the fraternity. Borradaile, reputed to be a man of great wit, was president not just of the Non-Fraternity Association but of a literary society and the junior class, earning the nickname "Boss." He carved out a career in chemistry and toxicology, finishing his career with the Veterans Administration. He then passed the bar exam without preparing for it and was admitted to practice law in Florida, though he never did. Boyd was so slight of build his nickname was "Teeny." He won the university's 1907 oratorical contest and went on to become a county judge. His son Clinton Jr. was initiated into Phi Tau in 1948, his grandson Mark in 1971, both at Alpha chapter, Miami.

The founders did not plan that their organization should become an actual fraternity. They wanted something different. Indeed, the second president, Harvey Brill, was considered a fifth founder by the others but was not listed as a Phi Tau after the organization became Phi Tau because he actually joined another fraternity later, as a doctoral student. He was a botany professor at Miami for many years and remained a Phi Tau ally.

After a few years the group decided to change its name to something shorter and snappier, and chose Phrenocon, which took parts of "freemen," "non-fraternity," and "commoner." They switched the "F" to a more classical "Ph" and the final "m" to "n" to sound better. Phrenocon had a house now, and began to adapt more of what fraternities themselves did, such as official colors (brown and white, changed at some point to Harvard crimson and white), flower (carnation), an initiation ritual, and later official crests and other symbols.

From Miami, new chapters were founded at Ohio University, Ohio State, Centre College in Kentucky, Mount Union, and the University of Illinois. The name changed to Phi Kappa Tau in 1916, at the fraternity's sixth national convention. The fraternal movement had picked up steam. By the time Cornell joined Phi Tau in 1930, there were 34 more chapters. Some began as Phi Tau and some were other entities that became Phi Tau chapters, like Cornell's.

✳ ✳ ✳

National headquarters lay on a street near campus, a newer building that inside resembled—as all fraternity national headquarters do—the base of a corporate empire. A fraternity is a business on one level, a belief system like the Salvation Army or Boy Scouts on another level, a network of relationships on still another level. From here, the staff monitored the chapters across the nation and the Phi Kappa Tau Foundation gathered hundreds of thousands of dollars for scholarships and projects.

The national staff faced a stern task: keeping track of the scattered chapters, which would soon number 90 after the colony at Indiana became a chapter. Three traveling consultants, a director of chapter services, a director of educational programming, the CEO himself, and administrative assistants—this handful of people kept track of which chapters had done their annual paperwork, reported pledges and initiates, raised money for Hole in the Wall, and were getting along well with their campuses.

The Foundation, as well as the chapters themselves, listed an impressive number of men who gave money year after year, long after college. Phi Tau meant that much to them, and they wanted younger men to feel what they had felt, learn what they did.

Phi Tau was a leader in one respect: it hired a woman for a key position, educational director. In fact, the character coaches and leaders at Leadership Academy were sometimes women, and sometimes they were men from other fraternities (LeGrand and Brian the IFC president served as character coaches). Phi Tau took quality people where it found them. The undergraduates did not always like this. In the residence hall rooms where the chapters met, they complained about having to talk about their creed with a woman or a non-Phi Tau. I thought they needed broader minds.

✶ ✶ ✶

After the men came back from either convention or Leadership Academy, I always waited to see how their ideas and enthusiasm would play out. They usually encountered apathy. I could see it at the first chapter meetings: one of the guys who had tasted the national scene would talk about it, and propose something he'd heard about from his community leaders, or try to talk about the creed's meanings. Several brothers made it clear they didn't care. The officers would figure out a way to mix some of what they had gained into our affairs, but it could be discouraging.

We had few Phi Tau neighbors: SUNY Oswego (70 miles away), Rochester Institute of Technology (about the same), Buffalo State (90 miles), and Rensselaer Polytechnic Institute (150 miles). Colgate, which was 90 minutes away, had a local fraternity called Phi Tau that had once been a national chapter and was petitioning to re-join us. We ended up hosting RIT for Phi Tug. Twice, encouraged by national headquarters, we hosted regional leadership retreats, the first at the outdoor education course and the second on campus. We got only a handful of guests each time, though one pair came all the way from the University of Akron and another group drove up from St. John's University in Queens. We liked national's faith in us, but the events were not greeted with joy. They demanded so much energy and help from the whole chapter, which was already focused on its own events and issues, that anything beyond us became a low priority.

Then Colgate staged a raid.

Men appeared at our front door late one night, saying they were from Union College in Schenectady. While a brother checked and saw that Union didn't have a Phi Tau chapter, other men from Colgate climbed onto a back porch roof and stole one of the big plywood letters we'd made for our first rush in 2001. Big Daddy climbed through his window and onto the roof with a baseball bat and they fled. Someone called the police, who told the Colgate men to return the sign. Two months later, I joined two national staff members in associating 36 of the Colgate men, all sophomores and juniors; the seniors, who had been behind the scavenger hunt, were not invited to associate. This would be a colony of Phi Kappa Tau for however long it took to prove they could make it. Some of them smirked when they heard I was from Cornell. Mostly I remember that they were tall and dressed as if they were all from Eastern prep schools. I drove home in a heavy snowstorm, through the valleys. I hoped we would at least meet the Colgate chapter, maybe mentor them, but the raid put an end to that. The guys said no, "they're a bunch of punks."

Sign stealing did not sit well with us. Jay's parents had donated two handsome green-and-gold signs, a large one in front of the house and a smaller one that hung from our front porch. The big one vanished one night, its posts pulled out of the ground, and we found it in the nearby gorge. Someone ripped the other sign out of the porch roof, chains and all. It re-appeared that summer, and we hung it higher. We blamed the thefts on enemies in the fraternity system.

We anchored the larger sign better in the ground, but a year or so later some fraternity sent a raiding party (probably fall pledges) who cut partway through the posts before one of our guys saw them and chased them into the night. Someone would finish the job two years later—we theorized that it was new pledges in that fraternity—and the sign was gone again. But by then we had a lighted sign made of concrete-like material, set down by the road, and the men did not see the need to hunt down the old one.

TWENTY-NINE
A President's Choices
(Fall 2002)

That fall new hostility erupted between cops and students in Ithaca. One night several Phi Tau seniors watched from the porch roof of a house they had rented as students milled in the street below me, forcing cars to stop. Someone called up that a student had urinated on a cop and another had thrown a bottle at a cop. For staid Cornell, this was anarchy.

The resentment levels rose in the next few months as students found it harder to have parties at their houses and the police increased their bar sweeps. In response the students elected a 20-year-old junior to City Council to represent Collegetown. He was the first traditional-aged student ever voted into local office. He would be replaced by another student (who was also a fraternity president), then both council seats from that ward would go to students, and then the county legislator seat would be next. Even with the students, the council passed a tougher noise ordinance aimed at quashing parties, inspired more by problems in the South Hill neighborhoods below the other four-year institution in town, Ithaca College, but affecting life on East Hill as well. Now police could shut down parties more easily, and students complained that police abused their power, ticketing them for even loud music. They cursed the city. All of this ill feeling joined the fraternities' anger at being hit with new rules every year. Now, besides being limited in their house parties, they couldn't have as many annex parties.

✳ ✳ ✳

After his father's death, Jacob shook off the problems, worries, and doubts that eat away at us. He tried to see the positive in every day, shrugged off little setbacks, did what he wanted to do. He went camping, took flying lessons, savored his polo friends.

As president Jacob was so tough after what he had endured that at times he did not sympathize with the men's more typical problems. But he was both businesslike and compassionate, and meticulous about working with Cornell's administration and other fraternities. He and I met once a week while he was president, technically because he was taking independent studies from me. He interceded when guys squabbled, encouraged guys that others gave up on, ran chapter meetings as firmly as he could (and was sometimes exasperated by their chaos), saw guys' development as people when he looked at the overall picture. He was well-spoken. When Jacob stood to address an auditorium full of men from other fraternities, it was almost like hearing a company CEO twice his age. Yet he regarded Phi Tau as just part of his life, and every Friday afternoon he and Train drove to Syracuse to shop, to get away from the brothers.

He showed a mischievous streak. One night, after drinking vodka, he turned into Evil Jacob, slipped into Jay's room, and dumped ice water on the sleeping Jay.

Jacob forgave me when, for his summer job at a financial services company, he sent me brochures and I did not read them (not really knowing they came from him). He handled the despair of the job search, patiently pressing on when other seniors sank into frustration. The lack of interviews and offers puzzled us, given his achievements, but he kept trying and finally landed a job that excited him.

Jacob took me to dinner, heard my complaints about students or my joys in owning a house. And while he often said how glad he was to have me as a friend, I was just as pleased.

He and I made the executive decision to de-commission the five fireplaces and little coal-burning fireplace at 106 The Knoll, after the men had a huge bonfire out back and seemed too fascinated by the flames. Jacob and I had both grown up in houses partially heated by wood stoves, so we respected fire but were afraid the men didn't. We held no illusions about how fast our mansion would go up if a fire ever broke out. We'd already been scolded by the fire department for having a real tree last Christmas. Student residences were not supposed to have real trees, especially not a tree like ours, so tall that it rose up from our foyer to the second floor.

* * *

Jacob's term was a perfect example of the choices a fraternity president must make.

A senior drank so much on his 21st birthday that he ended up passed out on the bathroom floor. Jacob faced the nerve-wracking decision of whether to call for medics. An ambulance's presence might attract police, which might lead to complications if guys who were not legally able to drink had been doing so. Yet medical personnel were the best solution to a medical problem. Jacob finally chose to make the senior stand and walk around, and he was OK.

The men liked to call things that were stupid or odd "gay," and joked about who might be gay based on how they dressed, how few women they knew, a strong interest in art. Some of them were more obsessed than others. I guessed it was natural when so many guys—even accepting guys—lived together, shared bathrooms, walked around wearing just a towel. Jacob called to say he was going to ask the men to stop the gay jokes and references, at least a few of the men who did it more than others. "Someone in the house might be questioning his sexual identity, and we don't need jokes about it," he said.

"Really?"

"Well, think about it: supposedly one in 10 men is gay."

For all of our talk about brotherhood and diversity, this was one hurdle we could not get past as a fraternity. Certainly we didn't lack for examples. Other fraternities at Cornell had openly gay members, although they were straight-acting. Phi Tau national made it clear that gays were welcome, and held discussions during national events about how houses should cope with having a gay brother. But the men in our house struggled with it.

In my travels I met alumni of other fraternities who were out (and it was OK, mostly, if they weren't obvious about it); a Cornell student who joined a fraternity because he hoped it would make him straight; a fraternity that made gay jokes during intramural sports but was rumored to have two members whose beds were pushed together; and a fraternity that filtered out gay or questioning rushees by having a brother pretend to be in the closet and share his "secret," so that the rushee confessed. I saw the birth of an organization for gay and lesbian Greeks at Cornell. But if word got out that a fraternity had a gay brother, the sales side of rush became that much harder.

I did not care too much about anyone's sexuality. I believed sexuality was biological and if someone wanted to keep it private, so be it, and I wished the men didn't care either, but it was a battle I could not win. Some fraternity men believed that no gay man could be a true brother. I thought he could be.

Jacob had guts. The men did stop the jokes, for a year or so.

* * *

Every fraternity has a few men who worry everyone else, with their appetite for booze and the stupid, even callous way they behave when drunk. While their drunken foolishness makes for good stories, it could grow into alcoholism, and maybe it causes too many problems. One of our men in particular concerned me. A wonderful guy, bright and funny, lover of literature, passionate about his studies in geology—he just shrugged off his own foolishness. Once, at another campus, he got arrested at a bar and proudly showed everyone pictures of himself in an orange jail jumpsuit. I didn't see what he should be proud of.

One night Jacob called to say this brother had hit a low point. "I've decided to try an intervention," Jacob said. I asked why. It was tricky to try and tell other people how to behave and live. Jacob said this brother had gone to Hitman's hometown that weekend and left pot where Hitman's parents found it. Then, two days later he wrote in an e-mail that he was going to have his way with a brother's hot younger sister. Jacob thought the men had had enough. If we were a fraternity that allowed fighting, those would've been fighting words.

"Should we talk to his parents?" I asked.

"No," Jacob said, "let's not involve them. I've been talking to fraternity and sorority presidents who have done interventions." The idea was to tell the brother or sister to shape up or move out of the house, while going to counseling. If nothing else, our brother needed to admit he had a problem and learn to control himself.

Jacob drafted a letter to the brother, telling him how things needed to be, and brought it to the executive board. One officer grew upset and said this solution was too harsh, but the other officers sided with Jacob. They thought the letter's language was too tough so Jacob revised it, and gave the letter to the brother. The brother cleaned up his act for the rest of the year. He did not have to move out of the house.

This episode showed me something, again, that I have seen ever since with our chapter: we have been blessed with strong leadership. Not all of our executive boards worked together well, and not all officers performed as well as they could, but we managed to find leadership.

* * *

As members of the fraternity, guys were always emerging, their interest soaring suddenly, even as other guys cooled off, just grew tired of the drain on their time and mental energy, or became involved with girlfriends. Guys tried to push pet projects and sulked when they failed. It was an old story in every fraternity.

That fall Mick, now a junior, decided to spend more time and energy on Phi Tau. He had been until then just a brother. Now he announced at chapter meeting that he had more time on his hands and was ready to play a larger role. Mild-mannered but quietly persistent, he became more visible and talkative, coming to the house all the time although he didn't live there. He joined a new organization, a college version of Lions Club, and spent more time on philanthropy. An English and anthropology major who planned to go to medical school, Mick was from the Midwest and, despite his Irish heritage on his father's side, had been raised Greek Orthodox at his mother's insistence. His faith was deep and steady. Before meals, he quietly said a prayer.

Mick was competitive. One afternoon I played a rare Beirut match, myself and Cage challenging Mick and Paulie. We played in the basement. I sank my first two shots, and Mick glared at me. Missing a shot, he punched the wall in frustration, making a hole. I said, "Too bad I'm a veteran. I just don't play with amateurs that often." Paulie answered by firing in his next seven shots. Game over.

Mick coaxed Lou, who disliked doing community service, into helping to manage a three-on-three basketball tournament for Big Brothers/Big Sisters. He tried to convince the sophomores that the fraternity would indeed be theirs sometime.

Ah, sophomores. No longer celebrated as freshmen newly arrived on campus or taken care of with course selections, they are seen but not heard. I was a sophomore once, and I felt so low, far from even a junior's status, that I asked my parents if I could spend a semester somewhere besides St. Lawrence (the answer was no, suck it up, kid). In a fraternity sophomores don't usually hold an exec-level office yet, so they have to be content with committee work or just speaking up at chapter meetings. Helping with rush for the first time, they must learn that they can't give a bid to everyone.

We always had cocky sophomores who demanded the chance to voice opinions. At times their opinions were worth hearing and considering. But they could be a little big for their britches. I saw myself in them, at 19, plotting my path to yearbook editor, unhappy with some of the moves made by officers in groups I belonged to.

It was a sophomore who was bold enough to ask something the Founders never would: why I'd never married. We were leaning against the upstairs railing and he asked. I had not thought about marriage much until, for some reason, lately this question had become part of a chorus in my head, urging me to do more with my life than I had in my twenties and thirties. I said a significant other and children had always seemed destined for other people. He looked at me as if to say, are you really an adult? I could tell him yes, I was maturing. Life no longer revolved around me. Middle age awakened me, seeing too many people who were alone in old age. So had Phi Tau. I didn't say this, it was too out there and these guys lived in a world of winners and losers. They were the generation where everybody was above average, everybody's opinion mattered, and we were in the Ivy League. I did not say, at least then, that this fraternity had shown me who I was as a man and I wanted more.

✳ ✳ ✳

Now speculation began about who might succeed Jacob.

Big Daddy, projected as president when he was a freshman, did not seem interested. I saw two juniors warming up for it: Barry, who often hung around after chapter meeting to ask Jacob about things he had done or said, and a brother I will call Xavier. I doubted that Barry would win, much as I liked him and appreciated his love for the fraternity. As alumni relations chair he had done well at updating our data base, at a time when we were steadily pushing to build this long-neglected side of our chapter. He was not a good writer, I needed to edit his newsletters carefully, but I thought he would be a good pediatrician someday. Barry was just too gruff in his speaking style, and regarded as tremendously stubborn. Xavier had made no bones about wanting to hold high office, since pledging last spring. Over the summer he had painted many of the rocks piled in our back yard and placed them around the front of our house, lining a sidewalk and garden. For some reason this annoyed the Founders. Then he butted heads with Barry over a check from an alumnus, which had been mailed to him. Xavier had his own ideas about spending it. The two argued out front of the house.

That was round one of their clash. Xavier brought his ideas to exec and the other officers backed Barry. That was round two. There was more to come.

THIRTY

Sex Talk

(Fall 2002)

Our risk manager scheduled the sex talk for a Monday after dinner. We were digging into dessert when our guest stood to speak. Usually a dinner speaker was a professor or alumnus or someone I recruited who might add to the men's appreciation of the world—travel, sports, public speaking, careers. But this was a Cornell junior, a member of Sigma Pi fraternity. Instead of being lectured by police or a counselor from the campus health center, as we were sometimes, this time we got a fellow Greek because he had developed an organization talk called Sexual Health Awareness Group—SHAG.

"I'm here to talk about sex," said the Man from SHAG, and everyone laughed. Grinning as if he were in on the joke, he pressed on. No chance he would get through this without giggles.

Fraternities are known as places to chase women, so they are also known as places for date rape, gang rape, false entitlement with women's bodies. Universities and national fraternities fight this through education. Cornell fraternities must be lectured about party management and alcohol consumption (from police), and about fire safety (from city firefighters). And they must get the "sex talk." The Phi Taus understood why. Women were safe with them, as even our wilder and more macho members would never do anything or let anything happen, but it didn't hurt to be reminded how to behave.

For a half hour the Man from SHAG reviewed the notion that a man needed to listen for a woman's saying no. He acknowledged that this could be difficult, since men and women spoke roughly the same way nowadays, and much was unpredictable.

I could relate. I lived in a world where women called each other dude and men called each other bitch. Men now said they had to "go pee" instead of the euphemisms for urinating that were used in my time. I didn't even know what college students called seeing a member of the opposite sex on a regular basis, because it didn't seem to be "dating." Maybe "hooking up"?

"I'm going to demonstrate the best way to put on a condom so that it doesn't break, and does what it should," said the Man from SHAG. "I need a volunteer." A brother stepped forward, smiling, and held up his right hand with two fingers extended. The condom stretched over hand and forearm.

"You wish yours was that long," someone called out.

A brother frowned at me and said, "Why are you here, Conroe? Why do you need to be lectured about this?"

I resisted saying something flip like "So I can judge your technique." I simply said it was part of my job. I had to sign the form from national headquarters.

*　*　*

The guys liked showing sororities that they were nice guys. Problem was, women didn't always like nice guys. They liked the bad boys, who radiated reckless disregard, the scent of money, supreme self-assurance. The Phi Taus wanted to be bad but weren't sure how.

The men rarely sought my opinion about women, perhaps sensing that a guy who had never married was not an expert on such things, or maybe not sure that it was appropriate to ask me. Nor did I try to be one of the guys by bragging or speaking as if I knew it all. That would have seemed silly and hollow. They lived in such a different world than I had. I read or heard about so many kids trying sex at 13 or 14. Kids heard and saw so much about sex at younger ages than in my time.

The sex talk was partly about being careful because seemingly everyone was so easy to offend, and so quick to complain about being offended. For citizens of a nation that prized free speech, what we said had become awfully scrutinized. Men needed to watch themselves. Things seemed easier for us in a way, since we were past the era when male students automatically faced suspension without due process if a female complained about something, but the burden of acting and speaking sensitively still fell on men.

I could think of reasons why men deserved it. I had heard the stories of gang rapes in fraternities. Occasionally I had heard stories in college, when men talked about having a "train" after a party. Sometimes it was the young woman's idea but other times the woman was passed out, half-aware, as men lined up to have sex with her. The idea made me sick.

*　*　*

A few fraternities at St. Lawrence had Little Sisters organizations. I was never sure what Little Sisters did—maybe serve as hostesses for some parties, make holiday cards and cookies for the men.

I was surprised to learn years later that one of the staunch feminists on campus—in a place where feminists could be counted almost on one hand, where many female students were shopping for a husband—was a Little Sister of Sigma Chi. She was a red-haired beauty, a New York City girl with a little wildness and adventure about her, and a lot of us men were infatuated. She told me recently that she had such fun being a Little Sister. I answered that many Greek systems have pressured their fraternities into phasing out these groups, because women attached to a fraternity was not politically correct anymore—they could appear to be like a harem. She was astonished. "It was nothing like that," she said.

✳ ✳ ✳

Phi Taus boasted of conquest, derided each other for ongoing failure, compared stories, helped each other meet women, cheered each other on, laughed over a couple of small-town guys who were addicted to Asian girls. A few of them liked to make wisecracks about their lack of success with women. I found this self-mockery a little unhealthy, and wanted to tell them that they would fill out, become better-looking with time.

They could make rude comments to women when drunk, but then women could hold their own. Phi Tau was known as a fraternity where women could feel safe. The pledge program had a section focused on giving a dinner party.

Female students of mine said they were friends with this Phi Tau or that one, and loved our house. Otherwise I didn't pay attention to any of it. I overheard the men assessing who was a pain in the butt, who was hot, who was cool, who was easy, without knowing names and faces. I did not keep track of who they were paired with.

"You'd recognize her if she was here," they'd say. "She dated X last semester. She's at all of our parties."

"I don't go to your parties," I'd say.

"Yeah, well, you've probably seen her somewhere."

One senior broke up with his girlfriend, who started seeing a fellow Phi Tau and housemate. This was supposed to be against any fraternity's code, but it was love and they married after graduation. A couple of other Phi Taus had girlfriends who didn't like being around a fraternity and demanded they quit us; one eventually did.

Like every fraternity the men wanted more hot women at their parties, and that wish, combined with a restlessness with some of the men in our brotherhood, fed what I came to think of as the Cool Brothers, the handful of brothers who wanted us to recruit more good-looking, socially adept men, not to transform us into a pretty-boy house but to add more face guys to the mix, men who would be front and center as host, who would be cool to hang out with. A couple of the Founders joined with a couple of the new men, and in time they became more vocal about wanting us to be cooler. I think they liked our non-hazing, leadership, and service sides for the most part. They did not think of themselves as frat boys but they were fratty, if that makes sense. Most of this is second-hand since they did not talk about the issue much in front of me. I pictured some brothers hearing this talk and wondering if that meant them. I'm sure hearing this hurt their feelings and then made them resolve to fight. The notion of making us cooler left me uneasy, because I liked the chapter as it was, a mix where it was OK to be a little raw and socially unskilled—like me when I was in college.

The Phi Taus talked about having a Sweethearts group, making women who were close to us—individually or collectively—a part of us. We advisors discouraged the idea, but the men heard about other chapters with such a thing, national headquarters encouraged it, and eventually we tried it. Seven women, mostly serious girlfriends or younger sisters, were asked one spring and then welcomed with a ceremony written by Hitman. They were not a harem by any means.

* * *

As Jacob's reign began to wind down and the Founders let go of this thing they had created, cracks appeared in us.

Phi Tau's election for the next chapter president left a split in its wake, for a while. Barry and Xavier were nominated. So, to my surprise, was one of the chapter officers: Rico, a Californian of Hispanic ancestry, who was capable in his office but quiet. Jay nominated him and Rico did not decline, a sure sign that Jay had talked to him.

I had come to like Barry immensely and hear his views on the fraternity. He always spoke up when he thought our chapter vision was in jeopardy. His interest in being a pediatrician had grown, he told us, from summers at a camp where he managed first aid for children. We talked about football. He said as a high school offensive lineman he'd been so much lighter than opponents' linemen and linebackers that he had to play dirty. He named two current Syracuse University stars, both bound for the NFL. "One time I went to the sideline and tackled a coach," he said.

Rico was a tall, low-key guy whose mother had smuggled him out of Honduras as a child, through Mexico to the U.S. Most of us never thought of him as even wanting to be president, but during his speech he informed us that in high school he'd been prom king and student body president.

I thought Xavier had a shot, but it was not to be. The brothers didn't mind ambition, but they wanted finesse. His rock landscaping had not gone over well. Neither had his clash with Barry. As we passed the gavel, where each man had a chance to speak about a candidate or about which way he might vote, I heard fewer comments in support of Xavier. Jacob said he backed Xavier, the only senior to do so. He passed the gavel to Vijay, who said, "I will vote for Rico, my brown-skinned brother." Everyone chuckled.

The Founders backed Rico and he won.

Barry shrugged off his setback and was chosen new member educator, a nice fit for his tougher side. Xavier and his backers didn't speak much to everyone else for a while. I could sit at dinner and see his table ignoring the other tables. I waited for him to get over it and for the rift to heal. Maybe that kind of tension was the reason our next five presidents were unopposed, as if the house somehow decided informally who it would be and avoided strife.

Mick, continuing his emergence, became vice president. He defeated Ken, Big Daddy, a couple of other juniors. The rest of the officers fell into place over the next few weeks. A sophomore, Dan, nicknamed Dice, had been the house manager for the fall, and now he became rush chair. The new exec board boasted only one Founder: Paulie, who agreed to serve a fourth semester as house manager as he prepared to graduate. Ken became social chair, Cage was philanthropy chair. Another junior became alumni relations chair, although he was equally eager just to serve on executive board and possibly change the chapter's direction. He was part of the Cool Brothers.

There was one other election surprise: brotherhood chair, the man who was supposed to promote unity, brotherly bonds—through drinking events, usually. The men decided to make this appointed semester position into a one-year elected position on the exec level. The hope was that being at exec level would cause the man to take the job seriously.

Lou had run for chapter treasurer as a freshman, to fill the fall semester vacancy as the incumbent studied elsewhere, and had lost to Joe. Now he was nominated for brotherhood chair. Worried because Lou never made any bones about his love for partying, Joe ran against him. Lou promised to have keg races (he was half-joking). Joe, who by then had served as philanthropy chair, treasurer, and vice president, and who didn't drink, promised a mix of wet and dry events. He said brotherhood was about more than drinking together.

They tied, with an abstention. Everyone looked at me to break it. They thought I was basically an undergraduate. But I rarely commented during elections and never considered voting. "No way," I said, "I will not choose your officers. Whoever abstained, make a decision." Lou won. I thought the swing vote might be Dream, who was Joe's close friend and fellow Founder but Lou's "big brother." Afterward a few of the Founders were in Jay's room. Jay, who had not gone to chapter meeting, told Dream he was nuts to vote for Lou.

"Well, I thought the younger men need to start taking over the chapter," Dream said. "They've been waiting."

THIRTY-ONE
Grading My Brothers
(Fall 2002)

Anxious, searching faces watched me slip around the U-shaped forma-tion of desks and to the front of the classroom. First day of class at Cornell, late August: tanned arms and shoulders, and relatively happy ex-pressions. While we waited for late arrivals I passed around copies of the syllabus, white sheets stapled together, a blueprint of the 15 weeks ahead. We looked each other over. This was my fifth semester as a lecturer and I was full-time and possibly—nobody knew for sure yet—getting into a real career. I already knew what was coming: students who wanted to be added, or had enrolled and might drop after hearing my policies. This was the science writing course writing about science for the public, so they were mostly senior biological sciences or engineering majors who hadn't written much for a few years. My class would not be a high priority com-pared with organic chemistry or fluid dynamics—one more battle for me.

A friend smiled at me from a corner: Hitman, the first Phi Tau to take a course from me. Four had done independent studies with me, and Big Daddy was doing one now, but this would be different. I would be grading Hitman, treating him like any other student. I would have to call him by his real name here, and instead of Conroe he would call me Scott. From 20 feet away, he seemed to be absorbing the sight of me too, in this setting.

The men had asked about taking courses from me, but I'd kept them out because they were too young; I reserved spots for seniors in the agri-culture college. The engineers in our house, like Hitman, were victims of a department policy that sent engineers back to their college, to take courses that fit them. But I welcomed the sight of a brother.

With other faculty I mentioned only my advising Phi Tau. Being part of a fraternity would seem alien to most faculty. Actually, many of my col-leagues seemed bemused that I advised a Greek society at all. People in academe see fraternities in particular as enemies of learning. They imag-ine places that breed cheating, pull guys' focus away from school, keep pledges from going to class, and use elitist and silly ways to choose new members and make them part of the organization. And they would be right some of the time.

The first weeks of class were always chaotic. None of us wanted to let go of summer. I put off grading as long as I could, for that was the honeymoon's end. The wait lists for my two courses, science writing and magazine journalism, grew and shrank as students pleaded to be on them and others bolted. A veteran now, I rolled with it. My standards had risen. I had caught some plagiarism, I had encountered attitudes, and while I liked many students and even befriended them, I started each semester as I did today, reviewing my syllabus a bit sternly. In science writing I was always anxious at first, where in journalism courses I felt in control. I was going to make students meet deadlines, learn to accept criticism, discover that writing had no right answers all the time, and otherwise enter a new world.

I greeted Hitman quickly, as I would any student I already knew, and moved on.

✳ ✳ ✳

A brother fumed over a "D" he did not understand. I let him vent.

A brother smiled when I snapped that his was Generation E, for excuse (I tried not to unleash my frustrations on the men, but I slipped). He said, "We learn to do it in high school. If we don't make excuses, our parents do it for us." I decided to push the men to be more accountable. Another brother added, "We are Generation E, for entitled."

A brother told me about professors who read from their own textbooks, which students were forced to purchase, or who droned through the same lecture as 20 years ago.

A brother heard me ask why students were such poor writers overall, at an Ivy League university. He said students rarely read for pleasure, and didn't worry about spelling or other rules when writing on e-mail, so papers were like a different language. Another one, a biology major, said they didn't write much after freshman year, except for lab reports. Were my standards too high? Should I relax my mistake limit and surrender to the realities of this century?

Technically I was not a professor at all. I was not tenure-track, meaning I was not expected to publish and do research. I possessed no doctorate, just 19 years of work experience. I had fallen into teaching. Besides 75 students each semester in three lectures and two labs, I had 20 advisees and a department committee position. I was just a hired gun for labor-intensive courses. I felt temporary. Yet I demanded to be taken seriously. I enforced deadlines, sifted excuses for absence and missed work, was disliked or appreciated, made sense most days, glimpsed some student brilliance, and tried not to feel like the high priest of a dying religion.

* * *

Scholarship was not written into our chapter's original vision, but we quickly had established ourselves atop both Cornell's fraternity system and the 90 chapters in the national fraternity—and stayed there for four years. Our grade point average stood at around 3.5. I never knew why; we didn't talk about academic strategy or plot ways to get A's. The guys just did it, with some exceptions who did not care about grades.

Hitman showed me this side of Phi Tau, that fall semester. He talked in class, met deadlines, and was irritated if I alluded to the fraternity or his nickname. He missed two Fridays because he liked to drink on Thursday nights, as did many of the men, but two absences were allowed. He wasn't there one Wednesday because it was his 21st birthday and he was out the night before. I said nothing. A couple of times I brought his graded work to the house, if I was going there for dinner.

I was not an ogre, with students. I flowed with the rhythms of student life to an extent, as seniors missed class to interview for jobs or grad schools. My policies allowed a little leeway. I just laid out my expectations and the punishment for not meeting them. But it was not so clear-cut, and Hitman interpreted attitudes and problems for me. An assignment that I thought was clearly worded left students puzzled, he said. I complained about seniors missing class, and he said employers often called at the last minute to summon them to interviews. I wondered why students procrastinated—I gave them a month to do a project and they waited until the final week to do it. He said it was the Cornell mindset, and he showed me the sheer volume of work students faced.

"All of you professors think the work for your class comes first, and you don't pay any attention to everything else we have to do," he said one day. "It's like you get together and plan how to bury us. You all have something due right before a break, and your tests and projects come at the same time."

I said, "There's no way we coordinate anything, and all of us operate with the same timeline for the semester, so we time things the same way. I can't do anything, really, but I'll keep it in mind." Tired of student excuses, told not to worry too much about their lives, I nevertheless appreciated his insights.

I hated that the GPA was used to measure Greek chapters academically, and I was not the only faculty advisor who felt that way. Students already were so obsessed with grades. They would say or do anything to get an A, and cry over a B+. But what else, administrators asked, could anyone use as a measuring stick?

We did not have the usual fraternity "study cabinet," the collection of old tests and papers. I opposed such a thing, since it felt too close to cheating. I had caught and punished students for plagiarizing. My own record as an undergrad was modest, a B average as an English lit major, but the work was all mine. I knew students wrote papers for each other and found other ways to help each other beat the academic system, but I could not do much about it. A study cabinet, I could.

Hitman was followed the next year by two more Phi Taus in the science writing course and one in magazine writing. The same thing proved true: they did not expect special treatment and I graded them as I would anybody else. I grew accustomed to seeing these men at dinner and chapter meeting, where I was a brother, and then in class. They adjusted on their end as well.

My students each semester always included fraternity and sorority presidents, rush chairs, treasurers. I asked them how rush went or about other Greeks issues. I asked athletes how their seasons were going, and musicians about their concerts, and thespians about plays. Students wrote, "He really takes time to know the student world" on course evaluations. Of course, every semester someone wrote, "He favors Greeks and athletes." Well, so be it. "He should talk more about his own writing" on an evaluation was followed by one that said, "He talks too much about his own writing. I'm a better writer than he is." Students respected me and disdained me, and I was neither as wonderful nor as clueless as they thought.

My Phi Tau students worked hard. You had to work hard at Cornell, to survive. The sheer volume of assignments, problem sets, tests, labs, and group projects was staggering. Every semester I watched seniors dragging themselves toward graduation, worn out and beaten down. Students would vanish for a week or two and say they'd been to counseling. The university was competitive even for an Ivy League school, everyone chasing that diploma that opened doors to power and prestige.

I wrote recommendation letters that helped students go to medical school, law school, PhD and master's programs. In the Phi Taus' behalf I also made the case to honorary societies, and to national headquarters for awards and scholarships. I altered futures.

While the tradition of faculty working with fraternities goes back to the 19th and early 20th centuries, faculty are right to see fraternities as unfriendly on the whole. Besides the study cabinet, fraternities can push men to miss class and feel apathy toward school. A man follows the pack, reluctant to go against louder, more assertive brethren. I heard faculty complain in particular during the spring pledge period, when freshmen fell asleep in class after being kept up all night, or weren't there at all, confined to the house. Then there were the risks to reputation. Fraternities got in trouble. Even when their problems unfairly reached the news media—and most news reporters were not Greek in college—it was difficult for an academic person to disentangle himself from the mess.

So why serve as a fraternity's faculty advisor? The question matters as many campuses require Greeks to have such advisors, and national fraternities and sororities see the alumni initiates (people like me) as a resource. Fraternities must connect better to society. They must be tamed.

Colleges have been looking lately for ways to link students and faculty outside the classroom, even when the two don't really want to be together so often. Faculty live in residence halls and eat in dining halls. They are recruited to support sports teams, clubs, and publications. But a fraternity or sorority falls in some other realm, with its Greek letters on a sweatshirt's chest, its ceremonies, its talk about prospects' coolness or dorkiness. Perhaps what it offers is less visible than the yearbook or student assembly.

Without that dimension of learning, the Greek system might not be needed anymore.

＊　＊　＊

Faculty who consider advising a fraternity or sorority should do it for several reasons: to see into student culture, if they are curious; to find friendship or a chance to mentor; to educate in ways they never knew they could.

I almost entered a career in student services. Perhaps it is in my blood; my parents befriended many students at SUNY Potsdam and lived in a residence hall for two years, in their fifties. So perhaps it was inevitable that I wanted to soak up the life of a student, when I turned to teaching at Cornell.

Obviously I could never know the men as they know each other. I wasn't there when someone acted like a drunken fool and his brothers forgave him, or for the road trips or spring break. But friendship was there, if a professor was open and kind, and saw beyond the parties. Not all faculty advisors got initiated, as I did, or wanted to, but it could happen. Some faculty might enjoy that.

I couldn't say that I was friends with all of my Phi Tau brothers. The years separated us. The men accepted the difference of my middle-aged life, and I mostly spared them knowing about it. In fact, if I had stopped by the house too much, they might have wondered what sort of life I had. And they left me behind when they graduated, because I was part of Cornell and the fraternity and both must be outgrown. I had to be content with the occasional e-mail or campus appearance. I can't say I always made the effort either, for every fall the house was reborn with a new mix of personalities and I let the graduates go. Ours was like any male friendship and, for the men I mentored, any student-mentor type of bond: laden with limitations and little betrayals, times of warm support and chilly indifference. We shared amazing moments, stories about each other, laughs, sudden insights. I walked with these young men for a few years when they seemed to grow and change every few months.

Finally, there was the teaching side to my role.

This was not like my courses. I did not grade the men. My lectures about their habits or behavior were brief and had to be well-planned, for they were resentful of criticism as only a man of 19 to 22 can be. But there were similarities. I had more impact on them than I realized. Just as a student once decided to go to law school because I praised his speaking in class, the Phi Taus listened to my most casual remarks as gospel. Just as students disregarded my opinions when I spoke from experience, the Phi Taus could be deaf to my deepest-held wisdom. As with the classroom, some days I should have talked more, other days I should have shut up. As with the classroom, I did not really see how much I influenced anyone's life.

I was forced to beware my moods. On days when I was just tired of students, it was best to avoid going to the house. The men might pull me from my sour mood with their silliness at dinner, but they might irritate me too. They laughed about skipping class, or compared notes on how to squeeze an A out of a course. It was their home and I was fortunate that they felt comfortable enough with me to speak candidly, as if I were not there. College was a game, and I was in their locker room. To push the sports metaphor further, I was like a referee sitting among athletes as they talked about referees' decisions. I had to hush and set aside my faculty self.

I helped the men deal with death, a parent's bankruptcy, an alcohol intervention, a party busted for underage drinking and the chapter president's resignation the next day, an officer who wanted to cut down on the number of gay jokes out of deference to someone who might be questioning his sexual identity, and the decision of whether to get a dog for the fraternity. Was any of this within the faculty advisor's role? Not when I started. But all of these situations, and more, did what the classroom always did: forced me to ask how wise I ultimately was, and how I might help young people understand.

Because I cared about the men and what they thought of me—I needed to care, to be effective—I did more than call upon my wisdom. I wanted to be wiser.

* * *

That fall semester with Hitman ended in the usual flurry of last lectures that I wished my students would remember, final projects piled in boxes outside my office, and students stopping by to thank me or ask for favors like extra-credit work (I usually said no, as they had plenty of chances to earn certain grades). Two students argued that they should be graded differently on their project than everyone else because "we worked together so well." Another, whom I had known since his freshman year, asked if I would raise his A-minus from a previous semester to an A so he could get into a certain medical school. No and no. Man, I hated it when students did that. I tried not to fixate on the grade grubbers and excuse mongers. I had some students who just worked at their writing, dreamed of getting published, or simply trained for jobs where they would communicate about science.

Hitman stuck his head in the door when he dropped off his project. There we were, student and teacher, in my office. I would assess his newsletter project (done with a partner) and determine his final grade. My grade would go into his GPA. It would be entered on his university transcript and be factored into our chapter GPA. I did not ponder the last two facts. I just thanked him and said I would see him at the house during the week.

THIRTY-TWO
Jocks
(Fall 2002)

"Come on, stripes, give us a break!"

Jay's yell cut through the sounds of men calling to each other, and of a mallet whacking a ball. Heads turned and people looked surprised, up and down the bleachers. Nobody raised hell at polo matches.

Phi Tau did.

Ten of us had driven just beyond campus to Oxley Arena, an indoor dirt playing field. Three Cornell players in red helmets and maroon short-sleeved shirts faced off against three blue-clad University of Connecticut players, while two referees watched. All rode ponies. A net separated the field from us.

The referees ignored Jay. The ponies and their riders raced back and forth, the men swinging their mallets to hit the ball from the dirt, toward goals mouths drawn on a wall. Jacob was one of the Cornell players, in what we interpreted as a defensive role—the other two took the shots. He had made the lineup last fall as a walk-on, after recovering from his broken leg.

We savored the chance to stand together and cheer. We did it at Cornell soccer games, for our brother who started at goalie, and of course at hockey games. But polo was sedate, calm, like golf.

"Hey, Ten, you suck!" hollered Dream.

The match was split into four periods called chukkers. Cornell led at halftime, by one goal.

UConn's No. 10 walked off the field, down the passage behind the bleachers, and out into the night, not looking at us. He came back with a dog on a leash, a pit bull sort of beast that had been tied out front and had barked non-stop. The fellow disappeared into the men's bathroom and came out without the dog. He had tied it to the sink.

"Ten, your dog hates you," Jay screamed as the action resumed.

Joe asked me if Jacob had been recruited for polo. I knew Jacob had begun riding horses back home on the farm. Ever the authority, I said yes.

185

Another senior, Jeff, said that wasn't true, Jacob had walked on while the others had been recruited. A handful of Phi Taus wandered in: Hitman, Andres, some of the newer guys like Xavier and Dice. Cornell went on to win. We all laughed and applauded and enjoyed our brand of rowdiness—no obscenities, just noise. One Cornell player named Senter was the president of his fraternity, and he told Jacob he envied our support.

Afterward Jacob greeted us from beyond the net, his face and beefy arms streaked with sweat. He said the coach loved our cheering section. Then he was summoned to a team meeting, and led his pony toward a big archway across the field from us, into the adjoining barn, his other favorite place besides our house.

* * *

Varsity hockey games were another place to spend time together. Hockey was the only sport Cornell students cared about, and the only one that charged admission to them. They lined up every fall for season tickets in Lynah Rink's student section, camping out all day and into the night in the Lynah Line. Phi Tau had a contingent of about 10 guys. Between classes I'd look for them along the quarter-mile line of folding chairs, blankets on the ground, card games. I'd find them studying or just hanging out. The hockey players were the only athletes that anyone at Cornell fussed over. The players really didn't have a normal student existence. They could drink in the bars only on Saturday night, all year, not just during the season. They were constantly meeting students who worshipped them, and they learned to handle it. Now the Phi Tau seniors knew some of them, because Jay, Train, and Jacob were members of Quill and Dagger leadership honorary and so were a few hockey players. The seniors ended up partying at the hockey house, and the die-hard among them needed to swallow their awe.

A few times I joined the men in the student section among the Lynah Faithful, if one of them wasn't going to the game. I was so used to being neutral as a sports writer that I seldom cheered for any team anymore, but I stood between Paulie and Barry, with Komo and Joe below me, and followed the customs. We held up newspapers while the opponent was introduced. We yelled that the goalie wasn't a black hole he just sucked. When he settled in his crease, we chanted "skate, skate, turn, bend over." We sang Cornell's alma mater, arms around each other's shoulders and swaying.

* * *

Big Daddy came barreling in from behind the line, held the football with both hands in front of him, and dove into the end zone: touchdown. The crowd—a gang of Phi Taus—shouted approval in the dusk. The other fraternity's team began to complain that it wasn't fair, this was flag football and what were they supposed to do to stop him? Big Daddy was 6-foot-2 and 220 pounds.

That fall of 2002, we actually won at intramural flag football, to our relief—nobody could say we were just nerds with high grades. Big Daddy, now a junior, had come into his own at quarterback, with a powerful passing arm and amazing speed and agility for a big man. We had a tremendous receiving corps with Jay, Hitman, Adam, and Magnus. Dream and Barry anchored the line. One sophomore, slightly-built but fast and slick, starred at receiver and defensive back. He was also our top player in soccer and hockey. We had a tenacious defense to swarm the opponent quarterback.

The men cared about sports. When we lost, Jay and Hitman and Big Daddy would retreat to their rooms, slamming the doors, and not talk to anyone for a while. I liked seeing us care about sports, even the intramural variety. It was a great way to build bonds and memories, out under the lights, in the cold, or in the late-afternoon sun. The best moments were when we triumphed despite the absence of some key player, who couldn't make it that day because of a test or review session. Intramurals was a last hurrah for former high school stars, and a chance for men who had not played a certain sport in high school, who maybe had been cut from the team, to try their hand. Flag football was so different from the regular kind that everyone needed to adjust.

We won that day and others, going 4-1 in our division. Dream served as captain and made out the lineups, while Big Daddy was the voice for strategy during the game and at halftime. To add levity, I took on the role of team owner of Phi Tau sports, e-mailing the guys after games with promises to whip the grounds crew into shape or trade away someone who wasn't performing. Our only loss before the playoffs was to Sigma Nu, the two-time champion, a jock house loaded with not just former high school athletes but former Cornell football players. They scored first but then Phi Tau pulled ahead by two touchdowns. I swear it had nothing to do with Dream's position as chief official, catching the referees' ears with his criticism from the sidelines, or with Dream's girlfriend refereeing and maybe giving us a favorable spot on downs. The Sigma Nus, surprised to be challenged, finally rallied and scored a few quick touchdowns in the second half to stop us, but we felt good.

In the quarterfinals we became the first team to score on Sig Ep, first-place team in another league. We lost in the closing minutes as Big Daddy injured his hand when someone blocked his pass. He spiked the ball and stormed off into the dark, to have his girlfriend drive him to the hospital. The Sig Eps thought he was a sore loser, until one of us filled them in. We finished at 5-2.

Soccer was a different story. We were awful. Only three Phi Taus had played in high school, and everyone else just tried. We had some fine athletes who would attempt to play goalie and would head the ball on defense. But they didn't know strategy. That year we did reach the softball finals, with Dream pitching, aided by an influx of athletic freshmen. I wanted to take a team picture but the men said wait until after the final, so in the picture most of them look glum. That would be the case most seasons in every sport: no picture until the season ended, so since it always ended with a loss, everyone looked serious.

THIRTY-THREE
Local Custom
(Fall 2002)

The men wanted traditions. Every fraternity had some.

We inaugurated a new one in November: throwing a guy in the shower on his birthday, or whenever he was careless enough to announce to the brotherhood that he would soon be a year older, or whenever someone learned about it and told everyone else.

Tradition is a strange concept in a fraternity. It is supposed to mean something done for years, but often it means something done for one or two years. A fraternity chapter has a short memory. This tradition stuck, and like birthday customs in many fraternities it followed a water theme. Some fraternities stick a guy's head in a toilet and flush, the classic swirly. Others pour ice cubes on him, or toss him into a tub of water designed for livestock. Phi Tau decided to throw guys in the shower.

The men ambushed a senior on his 22nd birthday. They grabbed him after chapter meeting, carried to the second floor (where all of the showers were), and shoved into the shower that had a bathtub attached. He was too surprised to resist. He just looked puzzled.

The men were better prepared when my 47th birthday arrived. We had our last chapter meeting of the fall semester the next day. Jacob presented me with a cake after dinner. Then he quietly warned that I was going to get wet, so I took off my shoes and put my wallet in my jacket. Chapter meeting dragged on for so long, I thought the men had forgotten. Then, as it ended, I heard Barry's deep voice: "Happy birthday, Scott." They pounced.

Barry took my right side and Hitman gripped my left shoulder. But the two of them weren't enough. I weighed about 190, unfortunately. On the landing before the second floor, Hitman yelled, "We need help guys— he's really fat." (In telling the story since then, I usually change the last word to "jacked.") *Wait until you reach middle age and see how you deal with it*, I thought. Someone else clasped my legs. I plotted a possible escape. "He's wiggling," Barry yelled as I thrashed. I was not fooling them. I was too slow to escape anyway. But struggling seemed like the thing to do, for entertainment value if nothing else.

Jacob darted ahead of what had become a procession: me being carried and a knot of grinning brothers behind us on the stairwell, taking in the sight of their advisor being treated like any other Phi Tau. (That became the pattern in later years: the president staying ahead of me and turning on the water, almost like a car with blinking lights leading an over-sized load down a freeway.) They stuck me in the bathtub and made sure I was wet. I just climbed out and came downstairs, to laughter.

The next year I thought again that the men would forget, but as the meeting ended Barry once more wished me a happy birthday. This time two sophomores, both 6-foot-3, joined him. One of them, Noah, was a bit gangly, not filled out yet, except that he was still damn big. He handled me easily. They chose a bathroom where the shower was large and didn't have a tub attached. At the door someone pulled aside the shower curtain and turned on the water. I braced my feet against the door frame, so they switched tactics and backed me in, over the shower stall's concrete lip, and sort of rolled me backward, making sure they didn't get wet. I made my head and shoulder tilt into the water stream—might as well make them happy. Then I stood up, dripping.

Noah wished me a happy birthday, looking me in the eye as if assessing how I was taking this. Thanks, I answered. A sophomore who had just been initiated in November smiled a bit uncertainly. Other guys looked satisfied. We had crossed some border, and I had allowed it, maybe.

I noticed one guy missing: Lou, who loved rough horseplay. I had assumed he would take part. Maybe he was afraid I would renege on my promise of a recommendation letter for graduate school (I would not have).

I listened for dissenters who thought my trip to the shower was not appropriate, and heard none.

Days like this reminded me how far I had come from my own college years, when I was overly sensitive, serious, and not sure how to take rough male humor.

Barry and Noah usually dodged the birthday custom because they were just too big and hard to carry. The guys did get Noah once, catching him by surprise at a sorority mixer, but usually they left him alone. When I asked one year if they were going to get him, he looked at me indifferently and a younger guy said, "Go for it, Conroe." I had no reply.

* * *

Belonging to a fraternity meant you were tested, watched, judged. Every little thing you did or said could come back to haunt you. Anything stupid—which covered a lot—would become a story told in chapter meeting. Worse, it could be brought up when a guy ran for office.

A chapter meeting was supposed to be a business meeting, with a framework of officer reports, old and new business, and my report, but it slowed down as someone commented, someone else made a joke, someone embellished the joke, and the chapter president finally pounded his gavel and said, "Guys, come on! Quiet!" The room would be quiet for a few minutes, then—if everyone was restless that night, or feeling witty—the chain reaction would start again. Long meetings were the worst: elections, changes in the constitution, the first meeting of the academic year in August, and the last meeting in May (when the seniors said their farewells and went through a ceremony to become alumni).

You had to develop a thick skin and try to laugh off your foibles. Otherwise the joke would never go away.

I was mostly exempt from this—mostly. The men preferred to leave me in my lofty spot, and I preferred to stay there. An advisor who liked being "one of the boys" too often risked losing respect, clout, or whatever quality made him effective. It might happen slowly, but it could happen, and then the advisor would have to work to regain respect, or at least wait until the fraternity's membership turned over.

At times my middle-aged life seemed so lame under their scrutiny. Everything lay ahead of them and they expected their lives would be perfect.

Away from campus with several of the men, whether eating out or gathering for some event, I stuck out. A waitress brought the check to me. A security man eyed us suspiciously until he saw me. The men always smirked and said, "Thanks, Dad."

My biggest problem was my sense of humor. The guys could take tough humor from each other, but if I tried it they looked stricken, stunned. Wisecracks that my fellow faculty or baby boomers laughed at drew pained silence in the Chapter Room. When the men did laugh, it was after a pause, as if the men were in the United Nations and an interpreter translated. And I was forbidden to try ethnic humor, as if my generation was not equipped. Vijay could yell at Nieraj, his fellow Indian, for sitting "in the white section" at chapter but no way could I make even the mildest comment about someone being Jewish or brown-skinned.

Vijay to a white brother: "You got a little white trash in you, boy."

Brother: "Well, your ancestors carried water jugs along the Ganges."

Vijay: "Damn."

Or, this exchange during a basketball game out front.

Sophomore brother, missing a shot: "Jesus Christ."

Jewish brother: "I guess."

Sophomore: "You wouldn't know."

Jewish brother: "Sorry. Sorry we killed your savior."

The Jewish brothers loved to make wisecracks about their religion, to us and to each other. They argued about points of Judaica, such as the dates of holidays or meanings of anything.

"We call this the Bread of Affliction," said a sophomore once, holding matzo.

Sarcastic reply: "Why, thank you, Emmanuel."

It was part of life in a family, I guess. How else would editors of Cornell's ultra-right, borderline racist alternative newspaper sit at dinner with a brother who was president of the umbrella organization for all Jewish groups on campus?

✳ ✳ ✳

I was not always too quick, sitting at dinner.

I tried to talk to a brother but he didn't say much. Quiet and cerebral, I decided, failing to realize that while he might be just that, he was also high.

One guy would pile some hip-hop riff on me: "Conroe, learn to be more gangsta. Yo, that course you teach, I've heard it's anthrax." Anything he didn't like was anthrax, that first year or so he was in the house. He really didn't know much about my course, he was just ragging on me. There was more ragging on Conroe now.

This being fall, the seniors were stressed out about the job search. Cornell students want to be hired long before graduation, especially in the financial or engineering majors. Seniors were updating their resumes and making the trek to career services. Soon they'd be waiting for interviews. I kept telling them it would be fine, the Cornell name would open doors, they had to just keep working. Offers could come two or three at a time; it had happened to me. One senior who majored in economics, which was in the expensive Arts and Sciences college, resented the number of interviews being picked up by a business major, who was in my less expensive public agriculture college. I said it was the team projects the business major did.

A sophomore asked my advice about women. "Conroe," he said, "I'm seeing this 23-year-old. We met on spring break. You think that's OK?" He was 19. I said sure. I wanted to say hell yeah, you're a legend now, they make movies out of stories like that.

A cluster of new brothers would mutter among themselves that our chapter needed to change direction a little, we had too many annoying guys—the Cool Brothers. Usually I looked at my food to hide my annoyance and thought of these guys as traitors or malcontents, wanting us to be more like a frat. We'd worked so hard to get here and they would screw it up, I could just feel it. My faith in what the Founders had established was absolute—maybe hopeless, maybe naïve, and maybe I was overreacting but there it was. But really these were brothers like any other, bright—at least two were aiming for medical school at the time—and decent guys. I liked them fine. I never disliked anyone in Phi Tau. They just had their vision and I just hated it.

✶ ✶ ✶

The hour after dinner was a good time to clean the house itself. The house manager or president might announce, "Guys, this house is a disaster, and we have a [rush event, alumni group coming, sorority mixer, take your pick] tomorrow, so let's get it looking awesome." He'd assign guys to duties: vacuuming, dusting, sweeping, mopping, taking a carpet outside to beat in the wind. Someone would reluctantly tackle the bathrooms.

If we had speakers sitting in the foyer, from a party, someone would put on classic rock or more current music—their tastes were as eclectic as mine—and we'd cheerfully (for the most part) go about the jobs assigned to us. The foyer would turn into an intersection where men hurrying to and fro practically collided, and guys snapped at each other to do something better or do something at all, because someone always drifted off into the chapter room to look at photo albums.

As soon as I touched a broom or mop I'd hear, "You don't need to do this, Conroe." I'd answer, "I don't mind." And I really didn't.

✶ ✶ ✶

Every semester we had a formal, right before finals time. I would stop by if I was in town, for a couple of drinks. I seldom had any date prospects who would want to spend an evening drinking with students.

The men who lived in Collegetown usually met the bus there, while the rest met the bus at 106 The Knoll. The men and their dates always looked so adult, so dolled up, the guys having actually shaved for once. The guys with girlfriends were calmer, the ones with dates they barely knew fidgeting a little. That year two seniors fixed up their younger sisters with Phi Taus, which was borderline appropriate. After dinner the booze kicked in and they danced until they were drenched in sweat, jackets tossed aside, collars open. The men got rowdy but not destructive, as some fraternities did.

As the senior had said a year ago, these were the times they would remember: the outrageous things they said and did, arms around each other's shoulders at the bar, laughter. Tensions fell away as rivals talked. We were still brothers, at least for that evening.

PART IV

The Spirit of Youth

(Or, Better Get Used to Change)

THIRTY-FOUR
Rebellion
(Winter 2003)

Before Rush 2003 started several of the newer brothers asked Rico, our new president, and Jacob for a re-vote on the issue of dry rush. The president's term carried into the rush period, for a smoother transition, but Jacob was letting go. These younger brothers said they had not been fully informed, when they had joined the older brothers last fall in voting to keep rush dry and abide by IFC rules. Nobody else followed the rule, they were certain. They also felt that dry events didn't truly represent us; we were not a partying house, but not a dry house either. The Cool Brothers thought we'd attract more recruits who were more to their liking, if we had booze. The Founders in this faction had wanted wet rush since the start.

The men discussed the issue one evening in the dining room and voted again, and this time wet rush passed. How much drinking they would use to attract freshmen, they didn't yet know. As a BoG member, I had to oppose the vote. Andres said, "As a National Council member, I must oppose this as well." Dream said that as rush chair he couldn't support it.

Out of duty, Jacob informed Pat Madden about the decision, and Pat told the new officers—and thus the brotherhood—that rush would be dry. By even discussing and voting on the issue, we were vulnerable to lawsuits should anything happen during a rush party. By being present for the discussion, I had opened myself to risk. After that I kept my distance more than usual that rush period and heard that the men had a couple of wet events, still not a wet rush.

That was the first sign that things were going to be different. The next one came after the association ceremony. We got 15 associates: 12 freshmen and three sophomores, one a transfer from West Point, one a transfer from the University of Washington. After the associates took their oath, instead of pouring champagne into glasses and quietly toasting, as we had done the year before, the men set up tables and had a Beirut tournament in the dining room, where we did not play Beirut. They did it quickly, as if someone had planned it, and if the associates thought it was odd they didn't say anything. Surprised and angry (as were a few brothers), I asked Rico what was going on. He just said it was the brothers' will and this was how he would be as president, going with the majority. *Great,* I thought.

I felt like a regular ol' fraternity advisor for the first time, forced to choose between what is law or policy (and maybe dangerous) and the guys' accepting me and listening to me. I didn't like this feeling. Our chapter advisor was quite capable. A director of research in engineering, he had once been in charge of the Greek system at a Midwestern college and knew a great deal. But he didn't come to the house more than once a semester; Jacob had to visit him at his office. That left me.

I supposed there wasn't much I could do. I realize I am saying that a lot, but I really did need to choose my battles. Drinking defined college life. In what had become a mantra of sorts, I reminded myself that whatever crises we faced were mild compared to other fraternities. I was lucky that this was at least a group I could reason with and that a core of men still believed in the founding vision.

Jacob, Joe, Train, and I decided that the house was on a collision course with some kind of crisis. Our chapter had become too big for its britches, as my grandparents would have said. We'd won awards, been told how great we were. Jacob said our parties were not competently managed. Well, the men needed to learn—that was partly why colleges still had fraternities. I just hoped our crisis, when it came, would not be too awful.

✶ ✶ ✶

The men weren't enthused about the storytelling hike the year before, but decided to try it again on February 9. They were willing to do something more than once before dropping it. This time Cornell Outdoor Education helped us have a winter version at Cornell Plantations, an expanse of gardens and open fields next to campus.

First we gathered in the house's foyer to divide everyone among the different cars and let the new member educator, Barry, make sure the associate members were there. Rico chewed out everyone for leaving the place a mess the night before. "I picked up before I went to bed, and this morning there were pizza boxes all over," he snapped. The men smirked at him.

The COE facilitators let us choose snowshoes or skis. I strapped on skis and followed the associates to a few stations where they heard about our chapter history. I hung out at one station with Rico. He was pleasant enough but tight-lipped; I couldn't get a feel for how he would do his job. This was difficult for me, spoiled by my open relationship with Jacob.

At the end of the event, the associates were blindfolded and led out of the field by the older brothers, or brothers carried each other. A few of the Cool Brothers declined, skiing ahead, looking unhappy at what they considered a touchy-feely exercise.

✷ ✷ ✷

With the years I've come to believe that the whole transition from the Founders to their successors could have been handled better. That's perfect rose-colored hindsight, but I pin the blame partly on my inexperience as a fraternity advisor. I was so used to the Founders not needing much guidance from me, relying on their collective wisdom. But if I could do it again, I would sit them down, and the younger brothers across from them or separately, and find out what was what.

Because as Jacob and Joe had predicted, the crisis arrived.

THIRTY-FIVE
Turmoil
(Winter 2003)

The house's next party, a week later, was broken up by Ithaca police after a girl from another college got sick and needed an ambulance. With a few words she unleashed a shit storm on us: She said she'd been given a date rape drug. Her friends told the police no, she was just really drunk, but she was underage.

Rico wasn't there and Jay took over, speaking with the cops, as if three years had not passed and he was still president. The officers said they wanted the names of whoever had purchased alcohol for the party—for underage students—or our president would be arrested. A lawyer advised Rico not to cooperate, that the police were probably bluffing. Until then I held hope that Rico would be fine as president, despite his rough start.

Who should make a surprise appearance the next morning but Tom, between assignments for the Navy and in town to see a young woman. We went to breakfast. I don't recall why I was in town unless Jacob had called me that morning to tell me about the party. Jay was standing in the foyer as Tom and I entered. Grinning, he told us what had happened.

Tom left immediately. "I can't believe it," he said to me. "This thing I helped build is going down the tubes." I assured him that we would get past this crisis, that it was a much-needed gut check for the men. I hoped I was right.

Before chapter meeting that day, someone told me to go to Rico's room on the third floor. I found him slumped at his desk with Mick standing next to him. "I'm quitting," Rico said. He could not do the job and he had too many academic pressures that were making him miserable. I asked if he was sure, because he was only three weeks into his term. Yes, he said. An hour later, as the chapter meeting began, Rico stood and told the brotherhood that he was stepping down, then retreated to the back row of seats, leaving Mick alone at the front of the room as acting president. I said we should thank Rico for his service to the fraternity, and everyone applauded, but only a few men spoke to him afterward. I felt badly for him.

200

The reaction to our getting busted by the cops worried me more than what had happened. Mick said we would be brought before the new IFC judicial board and probably be given social probation, meaning no parties for a while. We might be punished even worse. But, a couple of the guys said, the administration loves us, our national loves us, whatever.

"When is our next party?" Lou asked.

Blood pressure rising, I stood.

"Yeah, Conroe will back us," Lou said.

"No," I said sternly. I had one chance and I needed to be brief. "Fellas, this is not something to be shrugged off. This is a big deal. This is a pivotal moment for our chapter. You guys need to get your act together and decide where we go from here. You need to take a good long look at yourselves." I sat down.

The room quieted. Someone said yeah, guys, we need to take a good look at ourselves.

A couple of weeks later the city police arrested Rico. Two officers went up to his room and brought him down in handcuffs. He never gave up the names, and eventually the charge was disposed of somehow. But he disappeared from Phi Tau for the rest of the semester—stayed in his room, didn't come to dinner or meetings—and then quit us altogether that summer.

* * *

Mick pondered whether to run for president, while he did the job temporarily. A couple of other juniors talked about running but didn't. Barry was happy to be new member educator. Xavier might have had a shot, but he had not made peace with the seniors after his defeat.

Mick was chosen unopposed. For that two-week span when he was acting president, he prayed about what to do, and sought advice from me, Jacob, and Pat Madden. We said we were confident in him. In truth, we had no idea how he would perform.

I thought Mick was courageous. He didn't even live at 106 The Knoll but in a Collegetown place nicknamed the Mystery House, full of current and former lightweight rowers. Yet Mick was at Phi Tau every day, staying late to meet with guys. He carried a tough academic load and needed to get ready for medical school, but decided that instead of taking the MCAT in April, with most pre-med students across the nation, he would take it in August. That way, he could focus on being chapter president.

Dice became vice president, also unopposed. A Westchester County native who majored in government, he was already showing a deep interest in the house, having done a semester as house manager and then getting elected rush chair. Another sophomore was chosen to replace him as rush chair.

I worried for a while about the associate members. Unlike many fraternities, we didn't bar them from chapter meetings, so our associate class got an eyeful of our ugly side. From their seats in the foyer, beyond the Chapter Room's transom, they watched us argue about serving our punishment, whenever it came from the IFC judicial board, and debate who would be president. Everyone learns once they join an organization just how little it resembles its image, but this—the president quitting, uncertainty about who would succeed him, angry words against the founding vision that they were supposed to be learning—this was us at our worst. I feared the new guys would quit. Instead, they took part in the talks, even offered some key points and brought clarity to discussions that wandered in tangents. Whatever they said to each other about Phi Tau, they kept to themselves or passed along to Barry. None of them de-pledged. They just tried to get a feel for this strange situation.

✶ ✶ ✶

My relatively well-behaved fraternity chapter had become a moody, rebellious adolescent. Foolishly, I had expected the chapter to remain stable. The Class of 2003 seemed to be on their game those first years, their plan for us was obviously strong, and wouldn't we just continue on? We held together, yes, we did not fall apart as some houses might, but we seemed lost. Guys waited for other guys to take charge, and guys did their own thing without worrying about the rest.

Barry had his hands full as new member educator. He led the associate class that spring through readings about our chapter history, and he added a scavenger hunt to replace Hitman's history papers. He had the associate members interview brothers, about themselves and their involvement in Phi Tau, not every brother—there were a lot of them now—but a certain number every week. The associate project was painting the Newman Room walls and ceiling, and getting new furniture for it. Besides the storytelling hike, we used two COE events: building a bridge in a swimming pool and testing our strength on the indoor climbing wall, where everyone belayed each other and did their best to get up the wall at least part-way.

Barry lectured the new men about the re-founding vision, even as I now heard whispering that the seniors' vision for us was out of date, not realistic, something to be re-examined.

The seniors still held two lower offices: house manager (Paulie) and steward, Jay, who had decided to work on improving the menu in his final semester before he headed for his job at banking behemoth Goldman Sachs. We still called upon Jay. When it came time to ask the associates if they would switch from the campus meal plan to ours, he explained the reasons more clearly than anyone. I was disappointed that a younger guy hadn't stepped up to take over the house manager role from Dice, but everyone seemed content.

* * *

Life went on. I tried not to be a pessimist. The men were plainly debating for themselves which direction to take, and several of them, like J-Mac the engineer, Barry, and Mick, firmly declared that the founding vision was a solid blueprint, to be tweaked but not abandoned. They'd taken over the task of giving voice to the legacy.

National headquarters sent our assigned consultant, a 24-year-old from New Jersey, to intercede. I was relieved to see him, for he was dynamic and sharp, as a former chapter president himself. He held a retreat-style group exercise with the men, and wrote on flip charts, "What kind of chapter do you want?" "What would your ideal chapter look like?" "What do you think a poorly-functioning (under-performing) chapter is like?" The men said they wanted tight bonds among brothers, mutual respect for different views of who we should be, a sense of letting the past go while keeping whatever still pertained to us. A few said they valued parties and camaraderie above all else—no surprise there. "This is the way to go—a big discussion about the future," the consultant told me. "Anyone who thought I'd come in here like the sheriff, with my guns blazing, and start kicking butt, that's not going to happen."

* * *

The seniors let loose, as second-semester seniors will, and so some of the freshmen forever saw them as a bunch of drunks. They heard about the Founders during their pledge discussions of chapter history, about Jay's powerful leadership, and they saw the Founders slide head-first down the stairwell or do a beer funnel from the second floor. The ones who played softball with Jay and Dream and Hitman saw their competitive and athletic side as the team reached the intramural finals, but mostly they couldn't fit these partyers to the way Mick, Barry, or I portrayed them. Once rush was over, the seniors began to schedule their own parties and to pay less attention to Phi Tau.

The younger men asserted themselves more. Speaking up at a meeting, Jacob was greeted by a putdown from Rainman, who met his cold stare with an impish smile. The sophomores and juniors, overall, were tired of hearing from, and about, the seniors. One of them said our slogan "A Cut Above" sounded arrogant.

The seniors in turn questioned their successors' ability to keep the fraternity going. Worse, they made wisecracks about what they had accomplished the past few years. This was some psychological phenomenon I hadn't encountered before, a way of letting go that said, "We've done what was asked of us since we were freshmen, now we're enjoying life, so leave us alone." I tried to shrug it off as just one more new thing, but I was left bewildered.

"Try to look past what you see now and see them as they were," I told the new men, "as guys your age who were asked to do something really difficult and managed to carry it through."

This was almost an afterthought, but our nation went to war with Iraq. To me it was a new Vietnam and what was wrong with our president, who was of my generation—hadn't we learned anything back then?

Yet it was not a totally grim spring. The chapter played paintball and had parties. They had formal, a wonderful finale for the seniors. In the pictures from these events I saw guys put aside their differences and remember that they were brothers. I glimpsed a Phi Tau just beyond mine, because I was so caught up in my world of chapter meetings, sessions with the president, talk about problems and potential problems. This side, of drinking together and laughing, was almost denied to me—the price of being so much older and being an advisor. I was fine with it. I had already gone through college. I just wished I could know the men better this way, as we entered a new era.

THIRTY-SIX
The Value of Lou
(Spring 2003)

Chapter meeting was about to begin. As usual I placed a chair in the front, facing the president, vice president, and secretary.

My gaze roamed the room, noticing how fancier clothes re-cast everyone as adults. This was our monthly formal chapter. Then I spotted Lou and Ice, who had arrived at the end of dinner, missing the chaplain's words of inspiration. Well, at least they were here. Lou and Ice had never lived in the house, preferring an apartment.

Then I glimpsed, below Lou's jacket and tie, khaki . . . shorts. *Damn, here we go again. The man simply can't be like everyone else for formal chapter.* Lou knew the rules: business casual attire or at least a collared shirt for chapter meeting, formal once a month. But sometimes he didn't dress formally at all, showing up in T-shirt and gym shorts, saying he hadn't checked his e-mail for the reminder.

Mick the president and I stared at him. He stared back, his blue eyes saying go ahead, chastise me. His boyish face was expressionless. His blond hair was cut so short that he appeared almost bald—a tough look. Lou had wrestled at his Michigan high school, and I saw the edges it left in him.

I was annoyed. I liked people to obey rules most of the time, as I always had. I liked young men to attempt to grow up. I liked fraternity members to fit themselves to the greater whole. *Not that you would have,* my internal critic said. *You've always pursued your own orbit.*

Maybe I was jealous of the bad boys, for the way people often admired them.

Should I say something? If so, say it now, or wait until afterward? Or let the president and vice president talk to Lou? No doubt they had before.

Every fraternity had at least one Lou. He was not our only rebel, nor would he be our last. Anyone who thought men in a fraternity were all the same should have seen us. Like stones in a box, rubbing against each other, we had our squabbles. In our mix, the outspoken men who reminded us of our mission to be more than a "frat," were countered by the rebels who shook up things, like Lou.

I decided this battle should be left to Mick.

* * *

The Founders were responsible. That first real rush in 2001, they courted Lou and Ice and made them think we partied more than we really did. Eventually realizing their mistake, Lou and Ice nevertheless stayed, and yes, in some ways they did not fit. Besides tussling with the leaders over dressing formally, Lou didn't like doing the 15 hours of community service that each Phi Tau had to do every semester (although he wasn't the only man who resisted the idea). He stole street signs to hang in his apartment. We scolded him about it, mindful that our basement was lined with old street signs, stolen years before by men now in middle age. Lou was proud of his two arrests back home. He cultivated a party animal image and suggested that our parties have kegs. The officers would say no as he guessed they would. He just liked to push buttons, he told me.

Lou was like the nation's fraternities themselves, wanting the wild and woolly past that my generation enjoyed, resenting the politically correct present, open to reason one moment and then dropping reason in an instant. Even as I despaired over him, I could not imagine Phi Tau without Lou. Maybe it was that as a straight arrow who seldom disobeyed rules and did what was expected of me, I secretly rooted for guys who didn't.

* * *

From Lou, I learned that a fraternity has room for all kinds of men, who see in it and gain from it something different than I do. I asked myself if I was too rigid, if I imposed my sensibility on the men too much. I wondered if our vision for Phi Tau could be bent a little, if it was fun enough. From Lou, and guys like him who joined us later, I learned to forgive youth more often.

Lou reminded me, yet again, that many young people at Cornell were deeper than they seemed.

* * *

Sometime in the fall after Lou pledged, I saw him and Ice at lunch in the dining hall below my office and decided to get to know them better.

Lou, Ice, and classmate Ken—the ambitious fellow who would run for vice president as a freshman and president as a sophomore—had formed a trio who joined Phi Tau and stuck together to graduation and beyond. Ice shared Lou's rebel streak and love for partying but was quieter, and I never knew him as well. When I chose a chair at their table, they looked as if they expected me to chew them out or lecture them about the fraternity's wonders. But I talked instead about Cornell's strong wrestling team and the impact of the NCAA's decision to add seven pounds to the weight classes in 1997, after three college wrestlers had died and experts blamed the effects of cutting too much weight too fast after using a certain muscle builder. We discussed weight lifting and diet, a favorite topic of mine as I fought middle age. I established that I was not this disapproving older dude.

Weight lifting was a sound conversation topic for Lou too. He was not the biggest guy in Phi Tau, not as big as his classmates Big Daddy and Barry, or two of the Founders, Dream and Magnus. Nor was he one to go around shirtless. But patting his back and shoulders was like smacking rock coated with rubber. Despite having been a varsity baseball player and wrestler in high school, Lou never joined our intramural teams, but everyone knew where things stood in the fraternity. They really saw it after Lou won the intramural bench-press title for his weight, 170 pounds, putting up 325 pounds. That news passed through us quickly. He kept the title all four years, benching 350 as a senior. We liked to cite those numbers—170, 350—to other fraternities and outsiders who thought we were nerds. We forgave Lou his excesses because he proved our diversity. He was also, ultimately, a nice guy.

✳ ✳ ✳

One day I scolded Lou for being rough on a brother during some horseplay. He'd hit the brother, a scrawny freshman, hard and without warning. "You need to watch that stuff—you might hurt someone," I said, and he wrapped me in a headlock.

All my years around wrestling did me no good. I couldn't do what wrestlers did, I could just identify the moves by name. Besides, I did not bench press 350 pounds.

The side of my face crushed into Lou's chest, my eyes on the carpet, I'd been pulled off whatever pedestal the men let me occupy as advisor. It happened from time to time and I had to put up with it. I said OK, enough, and he let me go without a word.

I shook it off. No big deal. But I made a note to let Mick, whom he respected and to whom he listened, handle Lou problems from now on.

* * *

Lou was an electrical engineering major. Math and science came naturally to him. Writing did not. He once asked me to look over a paper about robotics and I did, as I would for any of the men, being careful not to write it for him but provide overall comments. We were at Collegetown Bagels, late at night. I asked how he was doing overall. Lou said he was carrying about an A-minus average. Really, I said, remembering that most engineering students struggled to pull B's. Lou had mastered the balancing act of booze and school, in a tough major.

He liked to solve problems. His solution to being paired with a terrified brother on that log 25 feet in the air, a year and a half ago, showed it.

Maybe it was not the intelligence but the emotion that caught me off-guard, how much feeling the crude man can have. I remembered Lou's being close to tears the night Vijay collapsed. And he was one of the Phi Taus who would greet me every semester with a rib-crushing hug.

* * *

Senior year, Lou asked me for a recommendation letter for graduate school: PhD programs in electrical engineering. He wanted to study Global Positioning Systems. This I never saw coming—Doctor Lou, even Professor Lou. "Will students get extra credit for doing more keg stands than the professor?" I said. He just smiled.

He told me that he'd been valedictorian in high school but had kept it a secret even from his friends. Didn't the school announce it at graduation, or in the newspaper? He said no.

I asked about the arrests he had bragged about. Lou said one was for being out past curfew in his town, and the other was for driving erratically one night when he was angry—over doing poorly on a test, maybe the SAT. He really was a Cornell student.

He was a bit thicker in the face by then, just a bit older-looking, as I could tell especially when I looked at pictures of him as a freshman at that tailgate, the red "E" covering his chest and stomach. He still didn't look like a college senior, really.

That year I'd wander into the Newman Room and see Lou lying on a couch, and just for a moment I'd consider ambushing him: leap on him and pin him. It would shock everyone. But then his shoulder would bunch up in his T-shirt and I would think there were less painful ways to get a laugh.

Lou was Polish, but in a fraternity that savored its ethnic humor, I never heard a Polack joke aimed at him. He was also Jewish, like one-quarter of the fraternity and one-quarter of Cornell, but he didn't seem serious about it and avoided the discussions of Judaica that occasionally broke out at dinner. Lou was spared any of this ethnic needling, or spared himself, and I don't know if anyone made comments about Asians in his presence since he was part of a sub-culture in the fraternity who always dated Asian girls. Another part of us that he belonged to: he was an only child. In a time when people of my generation were having one or two children, we had a few such brothers.

With Lou, I felt myself offering a different kind of teaching from the classroom. I really did want him to start dressing formally, as if it were a mark of adulthood. I really wanted him to be a leader. I learned my limitations as an advisor, too. He began to do more community service as a senior, but that wasn't my influence really, it was Mick's.

Lou came back for Homecoming after he graduated. He made sure I drank with him at the alumni bar tab—shots, no less. He put an arm around me and I put one around him. I patted that hard shoulder, and instead of letting go quickly, we stood there in the remembered warmth.

THIRTY-SEVEN
Recovery
(Spring 2003)

We did not have a strong goal anymore to unify us, since regaining our charter and winning awards, becoming a top fraternity at an Ivy League university. What could we do now? Once again we were the best in GPA among Cornell fraternities. Once again we were named an outstanding chapter. We were sending five men to Leadership Academy in the summer, including me.

One of the new brothers decided to live in the house the next fall, and his parents called me to ask about life in a fraternity. They were from Hong Kong and, although they had lived in the U.S. for 20 years, they didn't really understand what a fraternity was. The young man's father grilled me about what living in the house would do to his son's grades, and I said his grades would be fine. I said he would learn a great deal about himself. The father flew to Ithaca and toured the house with Mick. We assured him that this was a great place.

The Cool Brothers bided their time, waiting for the next rush, and they were more vocal. They said they were tired of un-cool people who could be annoying, say the wrong thing, follow them around, focus too much on obeying rules. They pushed and the rest of the men pushed back. We all knew that rush was too complicated and unpredictable to let anyone re-make the fraternity totally.

I hated the idea of recruiting guys because they were socially poised and good-looking. We would be like most other fraternities if we let ourselves think that way. But it was hard to argue when our parties were not attracting many women, and our reputation on campus was that we were a dry or service house, not in the same echelon as the fraternities that students flocked to. To endure once the Founders were gone, we might have to move more toward the frat end of the spectrum. Deep down, I suspected it couldn't hurt me to be more conscious of my appearance and physique. I supposed it was possible to find cooler men, or whatever the

Cool Brothers wanted, who were worth knowing. A dazzling man would need to show character, an athletic man would need to treat women well, a prospect who came off as cocky or shallow in rush could still get dinged.

Let me make this clear: the Cool Brothers were basically nice guys, at least to me. They were excellent students—two were thinking about medical school. They were and are my friends and brothers. They were not advocating anything evil. But I thought they might push the chapter onto a path toward frat-dom.

✶ ✶ ✶

Mick grew more assertive.

Like every president, he faced the great T-shirt test, where brothers nominated something borderline raunchy as a shirt slogan and the president must say no, we're not letting that be our public image. Mick said no to most of the brotherhood, on a slogan he saw as beneath us.

When brothers said we should have a new member program with more drama, maybe even try hazing, Mick said come off it. "You guys wouldn't have gone through hazing," he said, annoyed. "Come on, guys, be real."

When some of the average-looking guys grew enthused over the Cool Brothers' goal of rushing handsomer, cooler prospects and cutting back on annoying, anal retentive, shy guys, Mick said, "Those guys will never accept you. By the time you're seniors, you won't fit into your own fraternity."

When we ran low on turkey during a dinner for men who might rush our house, Mick took mine off my plate and put it back in the bin, staring me down. I didn't object; guests were more important than Conroe. I needed to lose weight anyway.

When the BoG felt that Jay had misused his power to purchase items for the house, Mick was the one who had to take the purchasing card from him and then endure Jay's curses.

I didn't meet with Mick as often as I had with Jacob, but he answered my questions about what was going on in the house. Barry reported that the brotherhood was kind of existing and not much more. The exec board didn't work as a unit all that well, so Train, Jacob, Joe, and Paulie organized a late-night scavenger hunt, to maybe build bonds as the officers worked to solve puzzles. It took the officers back to the room where the colony had met when I spoke to them in 2000. First the exec board had to build houses of playing cards. It was supposed to take a while, as the fragile structures kept collapsing, but here Lou the brotherhood chair showed his problem solving prowess again. He figured out how to do it within a few minutes: he folded the cards and fit them together strongly, to the seniors' chagrin. Later, the exec members returned to that room and were each given six clues to a puzzle, a story they had to figure out together by talking around the table—and Lou happily led the way. The officers' quest took them to the Schoellkopf Stadium, and finally to the War Memorial on West Campus where we had held our alcohol retreat and some men had been initiated in 2001. Train asked them to reflect on what they had learned about each other. It seemed to do some good.

Photographers came to shoot our composite portraits. Mick had grown his hair long, and for his portrait he combed it up like a fan around his head. There he was, for the years ahead, at the center of the top row. He would cut his hair in the fall, for medical school interviews, but for now it was a rare hint of whimsy.

＊ ＊ ＊

This is not the fraternity I joined, I caught myself thinking often that spring. Why had some of these men, the Cool Brothers, come to Phi Tau when we told them our philosophy?

Because they didn't want to be hazed, or because they liked certain aspects of our house and not others. Maybe they'd believed in what we were doing and then changed their minds once they became part of us, or had decided we were just too different and needed to be more like other fraternities, or had grown disgruntled with our straight-arrow persona. Maybe they thought we were putting on airs, saying we were different when they knew we weren't perfect by any means. Maybe they joined with the mission of changing us into a cooler fraternity—I had seen that before.

I might have been arrogant and narrow, to think that some guys fit and some didn't. We were bound to try different things, then keep them or go back to what the re-founding group had established. To try and preserve the way we were too zealously, when in a sense Phi Tau wasn't going to be mine as much as it had been, as the seniors left—I needed to reconsider my role.

Fool, you need to grow up a bit more, I told myself. *You need to learn forgiveness, instead of resenting guys who don't perform their office well, and resenting the cool faction.*

I was too deeply a part of the house. At the same time there were too many holes in my sensibility, too many things I wasn't sure how to deal with. I sensed that the newer brothers were puzzled as to who I was and why I was around so much, and I couldn't blame them. Mick said it was my imagination. I needed to pull back from Phi Tau and look to the future, as far as pushing my career along—I was now certain that my days as a lecturer at Cornell were numbered—and as far as finding a life partner, living a more balanced life, connecting with the house as it would be after the seniors graduated. I was 47.

I was, in many ways, like an alumnus now in my thinking. I needed to let go. "Take me with you when you graduate," I told Joe one sunlit afternoon.

But I was being a wimp. This was what I had signed on to do as advisor: guide, help the guys work through transitions. I needed some guts, some fresh wisdom.

Five guys de-activated that spring—a serious blow. We had lost two over the years, one to financial problems and one because he just decided he didn't fit, but five at once? The others didn't say, at least to me, why they were quitting us. Two didn't even want their names under "not pictured" in our composite. Men quit virtually every fraternity, but five at once was a large number, and what did it say about us?

Mick, Dice, Barry, and the other new officers planned how we could get back on track and recover. While we looked solid to outsiders, inside we were hurting. Somehow, in a pattern that has emerged every couple of years since, the guys decided to suck it up, get through whatever was holding them back (social probation, in this case), and face the future. At a key juncture when our three-year-old chapter could have tanked, we found a way to repair the damage and at least stay afloat.

✶ ✶ ✶

Our last chapter meeting of the spring was a time to wrap up business, wish each other a good finals time and summer, and say goodbye to the seniors. We passed the president's gavel, so each of us could say something to the seniors.

"Thanks for all you've done."

"You guys are an inspiration. I hope we can keep it going."

And so on, until the gavel reached a sophomore.

"Man, I hope you guys get laid a lot."

It was the seniors' turn. Most did not thank individuals, just the chapter as a whole. Jacob thanked me: "You've been a good friend." I nodded. He sounded halfway out the door.

The seniors left the Chapter Room, and we slid the doors closed and discussed who would receive the Meritorious Service Award. I thought five guys could get it, but who? Among the 22 men graduating were two

presidents, four vice presidents, two treasurers, three new member edu-
cators. The freshmen, who had not been around the past three years, listened as one by one I reviewed the Founders and other seniors and what
they had done. It was hot and we had just endured a long meeting. I realized that about 10 seniors deserved the award, even if some had not held
office for two years.

Finally Barry said, "I move we give it to the whole senior class."

"That's a cop-out," someone answered.

"Well, we have at least seven guys. Every senior played a role in this
house."

I hated to do it but I agreed, and the men voted to give the award to the
"re-founding class of 2003." The seniors sneered at that. I told Jay and Jacob
they were both prime candidates, and both said they didn't deserve it.

"Oh, hush," I finally said. "We're giving it to all of you and that's the
way it is."

The Board of Directors gave the Skull Award, for improving life in
the house, to Paulie. He had been rewarded for the abuse he put up with
as house manager.

THIRTY-EIGHT
Departure
(Spring 2003)

We gave up waiting for Magnus and walked away from 106 The Knoll, the eight graduating seniors in their black robes, mortarboards resting on their heads, and me in a red polo shirt and khakis. The morning was cool at almost 8:30, and promised a warm, occasionally sunny Commencement Day.

The guys reminded me of boys heading to school on the first day of a new grade, anxious, pleased, giddy, certain they were a little older. Some would be making more money than I did. They were graduating from Cornell and leaving it behind, me with it, and between that and my 30th high school reunion in two months I hardly knew what to feel. Old, I guess. Working at a school is like standing on a rock in the middle of a river, as the current carries people to you, maybe you touch them, and they sweep past. Students vanished into the world just as I grew to know them. Now it was happening to the seniors of Phi Kappa Tau, and I was determined not to show them how much I'd miss them.

"The big day," I said to a Founder, Jeff, as we headed down the tree-lined street toward a bridge to Central Campus. "The college grad."

"Shut up, Conroe," Jeff said, "don't remind me." His dark eyes bored into mine, sober and haunted.

"Oh, you'll be fine," I said, summoning a favorite old-guy refrain. "This is part of life."

"Shut up."

Yeah, I get it, I thought. *You're wondering if you'll remain friends, and I can't say, nobody ever can. You'll lose and keep each other, at the same time.*

The guys looked presentable, as if they had not stayed up most of the night before, clinging to what remained of college. Most had even shaved. Their eyes seemed to focus, pretty much. Joe caught my eye.

"Conroe," he said, "we need you to keep alive what we started. Remember that. Don't let the guys forget us or what we set out to do."

215

"I'll try," I said. Maybe Joe wanted to say this now, before Commencement ceremonies and his family devoured the rest of the day. But I knew what he meant.

The bridge across Fall Creek Gorge lay suspended between cables, above a 150-foot chasm, and it shook and bounced slightly as we strode across. The creek roared below, in spring flood, and cars rumbled on the next bridge down, against a glimpse of the valley that cradles Ithaca. Time to do my thing; I put my Nikon between me and my friends as they reached the bridge's midway point, accelerating to a few steps ahead of them, turning and framing it.

"Let's throw Conroe off the bridge," said Jay, brusque and crude and dynamic Jay, soon to be slaving on Wall Street. They laughed. I snapped the shutter: Jay, Jacob, Joe, Paulie, and Dream out front, and behind them somewhere, hidden, Hitman, MacGyver, Train, and another Founder, Komo. Jay grinned wide. We were past the days when he was president of something barely more than a club that wanted to be a fraternity.

I was not the same man I had been when I met the Phi Taus. Now this stage of my brotherhood was ending. The guys who had pulled me in were off to jobs, graduate school, new directions, and I would rarely see them and they would soon be different men, it was the way of things. I would need to prove my worth to a fresh wave of teenagers every year. The thought tired me.

✷ ✷ ✷

Magnus caught up with us as we turned left from the bridge to the wooden steps that led up through a patch of forest to Central Campus. Magnus: our resident mystic. Andres came right behind him, having decided to walk to the Arts Quad with the seniors from The Knoll instead of his classmates who lived in Collegetown. Then Andres came up behind us. Someone spouted a triumphant story of a final grade changed after negotiation—pleading, whining. For a moment I was irritated. I would never get used to the ways students plotted for higher grades. My own final grades were done and I could defend them. Let it go.

I felt like crying or something, so I tried to beam with pride every time the guys looked at me. Just froze my face into an atta-boy, jaw clench of approval. The only one who truly saw through it was Jacob, my fellow Northern New Yorker. I was going to miss him enormously, when he moved to Memphis in a month for a sales job. He sensed it, could do nothing to ease my feelings, looked annoyed at times lately, so today I smacked his shoulder and said he'd have a Southern accent soon. He grinned.

The men can become like your sons, I had been told when I agreed to serve as faculty advisor. And I had thought no, I understand such things but not me, uh-uh. So of course here I stood, practically ready to pat the guys' heads.

✳ ✳ ✳

We crossed the street next to the art museum, slipped between two of Cornell's oldest buildings, and looked across the Arts Quad, where the 5,000 graduates were lining up for the procession to the stadium. Sunlight flashed between the oak trees around the green quad, only to be swallowed by gray haze. This joyous day was the world, the war in Iraq forgotten. The men gathered on the steps of a library, across from the platform where the university president and trustees would wave everyone on their way. We were joined by other Phi Tau seniors who lived in the house in Collegetown. Now 14 of the 18 seniors stood there, the others not on the quad yet or, in one case, not coming at all—just wanted to pack his room and go. In a sense they were a portrait of courage. A fraternity that wasn't built on drinking and chasing babes and making pledges do pushups or stay awake for days on end? Right. But they had done it. Back at the house lay a broken water cooler, victim of some wildness last night. Yet, as fraternities went, as young men went, they were no problem.

Look at you, I thought.

I met you as you worked out what a fraternity was, what you wanted yours to be, how much you could or should be like the cool houses that seemed to have it all.

You feuded and patched things up, felt crushed by losing an election, sat there dazed with a slight smile after you won, told everyone that a Phi Tau didn't behave the way some of you had, stopped a movement by the house rebels to do something inappropriate or stupid—a T-shirt slogan, a theme for a sorority mixer—by reminding everyone who you were as a fraternity.

You learned to manage parties in the age of the lawsuit. You caused trouble, and guys did an intervention. You punched a hole in the wall, tried drinking from a funnel from the second floor of the house, and did who knows what on road trips to Montreal. I wasn't there for these things but I heard about them later.

You threw me in the shower on my birthday. Conroe was not immune.

At your first rush events, you fretted that nobody knew about us, no freshmen would stop by, and nobody would find a fit with who we were. You moved into a house and learned to share bathrooms, do chores around the house, and get along—you, mostly from families of two children, not the larger families of my time. You played in a rock band, reached the quarterfinals of fraternity intramural football and the finals in softball, heckled Cornell's opponents in the normally staid setting of a polo match. You researched the Arctic tern, the gray wolf, neuroscience, and biological engineering. After you achieved the highest grade point average among Cornell's fraternities and Phi Tau chapters nationally, you were proud but wondered what it said about you; milk this with parents and alumni but downplay it with freshmen who might rush. Struggling in organic chemistry, fluid dynamics, financial systems, or group projects about anything, you turned to each other for help. Or you got A's without going to class much.

* * *

You decided how to be men, in your time. All the while, without knowing it, you pushed me to decide how I could be a better man.

Unless you're made of stone, being among other men in a fraternity can teach you so much.

You reinvented our chapter. There is no other word for it. Where some colonies revert after a couple of years to the culture that got them banished originally, you stayed on course.

* * *

A few Phi Taus didn't have jobs yet and were trying to quell their panic. The others were scattering: engineering sales in San Francisco (Hitman), graduate school (MacGyver, Paulie, maybe Magnus), law school (Jeff), medical school (Nieraj), company management (Dream), financial companies (Vijay,), advertising (JB), sales in Memphis (Jacob), neuroscience research in Boston (Komo), the Four Seasons in Washington (Train). I had tried to assure the ones without jobs, in my best old-guy way, that they would find something. I had tasted both ends of the job hunting spectrum. I stopped there, not wanting to describe how life might unfold. I did envy them for going to a workplace more stable in some ways than during my earlier careers, when men felt neutered or at least less important.

The Phi Taus were to march last, in honor of their fundraising abilities in the annual alumni phone-a-thon, but they didn't know where they were supposed to be. Jay strode off to ask someone, still the guy they turned to even at the end. He returned with the news that they would walk behind the graduates of the College of Arts and Sciences, so we made our way to the front of a venerable stone building with wide columns. Seniors were posing on a statue of Cornell's first president, seated on his throne across the quad from a statue of Ezra Cornell himself. We could see the red and white footprints—painted by a fraternity every year—that connected the two. Legend said if a virgin crossed the statues' path on Halloween, they would stand, walk to the center of the quad, and shake hands. I drifted among the hundreds of robed seniors, greeting some who had become my friends, watching others turn away or just not bother to say hello, soured by a grade less than an A or simply done with me. I usually knew about 250 students in any senior class. I'd written recommendation letters for some, drunk beers with some during Senior Week. I heard their joy and saw their anxiety. I smiled, nodded at them as if to say congratulations and welcome, you have done well, now you are adults.

"Conroe!" a couple of the Phi Taus called, as if to say "look at us." They beamed for my camera. I said they were like rock stars today, with entourages and fans. The hugs would come later, as would conversations with parents, dinner with Jacob and his mother, goodbyes fast and imperfect. No matter how many years I had done this, here and elsewhere, I still ached.

These guys were passing through, I was here, and I would be here a while yet. Our paths diverged, as they geared up for the plunge into career and maybe family, hacking a trail, and I had already cut one trail—done the career thing too deeply for my own good—and neglected the other.

Eighty yards across the quad, other groups of seniors waited for the procession to flow past them, an African-American group and a fraternity that always tried to be last, all of them ready to claim the spot at the end. "See you guys at the house," I said, and crossed back to a place near the library steps, just before the president's platform. I had loved this spot for several years, since graduate school, this lip where the Arts Quad overlooked the valley's steep west side and a patch of Cayuga Lake.

The procession had begun. Seniors strode past me, waving to family, glancing around as if to absorb it all, talking to each other, looking stunned. Around the quad the black-robed figures moved, doctoral students and then veterinary and MBA, labor relations and then engineering and then the agriculture college—the colleges, it looked so slow from across the quad but was actually quick, and then the guys were passing me. Jay raised his arms like a champion athlete. Some of them smiled at me again, Jacob and Andres and Joe and Paulie and Hitman, and they were gone.

THIRTY-NINE
Summer of the Future
(Summer 2003)

"**C**'mon, Charlene! Do it!"

Barry Mask grinned at the men from Auburn University's Phi Tau chapter and launched himself from the diving board. In midair he pulled his legs under his big frame and grabbed them. He hit the pool's surface so hard that waves and sheets of water erupted in all directions. The couple hundred people watching in Miami University's recreation center cheered. This was the Olympics part of Leadership Academy, second from the last night of the week, a chance to unleash energy for the men who had spent hours discussing chapter management issues and our creed's meaning. Barry, an alumnus of the Auburn chapter, in his early forties, was here as a character coach in charge of seven guys. Eight undergraduates were here as well, for their chapter was a finalist for the Maxwell Award as outstanding chapter.

And Barry had volunteered for the cannonball competition.

His guys called him Charlene because on opening night the undergraduates were treated to a hypnotist performance. The man had hypnotized Barry and convinced this man, well over six feet tall and 200 pounds, that he was a woman. He laughed it off.

I was at the academy as part of the advisor's track, spending part of each day with other chapter advisors as we examined some of those same chapter issues and the very nature of college students. For part of every day, if we chose, we could hang out with one of the four communities and take part in their discussions. I was hanging out with Community B, where one of our rising sophomores was a member. Another sophomore and a junior from our chapter were here, plus Mick.

The Olympics consisted of basketball, volleyball, dodgeball, and swimming races where the swimmers wore sweatshirts to wear them down. There was also a climbing wall, and one of our sophomores was showing his mastery of that.

Auburn's chapter was on the rebound after a period on the edge. The cinderblock house had a new front foyer, the Phi Tau crest embedded in the floor, and a new library. In many ways this chapter was not like ours. They did not have a cook; their kitchen was tiny, their meals catered. Their main rush was in the fall, when they pulled in about 25 freshman pledges. They ate, met, and watched TV in a big room on the house's first floor. People camped out the night before football games. In other ways, they were much like us, trying to reach for a new future. Their president was a confident senior who clearly led them decisively and competently. I sensed that he was a strong force in their resurgence. Barry Mask, though not a formal advisor for their chapter, was a part of them, a man of energy and humor who visited the chapter frequently and was a domain director, a national rep who advised several chapters in his region.

Barry did not win the cannonball competition, but he grinned as he strutted back to the stands. The men from Auburn thought they were a longshot for the Maxwell, going against Bradley (a chapter that raised $30,000 for Hole in the Wall every year through a haunted house) and Cal Poly-Pomona. But they would win it, and we would take note. The Maxwell was now in our thoughts as well, some of us anyway, for we needed a new goal.

* * *

The verdict was clear from the other advisors in the conference room: I was too close to my chapter, too involved. An effective advisor needed to maintain distance.

We were meeting again, studying team-building exercises that our chapters might use. I had told the others about watching the men vote to have wet rush last January. They were appalled.

"You put yourself at legal risk by being there," said one of them. "You need to stay clear of anything to do with drinking. You could be in as much trouble as the guys, if anything happens."

Oops.

The advisor track was great but I wanted to meet undergraduate brothers and hear about their campuses, their chapters. So I did.

I heard about chapters as small as 15 men or as large as 80.

I heard that most Greek systems were one-third the size of ours, and that Cornell's Greek affairs office—with a staff of 10—offered us far more support than chapters elsewhere got.

I asked Mick what he was learning. He said men were comparing notes on hazing. Our national would have loved to get rid of hazing, but the fight was tougher than our fight at Cornell—across the nation. The national staff tried so hard to convince young men to be careful, look after each other, do things for the right reasons. The chapters needed to mind themselves. The national did what it could by having this academy and the regional conferences.

* * *

One day we all gathered in a large room and ate a picnic lunch at long tables that held dozens of us. A huge screen covered one end of the room, and before it stood one of the National Council members and academy directors, Steve Rupprecht. And he showed us a video about the Hole in the Wall camps, our national philanthropy.

On the screen Paul Newman spoke about what it means to a child with HIV or sickle cell anemia or cancer or kidney disease or any number of things to go to camp for a week, as other children do. To get out of the house, to be somewhere where a wheelchair or help taking a shower or a blood transfusion before a hike in the forest was not unusual. A woman spoke about what camp had meant to her son before he died, how much he looked forward to it for a whole year, the friends he made, his laughter.

Steve then summoned two Phi Taus to the front. They were among the dozen or so Phi Taus who had volunteered at one of the camps. "I can't put into words how this changed my life," said one. "These kids are so tough. You hear them sitting around, comparing surgery scars and laughing about it. They face so much in life and all they want to do is be kids." The other guy offered a story as well. They both asked us to consider volunteering.

We listened quietly. We felt the power of what this experience had done for them, it lay in the cracking of their voices, the way their faces looked so longing to have us feel what they had. Most students I knew looked to summer for internships or jobs, that all-important experience that made a resume sing. Not many people could fathom spending a week at such a camp.

Then we had a Jello-eating competition, with one Phi Tau from each community. We cheered for our man. The images of that camp, of Newman, stayed with us.

* * *

A limb grew between two old trees near the entrance of the Double H Hole in the Woods Ranch, a sleep-away camp in the Adirondacks not far from Lake George. The limb and trunks formed a huge "H" that, the camp staff insisted, stood for health and happiness.

That day the Double H looked much like any camp to me, with buildings for arts and crafts, science experiments, animals, cabins, and a medical building. Children's laughter drifted on the breeze, which smelled of pine. There were playing fields, hiking trails, and a rope bridge high in the air. A small lake awaited kids who wanted to fish and canoe.

But the lake was not for swimming, for it was too cold and laden with bacteria. Campers swam in heated pools. The medical building, named Paul's Body Shop, had a volunteer staff and refrigerated areas full of medications and blood for transfusions, for the campers had hemophilia, AIDS, sickle-cell anemia, cancer, kidney ailments. The campers themselves might look like other kids, but some were in wheelchairs, and some could not do much on their own. On this cloudy afternoon, as a breeze stirred the trees, a game where everyone tried to tag out someone on the other team swirled through a grassy area, and one boy was carried on a young man's back.

This was a Hole in the Wall camp, the second one after Newman's first in Connecticut. The Double H had been a rundown place purchased by a local entrepreneur, Charlie Wood, developer of the nearby Great Escape theme park.

Darting among the kids with other counselors was a dark-haired guy: Dice, our chapter vice president. He was here because, Phi Tug and our other fundraisers aside, he wanted to experience this side of our philanthropy: the target people. Two other counselors here were Phi Taus from Washington State University and Missouri's Truman State. The rest were college students majoring in something related to kids, such as adaptive physical education or pre-med, or who just wanted an adventure of the soul. Dice had decided to work here for seven weeks. His internship last summer with a law office—he was toying with law as a career—had not satisfied him and he didn't want another office position. The Double H's development officer had visited our chapter. Dice had hated sleep-away camp as a boy, but this sounded different, a test of sorts, something a liberal arts major was not going to see otherwise.

"Hey, Scott," Dice said. He took a break from the game and joined me on a picnic table next to the field. He looked at home. The first day, he'd been so on edge, wanted to please everyone and not offend anyone. It was exhausting. It took a while to get past that. He pointed out that the field was ringed with small evergreen trees. "They're in memory of kids who are no longer with us," he said.

Every week Dice worked with eight to 13 boys aged 12-16. In the morning he awoke the ones that needed more help with showering, or required their wheelchair or a trip to the Body Shop. Then he awoke the other campers at 8. First the kids had two activities, like fishing and arts and crafts, or drama, or nature talks. After lunch they had more of the same or a special event, maybe a trip to Great Escape. The campers were from cities, mostly upstate New York but New York City and Philadelphia too. There might be a contingent from Russia or Israel.

Some campers were high-maintenance and some fiercely independent. Accustomed to being stared at, maybe even teased by other kids, if they got out of the house much at all, they found release here (as did their parents, who got time off at home). Dice found that the kids didn't trust him as much this first year, as he helped them; that would take time. Late in his stint here, he was wearing out, and he'd have only three days between camp's end and the start of classes at Cornell, but he loved it.

✶ ✶ ✶

The seniors were scattering. Jeff and Paulie were staying at Cornell for law school and engineering master's work, respectively, and were getting ragged about it. Everyone wanted to put Cornell behind them. Jacob had remained at the house for a month before heading south, and he was relaxed but anxious to move on. Magnus was contemplating ways to work in the wilderness. Joe had landed a financial job in Manhattan. JB was going to work in advertising and dabble in music. Andres was going to write a novel and figure out what was next. Several of them would live in Hoboken, NJ, a rough town being reborn as an attractive place for young people. Adam and Dream were working for a uniform company. Hitman headed to the Bay Area.

My first job had lasted eight months (I was let go as the little newspaper sank) and I had liked it but it would've worn me out. From there I had gone on through my life, as they were about to.

I had an epiphany: I tended to befriend too few of the men, an old rut. I needed to know more of them, as they allowed me.

✶ ✶ ✶

Dice and I watched the game. A male counselor lifted a boy from a wheelchair and onto his own back, and carried him among the running kids. The counselors alternately needled and coaxed the children into trying, accepting defeat, being modest when they tagged someone.

Dice was about to be a junior, entering his second semester as chapter vice president. Though sharp of wit, sometimes cynical, he was kindhearted as well, and was a fine writer. He was thinking about running for president, but Mick was pushing him to serve as alumni relations chair instead. We needed to make big steps in that area. We hadn't noticed yet, but our 75th anniversary as a Phi Tau chapter was approaching in two years—a nice opportunity to pull alumni back to Ithaca. Dice was about to become the uber-Phi Tau, the man who made our chapter run.

He had stories, of course. He said one really rough kid was 14 but looked eight; he had cerebral palsy. On top of that he had something like Tourette's syndrome. He wore a helmet all the time and sat on his hands so he wouldn't hit himself or put his fingers down his throat. "But he was mentally aware, we could communicate," Dice said. "We'd try to give him a shower and he was writhing around. We had to stop him from banging his head. I thought about his parents, who have to deal with this every day."

When Paul Newman visited the camp every couple of years, the movie star and entrepreneur spent time only with the kids. One time he let them punish him for breaking a camp rule—he put his elbows on the table during dinner and had to run laps around the building as a result. But he always had his picture taken with Phi Taus. We never knew what Phi Tau itself meant to Newman, for he had been initiated a lifetime ago (60 years) at Ohio University and did not attend national events. But he gave generously to the Phi Kappa Tau Foundation, which offers scholarships of $1,000 and up for brothers, and he sponsored brothers for Leadership Academy.

After that summer, Dice became one of those Phi Taus who encouraged men to volunteer. He showed a DVD about the camp during a chapter meeting, so the men could hear Newman explain why he founded the camps, and parents talk about their children. He had staff come from the Double H to talk to the men, during dinner and at a regional conference we sponsored. But several guys would volunteer, mostly pre-meds who wanted experience working with people who had serious physical problems.

But brightening a resume for medical school didn't explain it all.

One winter week and then one summer week, a Cornell brother named Comron volunteered at Double H. Convinced by Dice to try this, in a conversation at 106 The Knoll, he wanted to do something that would help others and be enjoyable for him, as well as helping his chances for medical school. As a Phi Tau, Comron sometimes went his own way, rebelling against authority, especially as a pledge. But he relished community service, whether the chapter's events or ones he found on his own.

Comron was a bit concerned about the summer session because the children would have hepatitis C and HIV. He got over his anxiety, which helped when he got to medical school at Columbia and worked with people ill with those diseases. His comfort zone disappeared. He found himself on a platform 50 feet in the air—the high-elements course, like Cornell's, which our chapter had not tried in a couple of years. He put the kids in belaying harnesses so they could walk on the ropes bridge. Being so high up, on a tiny platform, while being responsible for putting the kids into their harnesses was stressful, but fun at the same time. Then there were the campers in his group: they suffered from sickle cell anemia, hemophilia, cancer, and HIV. The campers with HIV were mostly unaware of their condition. Most of the kids came from very low socioeconomic backgrounds and brought a lot of baggage, which the counselors tried to make them forget. A boy said his mother drank all day. Another boy told Comron about gangs like the Bloods and Crips, while holding a toy like a gun. This was not something Comron expected when he pledged Phi Tau.

He once helped a boy in a wheelchair, aided by a young woman. The boy defecated on himself. "We had to take him back to his room and clean him off," Comron told me. "So I'm in a room with him naked, helping the girl clean him. You would think this would have been the most awkward situation of my life, but it was surprisingly not. The girl and I just cracked jokes the whole time to lighten the mood and told him we did that all the time. Obviously he knew that was not true but it got the point across that we didn't think there was anything wrong with what happened. Afterwards, though, I felt really depressed about his situation. That sort of experience helps put your priorities in order."

Comron also was inspired by a girl with cerebral palsy who wanted to ski. "We fitted her with upright supports so she could ski standing straight up. Although she had virtually no motor skills, she was able to ski by holding onto a handle bar, which I supported as I skied backwards in front of her down the hill. The girl had a great time, which made me have a great time, but more than either of us I think her mother was happiest because her daughter was getting to enjoy life."

Would I ever volunteer? I would have to climb out of my little comfort zone enough to work with kids, sick kids who wanted—fiercely—to enjoy what other kids did. Any feeling I ever had that I was an outsider, any anger I held with not getting a promotion or with students whining about grades—any of that paled beside this. I decided I would try it someday.

Of all the things that came from our chapter's starting up again and rebuilding itself, this might be the best and the most unexpected: not part of a fraternity at all, technically, and yet reaching to our hearts and character and sense of brotherhood as much as anything we did.

* * *

I rested that summer in the parts of my life that were not Phi Tau. My job: going OK, my chair impressed with my continual push for improvement and with my evaluations. Social life: not bad, though Cortland was tough on outsiders. The men leaving and the men coming back in the fall stopped being Founders, Cool Brothers, rebels, leaders, whatever. Not like friends my age but I had something with them, that I knew. Life had shown me the power of shared pasts.

One afternoon I hiked in the gorges, showered at the house, took a nap in the Newman Room. Lou was there for the start of summer, looking for a job. He had set his mini-fridge full of beer in the doorway to the room. I had suggested he move it and he had ignored me.

A brother popped in, home from his lab job. He was a chapter officer I'd been meaning to speak to, who could be performing his office better. He did the basics but was not enthused; he'd wanted a different office, settled for this one. Was summer the time for a chat, or should I wait until fall semester? Guys sometimes decided on their own that they could improve. I was an optimist.

Being us at our most noble took work and will.

He smiled in greeting. He was 20 and figuring out what he wanted, who he was, nothing more. He said, "Conroe, you want a beer?"

"Sure," I said, and he fetched two cans from the kitchen (apparently Lou's beer was his own). We watched something on TV. I asked, "What about medical school? You going for it this fall?" He said he wasn't sure, and that hot afternoon we were just two brothers.

The fraternity would not sit still but moved through stages, and it always hit me, hit any of us, with the unexpected. Dice and Comron and the others among the terribly ill children—that image is as real to me as remembering Phi Taus at a formal or a chapter meeting.

Those images stand next to each other in the photo album of my mind: children laughing and forgetting their awful physical lives, young men and women laughing and pulling on a rope. Pulling together as best they can, arms and shoulders and legs straining against something, somebody, that wants to pull them where they don't want to go.

Epilogue

Three young men faced an awards committee and described why their Phi Tau chapter should be chosen most outstanding among the 90 chapters nationally for 2006, which happened to be the national fraternity's 100th anniversary.

They stood straight in dark blue suits and pants with white shirts, and they spoke without notes, backed by Power Point images. One of them barely concealed his nervousness. Another, a rising sophomore, wore someone else's suit (he favored more colorful clothes) and had removed his diamond earrings. A pink necktie lay against his white shirt, as if he would not totally surrender himself to the demands of this occasion.

We were the third of six finalists for the Maxwell Award. I wanted us to win. Badly. This was our third year in a row as a finalist. If we didn't win, life went on—an award is always nice but getting it is a crapshoot and either way, you put it on a shelf and get back to work. But we wanted this.

I was back at Miami University, this time for convention, seeing us talk in this conference room at the student union. The panelists were from the Midwest and South, familiar faces: Todd Napier, who had been national president when we got our charter back; a young man from Kentucky who worked in state government and whose chapter had won three times; a young man who had served with Andres on National Council.

The three each talked about an aspect of our chapter. The president, a senior of Chinese descent, a materials science major who designed cartilage tissue, spoke about our aim to develop the whole man. The vice president, a senior of Indian heritage busy applying to medical school, outlined our leadership on campus. The sophomore explained last spring's new member program: no hazing, a community service project, a house improvement project, and an emphasis on being a gentlemen, complete with etiquette dinner for associate members and two sororities. They were poised but low-key, which meant they had listened to me. *Thank you, thank you.* Last year, I said a week ago, we came across as too Ivy League. We strutted. We couldn't help it, Cornell trains you to be that way, but I said we should tone it down. The men were irritated with me but they did it.

Six years had passed since our chapter re-founded. We were 62 strong, and it was harder to get a bid from us. Last rush, the men identified an unprecedented 40 solid prospects, offered 26 bids, and signed 15. We gambled on guys who might go elsewhere, and in some cases lost. A couple of other freshmen were forbidden by their parents to pledge a fraternity. Many of our men said they had not planned to join a fraternity. The campus knew us better. Awards covered our chapter room wall. Our men were, in general, more adept socially, and they had more parties than the Founders. But this trophy would validate us.

We were not perfect. We had our squabbles and divisions, and we were restless as ever with this higher path to the point where every year we moved a bit more toward being a "frat." But we looked at ourselves, debated who we were, and our leaders—we'd found many solid leaders over the years—pushed us onward. There was no sign of hazing, we still did our community service, we were worth knowing, and I was still glad to be associated with us.

Pledges, interviewing me in the spring, asked what the fraternity was like back in my day, meaning the 1970s. I said my day was just a few years ago. I took them through my history with the fraternity and said what it had meant to me, that I learned so much from being among other men. I became more forgiving and tough and humble. I acknowledged the oddness of being in a fraternity in my forties. "If you get one-tenth of what I have gained from being part of this house, I will be happy for you," I said.

The committee fired questions. Our GPA had fallen from No. 1 at Cornell to No. 21—why? The men said we were not sure, it was still 3.189, not bad. We had more engineers these days, and maybe the seniors had not cared this spring. Why had the sophomore joined? "They seemed genuine," he said, "and did things for the right reasons, not to pad their resumes." I watched from 20 feet away, with several other men from our chapter and Pat Madden, our alumni chair. The other finalist chapters were impressive in their own right, their campuses different from ours, their Greek systems smaller, their stories mainly about rebuilding. We were not a lock.

The award itself would pose a challenge if we won. It might leave us complacent. Awards could do that. We were going to be a young chapter this year, dominated by juniors and sophomores. I had become more of a traditional advisor, like it or not. The new men joining us did not see me as the Founders had but as more of an authority figure. They did not hold each other accountable to the same degree as the first few years; hardly anybody apologized to the chapter for their actions or criticized each other. Yet whenever I worried that we were headed down the slippery slope toward frat-dom, the men found a way to get back on track.

My teaching job was ending in five months. I would probably leave Cornell and return to writing and editing. I was angry at myself for hanging on when I knew my teaching was a job, not a career. I savored having the Cornell name attached to mine. And the chapter needed to find someone else to serve as faculty advisor. So much change.

The men finished. Time for some other chapter. I congratulated them. They were pleased that it was over.

* * *

The next day the winner was announced at an awards luncheon, outdoors under a huge tent. The trophy for top GPA, which we'd won for four years, went to Case Western. We were still third.

We just waited.

National President Bill Crane's baritone said the Maxwell Award this year was going to a chapter that had campus leaders. Well, we all did. Then he spoke of a new member program with an etiquette dinner . . . and I looked down, so happy, so relieved.

We smiled around the table at each other. Up front we faced the gathering—the trophy would be presented the next night at the annual Brotherhood Banquet—and then formed a circle, arms around each other's shoulders. I stopped just short of crying. Men from Cal State-Long Beach, another finalist, came up to greet us.

Even before our win, other Phi Taus asked us how we did things: attract and retain new members, manage our affairs, collect dues. Why had we remained strong where so many fraternity chapters messed up, were punished, must re-structure? We explained that we had re-structured six years ago, we'd just avoided tanking since then. The men were modest with other Phi Taus, glad to know them and hear about their parts of Phi Tau Nation. Three of them had been to Leadership Academy last summer and remembered men they had met. So did I, for I had served as a character coach at the academy. So had Pat Madden. So had Brian the former IFC president and anti-hazing crusader, who had finished his Peace Corps stint and worked for two years at Cornell as an assistant dean of students, advising IFC. He had also volunteered at a Hole in the Wall camp. Brian was practically a Phi Tau.

If we could offer anything to other fraternities, we were glad.

Dice called in, and they told him the news. The men began to send out the word via text messaging. "About friggin' time," replied one May graduate.

I called Brian, and Tom, who had finished his four years in the Navy and was enrolling in business school. He had toured the North Atlantic as communications officer on a ship. Sometimes he had the bridge. "Picture that, millions of dollars in taxpayer money in my hands," he e-mailed me. Tom was pleased.

I called Jacob. He lived in San Francisco now. He had not enjoyed Memphis, had re-located to Hoboken, and then had come out of the closet as a gay man. The Founders were dealing with that in their own way. Some would not talk about it. Jacob had joined the Board of Governors, but he quit. I exchanged e-mails with him every couple of months.

* * *

I had visited Jacob once in Hoboken, in the spring of 2004. Komo had come down from Boston, Joe in from Long Island, and Train up from Washington. They let me have the couch while they slept on the floor.

We rode the subway to the site of Ground Zero, which was empty and eerily quiet, as if we didn't dare to speak much in the presence of such horror. Then we walked and took a cab to a place in the East Village called Corner Bistro, famous for its hamburgers. I didn't really want burgers and fries, but what the hell. The guys ranted about their jobs and how they were already looking toward the next career move, or the next career. Some of the other Phi Taus—like Vijay—worked insane hours on Wall Street, to build up money and then do something else maybe. Then the conversation shifted to other Cornell alumni in the city, for Manhattan was like Cornell Part II. We might as well have been in Collegetown.

But we were not. I quietly listened, marveling at how much older the guys seemed already. They remembered I was there and asked about Phi Tau. I told them we were sticking with the original plan but tweaking it, questioning some of what they did. I worried at times but tried to remain optimistic. They listened, and were interested. Then someone said his job sucked and they were off again.

The men left Cornell behind and me with it. When they did come back, I was sometimes too busy or distracted to see them.

I was on fence patrol at Slope Day that year when my cell phone rang. It was Mick. He had Hitman and Magnus with him, and they wanted to see me. I told him where I was. Slope Day had a fence around it now because Cornell wanted to manage who attended, and because we had bands playing again and they wanted concert-style security. The fence was a pain. As we talked, I kept my eye on a jock fraternity that wanted to jump it. Someone opened a gap in the gate to allow students to leave, because the nearby wider gate into the slope was jammed with people. Naturally students tried to come in through the gap and I was not prepared for them, I did not have a stamp for their hands or time to check their ID. So our conversation with my three brothers went like this:

"Magnus, you look good. How's life?—No, miss, you can't come in this way."

"Great, Conroe. I think I'm going to veterinary school."

"Nice! Life here is the same.—No, miss, I don't care how much your dad pays for you to go here."

By the time I got to 106 The Knoll later, everyone was drunk and I was exhausted. I talked to the alumni as much as I could.

✶ ✶ ✶

Now, two years later, Magnus was at vet school and Mick was at medical school. So was Barry. Lou and Ice were doctoral students in electrical engineering. Ken worked on Wall Street, Big Daddy in Philly. Train had moved to Boston to be a hotel consultant; he shared an apartment with Komo. Paulie was back on Long Island, in environmental engineering. I caught up with them occasionally.

I left a message on Jacob's voice mail. He had let Phi Tau drift from his life. I hoped he would come back someday.

That afternoon I thought of the Founders. They would be pleased. I saw Gabe and Winky, the staff members who had worked with the Founders on the colony. Both men now worked in sales. Gabe owned several companies near Lexington, Kentucky.

✶ ✶ ✶

Saturday evening's banquet was in a gymnasium coated with elegance, the tables set with different glasses for different drinks, and more than one fork. Giant screens flanked a stage that had been decorated in a starry motif. We saw montages of Phi Tau history, and heard tributes from U.S. Senators George Voinovich of Ohio and Mitch McConnell of Kentucky, and former astronaut Leroy Chiao—all Phi Taus. The nine of us from Cornell filled a table at the center of about 870 well-dressed people. We drank water and wine, and dined on prime rib, except for a vegetarian and a vegan among us.

Finally Bill Crane said our name. We rose and made our way to the stage. I was last and slipped to the edge of our group, next to our great ally Don Snyder Sr., our 1950s alumnus who had served as Eastman Kodak's chief financial officer. Our chapter president beamed as he held the enormous silver trophy. I glanced at the hundreds of people applauding us, for when had I ever stood in such a spot and when would I ever again? I sneaked a look at one of the TV screens, to see us.

People congratulated me as we find our way back in the semi-dark. Bejeweled women and tuxedoed men said well done, nice job, and I said thank you, we are very glad.

We set the trophy on a chair and the guys said it looked like the Stanley Cup from the NHL. We were just warm with our own thoughts and gladness for each other. We covered our joy, aware that men were studying us from other tables.

The speeches and snippets of history went on. The love that men held for this fraternity shone on us. Well, I loved it too but I tried not to be too sappy about it. My Irish nature leaned toward the dark as well as the joyous. Some days the chapter embraced me and some days it ignored me. I was no more important than any other part of us. My six years gave me credibility and leverage, for I was on my eighth president, ninth vice president, sixth spring pledge class. Yet even now if I said the wrong thing too often, stopped trying to connect, I could be done. A fraternity values older men but only so much. Being part of us was a joy and a chore, mostly a joy: a relationship.

The men would be shocked at how much I had grown up because of it.

"Mr. Bill" Jenkins held his Candlelight Ceremony, and asked our chapter president to represent one of the national Founders. The reception afterward offered endless desserts and a chocolate fountain. We carried the trophy into the lobby and set it down. It weighed about 25 pounds.

I spotted Gabe and Winky and the national consultants who had come after them, one of them the fellow who had talked us through our social probation problem three years ago. "This is your award too," I said.

We climbed on a bus for the ride to the residence halls where everyone was staying. Someone gave the trophy to a senior of Filipino heritage and he joked, "Sure, give it to the brown guy to carry." I thought of a reply but stayed silent. I was not allowed to do ethnic humor.

Men from other finalist chapters were on the bus. They looked glum. We enjoyed the moment among ourselves. We had felt as they did, two years in a row.

* * *

One fall we lost the football quarterfinals in a pounding rain. At the end we were a few yards from the end zone but could not punch the football across. The rain and mud were ruining our speed and passing ability, and our opponent was too good or too lucky, intercepting us, plucking the ball from the dim air under the lights.

Our quarterback took shelter under my umbrella, one of three on the sidelines of this intramural flag football game. He was a bit taller than me, about 5-foot-9, a senior who looked like the biochemistry major he was—scholarly and intense—and the jock he also was, with big forearms that echoed his favorite sport, baseball. Drops of water coated his glasses as he calmly watched our defense.

"Any dry shirts around here?" he said.

"Yeah," I said. "Hold this." I handed him my umbrella, he handed me his glasses, and with just a bit of regret I pulled out the flap of the brand-new dress shirt I was wearing and pinched the glass between the fold of cloth. Only a couple of us had dry shirts, so what the hell. Papa Conroe.

* * *

Brian the former IFC president hated hazing as much as ever, and butted heads with the fraternity leaders. I grew to know him better. He enrolled as a graduate student at Tennessee, to become a school counselor and maybe a football coach.

St. Lawrence had two fraternities where it had seven in my time: ATO and Phi Kap. The university president said that one chapter was suspended, Beta Theta Pi, and would return in the fall of 2008. He did not say the same about his own fraternity. Four sororities remained. By December, Phi Kap would be gone too, having broken too many rush and procedural rules over the years. That left just ATO until Beta, its uneasy neighbor, came back.

I saw the Betas from my time at alumni and athletic events. The lawyers among them who lived in Syracuse liked to laugh about how they had to argue cases before a Family Court judge who had belonged to ATO, their despised neighbor. "We have to argue in front of a Tomato," they said. The judge just smiled. It was all so long ago.

SUNY Potsdam's Greeks struggled. One fraternity shrank to two brothers and lost its house. The alumni said they might ask me what to do as they re-colonized.

* * *

We had the same mix of races and religions and home states, the same characters, like the athletically gifted Latino fellow who usually wore a blue zoot suit instead of a coat and tie. We had Asia Max and Jewish Max. We had a brother of Turkish descent whose family came from Cyprus, which made it all the better when he dressed up as Santa at our Christmas party one year. Guys served as resident advisors, editors of the campus newspaper and magazines, Student Assembly members. We had a blond California surfer and skateboarder, and hard-edged, forthright military men. We had our first Australian, after sending guys to Australia for a semester here and there. He transferred to Cornell just in time for rush, didn't know what a fraternity was, and decided to try us.

On the anniversary of 9/11, a few of us gathered on the Arts Quad and talked about that day and the importance of life. Our candles sputtered in the dark while we cupped our hands around the flame. The vigil started a year after 9/11 and was continued by Dice.

For our 75th anniversary in 2005, Dice organized a weekend celebration that brought back 90 alumni. The Founders gave Tom a hard time about a mustache he'd grown. An alumnus from the 1970s heckled our guest speaker, Dean of Students Kent Hubbell, and some 1980s alumni talked through his speech. Different times in our chapter history show different attitudes toward what we value now. Mr. Bill came from Ohio and did his Candlelight Ceremony.

I started a speaker series, to supplement what guys learned in the classroom. Professors in my department came to our house to talk about sociological research into cell phone and e-mail use, and finer points of public speaking. A photographer who roamed the world with his wife, a United Nations official, showed his photographs from Asia and Africa, and told the stories behind them. Former Yankees pitcher Jim Bouton, author of the 1970 classic book *Ball Four,* came to our house to discuss professional sports, writing, and his fraternity memories from Western Michigan.

The city building department failed our house on numerous electrical and safety violations. I worked with the contractor and inspectors to bring us back into compliance. Such is the life of an alumni board member.

One spring evening we hosted my former sports editor from Syracuse, the man who hired me in 1984 to cover high schools. He was a columnist now, nationally known, had covered 14 Super Bowls and many basketball Final Fours, pretty much everything. Before dinner he paced our chapter room, asking me about fraternities. His college didn't have them, and if it had, he wouldn't have been interested.

"What's this?"

He pulled a booklet off the top of a shelf and began glancing through it. With a start I recognized one of Phi Tau's ritual books. I snatched it from his hand, saying he couldn't read it.

"Come one, you're not serious," he said, laughing.

"I'm totally serious," I said. "Only we can read this."

Later, as he told the men stories about sports, he looked at me and said, "What do you guys think of this guy?" The men were quiet. He pressed on: "What do you say, Scott? Are you a frat boy now?"

"No," I said, "a fraternity man."

The room erupted in cheers.

* * *

I ran into Chef at a supermarket and learned that he didn't cook for Zeta Psi anymore. He had had a falling out with the chapter and was fired, after 13 years. He blamed himself, but hearing this reminded me that any older man's roots in a fraternity go only so deep. It doesn't take long for the men to decide they don't need you. I could wear out my welcome.

Our chapter is like the fourth generation of a family business: the man who founded and built it with work and luck is long gone and the current generation enjoys the results while wondering how to stay on top. These few years since the Founders graduated are like two generations. The men know a few names, like Jay's, but otherwise 2000 to 2003 is long ago. They were in seventh, eighth, ninth grade.

I needed to get away from Cornell itself and catch up with the alumni in the world, so I did. There we were, just men now, out in the world and drinking beer and talking. As alumni the Founders and the rest of the Alpha pledge class had forgotten how anyone performed in office, their tussles over money, their many clashes. If not buddies, they gave each other a chance, buried old feuds. I saw why men often said they learned so much from a fraternity but could not always give me examples: they absorbed the lessons but let go of the details.

* * *

As my teaching job unraveled like a ball of thread in the fall of 2006, Phi Tau quickly found another faculty advisor: David Dittman, an accounting professor who had been dean of the School of Hotel Administration. It showed how much the faculty advisor's role had grown since the colony asked me to do it. Dave went to Notre Dame, which doesn't have fraternities, but was eager to learn about us. The final semester was a great test of my maturity and of the lessons I learned with Phi Tau. Tough as it was to focus, in the classroom I actually tried some things I had not before, and had a good semester.

My paternal grandmother, Frances Barden Conroe, died in April 2006, two weeks shy of 103. We thought the end had come a couple of times. She even went on Hospice. But she endured, and told everyone she had flunked Hospice. My siblings' children grew and showed their talents. My parents headed toward 80. They traveled somewhere in the world a couple of times a year. I expected to move to their area at some point, to be there when they needed help. They did so much for me these past five decades that I was glad to pay them back.

The week of my 51st birthday Phi Tau had a reception and dinner for me and Dave Dittman. I wasn't leaving the area, so it wasn't that tearful, but never had someone held a dinner for me—serving prime rib, no less.

The men were not all there; it was the first day of finals week and some of them had academic obligations. "They know you aren't going anywhere yet," said the chapter president. But that evening I basked in their warmth. The president and president-elect spoke of me as a great resource (I felt like a library or something). I was going to serve as interim chapter advisor, and since nobody had held that position for a couple of years, set about re-establishing it. I couldn't do what LeGrand did, although in some ways our situations were parallel—like the colony, the chapter would be young, anxious to have fun, and small since 10 brothers were going off-campus for the spring. The Maxwell Award glittered in the Chapter Room among brown wood and books. Could we win it again? The fall had been rough, the mood grumpy, the work ethic missing. I just wanted us to remain a solid fraternity.

Every table had an adult. My colleague Brian Earle, who taught business speaking, sat with a brother who had been his student and one who would be, while next to him sat a sophomore whose father was in Brian's own fraternity at Cornell when Brian was faculty advisor. Two brothers' parents were there, and an assistant dean of students who had been our ally since she worked for Cornell Outdoor Education and we were trying that instead of hazing. At my table was Bob Cundall, the alumni board veteran, an engineer, and he debated with two engineering majors about what awaited them in the workplace.

The workplace. I had to find a job or start a business. I wanted to matter more. I wanted to make more money. Maybe I would find a job I didn't care about much and focus on writing. I had paid off my mortgage.

They all stood and applauded me. I made a short speech about how ironic it was that fraternities, having grown from defiance against professors, should get past that and value us. The president and alumni relations chair presented me with a watercolor painting of the house, made by a junior's grandmother.

No, this thing should not be too large in my life, but it should be large.

I want the men who founded that colony back in the spring of 2000 to understand the power of what they did, the legacy they left, the sheer achievement of it. I am bound to them. They gave me a white card that invited me into their company, and I fell deep. What that meant, we are still discovering.

I do not want us to become a frat.

I am still heard and I am still ignored. I can be pretty wise. But other days, I am still full of crap.

Appendix

A Q&A Session about Advising, Stages of a Fraternity, and Other Matters

Question: What major points would you stress with a colony that is trying to become a chapter, or a chapter that wants to be different from the "frat" path?

Answer: This sounds pessimistic, but when a colony or fraternity is doing well, watch out. We seem to reach great heights and then quickly fall a little, sometimes within months. Young men can get cocky and careless. Being good might get boring for them, they feel they're missing out on what wilder fraternities are doing, or they just get restless. So, a colony or fraternity needs to be consistent, strong, find guys who believe in what it's doing, and encourage everyone to keep believing. When they are doing well, older people should tell them so—alumni, administrators, other Greeks.

I've noticed that colonies don't do well if they're established only a year or two, even three years, after the original chapter folds. They seem to go right back to cultural patterns that got them in trouble in the first place. Also, colonies that begin with really strong leaders can struggle after that leader or handful of leaders graduates. We went through that, to an extent. I would try to have a structured transition, if I were an alumni board chair.

Q: What central idea should an adult working with a fraternity keep in mind?

A: These are young people, growing up, making mistakes. Try to laugh a little. Try to help them learn from mistakes. Do not confuse their poise and confidence with wisdom.

Q: What can an advisor do when they make mistakes?

A: Encourage the fraternity leaders to be tough, vigilant, compassionate but also aware they have jobs to do. Try to be proactive. That's difficult because we want young people to learn on their own, we don't want to be too involved, and they don't always see a problem coming as we do. If you must be reactive—and you can't always see a problem coming, situations just happen—try to get the facts and remain calm.

Q: How do you decide when to get involved in a situation?

A: I weigh what the president and vice president want me to do, with what the alumni board expects, what the law says, and what I have seen before. Do I let the men figure things out, or see potential for disaster and act? If I am too assertive, there could be a backlash. Young people often think they know best and resent being told what to do. Talk too much and the men will tune me out. Talk too little and they might think I am ineffective. It doesn't take long to wear out your welcome. Of course, there is no manual for all of this.

Q: But haven't you established yourself, after seven years?

A: Yes and no. Seniors and juniors may remember times when I have helped and may regard me as part of the house, but new men know little about me. College students come and go rapidly, and the turnover in a fraternity is complete every three years. There's always the chance that an emerging leader of the house might think I'm not valuable, too.

Q: Does age matter with an adult who wants to work with a fraternity?

A: There are times when I wish I were younger, because maybe a 20-year-old will listen to a 35-year-old. A baby boomer might seem too stuck in the past, or hypocritical—my generation has made its mistakes. But do the men think a younger advisor will see things their way and agree with what they want to do, when an older person would not? If so, they have to remember that's not an advisor's function. I think personality and experience might be more important than age. No question, I have gaps in my sensibility because I was not part of a fraternity in college.

Q: You were faculty advisor, then a combination of faculty and chapter advisor, then interim chapter advisor. How are the roles different?

A: The faculty advisor focuses on academic matters but is also a resource for other areas of fraternity life, such as officer development and counseling. That happened to me—my role was not clearly defined and it grew as the men and I got to know each other. The chapter advisor focuses more on chapter management, officer development, and counseling. He (or she, if a chapter can accept a female in this role) works more with national staff and college staff. In many cases this person is the "bad guy," warning the men about problems and consequences.

Q: How do you convince fraternities to follow higher standards of behavior?

A: It is difficult. College-age men don't like to be preached at and don't always like being held up as a model. They value the fine art of acting out against adults, of enjoying youth and the relative freedom of college, when society forgives them more readily. One thing to do is convince leaders to encourage higher standards. Go to the other end and talk to pledges about it too—ask them if they see something they don't like and remind them that they can start working for change. Unfortunately, with men you often have to resort to threats: loss of charter, legal trouble, social probation, that kind of thing. That's been the case when we try to fight hazing.

Q: Why is it so difficult when it would seem that a fraternity would want to be a strong, positive entity?

A: Partly because men see other fraternities getting away with hazing, party violations, and boorish behavior, so they wonder why they should hold higher standards. They have to think about why they joined in the first place. Plus, having higher standards can seem like pleasing the college and national staff too much—kowtowing to The Man. Students like to rebel. Alumni sometimes feed that view, telling the men to stop being wimps and have fun.

Q: A lot is being written about the Millennials, the current college generation born since 1981. What do you see happening?

A: I don't work in student affairs on a day to day basis, and I hate to generalize about a generation as people do with mine. These students are enormously sophisticated with technology, which helps them manage rush and the fraternity, discuss house matters via e-mail, find information, and publicize themselves via web sites. They can confuse being informed with being wise, but then, in my time young people tended to be more confident than they should have about what they were doing. How much is generational and how much is youth? And I'm at Cornell, so these are achievers anyway.

They do not hold each other accountable at times, or criticize each other, and they have a difficult time with criticism, perhaps more so than previous generations. Everyone was above average as they grew up, everyone's opinion mattered, and everyone was heard even if they should not have been. They do not clean up after themselves too well, but maybe that has always been the case in fraternities—I don't want to fall into that trap.

Certainly the pressure on these men to get high grades was (and is) far greater than in my time, so they face more pressure and sometimes crack.

How will this play out? We don't know yet. My chapter is aware of how its generation is perceived and the men often try to defy that image. Every brother is different and goes through different stages.

Q: And beyond your chapter?

A: I hear a lot of concerns. Other advisors say their men are so used to adults doing things for them that they are slow to do what needs to be done—paying bills, handing in reports. They cannot accept punishment for their actions. Their parents did not punish them and maybe protected them from being punished. It's not true across the board, and as with so much about this generation, we will have to wait and see.

Acknowledgments

I must start by thanking the men of Phi Kappa Tau's Alpha Tau chapter at Cornell University, who brought me into the fold and continue to offer me support and brotherhood. Many of them spoke to me for this book and corrected my errors. Any errors that remain are mine.

My thanks to my editor, David Bischoff, for his guidance. For reading early versions of this book, and their many suggestions, I thank Dan Schiff, Brian Strahine, Jeff Bank, Gary Ingraham, Mike Paestella, and Seth Center.

I am grateful to Phi Taus who encouraged this project, including Barry Mask, former National President Jay McCann, and national ritualist Fr. Nick Rachford. Our fraternity has superb leaders in President Charles Ball, Vice President Bill

Macak, and CEO Steve Hartman.

Places that put up with me as I wrote: in Cortland, the Blue Frog Coffeehouse, the Bagel Shop, and the Dark Horse Tavern, where people scribbling in legal pads is not a common sight; in Ithaca, Collegetown Bagels and Benchwarmers; in Potsdam, The Bagelry, Strawberry Fields Coffeehouse, and The Greenery at SUNY. Maybe Maxfield's too. In Manhattan, I found Bryant Park a nice place to jot a few notes at the end.

My family has put up with my writing projects since I was in fifth grade. I thank Barbara and Bruce Conroe, David and Dianne Conroe and their extended family, Aura and Jamie Moore and their children; Laurie and Jim Mousaw and their children Jenna, Kaylie, and Ryan; John and Robin Conroe and their daughters Emilee and Allison. I thank my many other relatives named Conroe, Moore, Beall, Buff, Dale, Gantert, Forsythe, Mead, Davis, and Gerace. My heart will always have a place for those gone but not forgotten: my grandparents Irene and Furman Holme, my grandparents Irwin and Frances Conroe, Aunt Connie Conroe, Uncle Gordon Holme, and my cousin Dorothy Dale. Their love of books has flowed through my life. Grandpa Conroe's love for his fraternity, Klan Alpine, caught my attention when I was a boy—and look what happened.

Bibliography

Baird's Manual of American College Fraternities (20th ed.) (Banta, 1991)

Ball, Charles T., *From Old Main to a New Century: A History of Phi Kappa Tau* (Heritage Pub., 1996)

Bishop, Morris, *A History of Cornell* (Cornell University Press, 1967)

Bohmer, Carol and Andrea Parrot, *Sexual Assault on Campus* (Lexington Books, 1993)

Bruchac, Joseph, *At the End of Ridge Road* (Milkweed Editions, 2005)

Chickering, Arthur W. and Linda Reisser, *Education and Identity* (2nd ed.), (Jossey-Bass, 1993)

Colton, Larry, *Goat Brothers* (Doubleday, 1993)

Douglas, Kirk, *The Ragman's Son* (Simon and Schuster, 1988)

Faludi, Susan, *Stiffed: The Betrayal of the American Man* (W. Morrow and Co., 1999)

Hoekema, David, *Campus Rules and Moral Community* (Rowman and Littlefield, 1994)

Horowitz, Helen Lefkowitz, *Campus Life* (University of Chicago Press, 1987)

Kluge, P.F., *Alma Mater: A College Homecoming* (Addison-Wesley, 1993)

Kuh, George D. et al., *Involving Colleges: Successful Approaches to Fostering Student Learning and Development Outside the Classroom* (Jossey-Bass, 1991)

Land, Brad, *Goat* (Random House, 2004)

Leemon, Thomas, *The Rites of Passage in a Student Culture* (Teachers College Press, 1972)

Nichols, John, *The Sterile Cuckoo* (McKay, 1965) (fiction)

Nuwer, Hank, *Broken Pledges* (Longstreet Press, 1990)

Nuwer, Hank, *Wrongs of Passage: Fraternities, Sororities, Hazing, and Binge Drinking* (Indiana University Press, 1999)

Sanday, Peggy Reeves, *Fraternity Gang Rape* (New York University Press, 1990)

Sanderson, James Gardner, *Cornell Stories* (Charles Scribner's Sons, 1898) (fiction)

Somers, Christina Hoff, *The War Against Boys* (Simon and Schuster, 2000)

Wolff, Geoffrey, *The Final Club* (Knopf, 1990) (fiction)

The Fraternity and Sorority System Strategic Plan, Cornell University, January 1997

The Report of the Committee on Residential Life, Hamilton College, March 1995

Strategic Vision Statement, St. Lawrence University, 1993